Fifty Years of EU–Turkey Relations

The publication of this book marks the fiftieth year of Turkey's application to the European Economic Community for associate membership, and evaluates EU–Turkey relations in a historical perspective.

Examining the evolving approaches of Turkey and of the EU towards each other, the volume focuses on the 'delay' in Turkey's accession to the EU, and explores the characteristics and reasons of this delay in political, economic, security, ethical and sociological dimensions. By shedding light on the main actors and changing parameters in these relations, the book reveals achievements as well as failures of Turkey and the EU in their mutual relations.

Fifty Years of EU–Turkey Relations will be essential reading and a lasting reference volume for policy-makers and academics interested in EU–Turkey relations, European politics, European Union enlargement or international relations.

Armağan Emre Çakır is an Assistant Professor at Marmara University, Istanbul.

Routledge Advances in European Politics

Fifty Years of EU–Turkey Relations

A Sisyphean story

Edited by Armağan Emre Çakır

Routledge
Taylor & Francis Group

LONDON AND NEW YORK

First published 2011
by Routledge
2 Park Square, Milton Park, Abingdon, Oxon OX14 4RN

Simultaneously published in the USA and Canada
by Routledge
270 Madison Avenue, New York, NY 10016

Routledge is an imprint of the Taylor & Francis Group, an informa business

Typeset in Times New Roman by
HWA Text and Data Management, London
Printed and bound in Great Britain by
CPI Antony Rowe, Chippenham, Wiltshire

British Library Cataloguing in Publication Data
A catalogue record for this book is available from the British Library

Library of Congress Cataloging-in-Publication Data
Fifty years of EU–Turkey relations : a Sisyphean story / edited by Armagan Emre
Cakir.
    p. cm. – (Routledge advances in European politics ; 69)
Includes bibliographical references and index.
1. European Union – Turkey. 2. European Union countries – Foreign relations
– Turkey. 3. Turkey – Foreign relations – European Union countries.
I. Cakir, Armagan Emre.
    JZ1570.A57 T92 2011
    341.242´209561–dc22

ISBN 10: 0-415-57963-5 (hbk)
ISBN 10: 0-203-83642-1 (ebk)

ISBN 13: 978-0-415-57963-6 (hbk)
ISBN 13: 978-0-203-83642-2 (ebk)

Contents

Illustrations

Figures

Tables

Contributors

Dr Pınar Bilgin is associate professor of International Relations at Bilkent University, Turkey. Her studies concentrate on critical approaches to security, Turkish foreign policy and EU–Turkey relations.

Dr Armağan Emre Çakır is assistant professor at the European Union Institute of Marmara University, Istanbul. He is the chairperson of the Department of Politics and International Relations of the European Union. His research focuses on theories of European integration, and EU–Turkey relations.

Dr Ebru Ş. Canan-Sokullu is assistant professor at the Department of Political Science and International Relations of Bahçeşehir University, Istanbul. Her research centres on transatlantic relations, European and American foreign policy, European Union, public opinion, electoral and modern political behaviour, and political psychology.

Dr Thomas Diez is professor at the Institute for Political Science at the University of Tübingen. His fields of interest are international relations theories, theories of European integration, ethics and European integration, religion and European integration, border conflicts in the EU, and postmodernity.

Dr Çiğdem Kentmen is assistant professor at the Department of International Relations and the European Union at Izmir University of Economics, Izmir. Her research areas are public opinion, voting behaviour, institutions of the European Union, and Turkey's membership of the EU.

Dr Tevfik F. Nas is professor at the Department of Economics at the University of Michigan-Flint, USA. His areas of interest are macro-economic theory, public choice, public policy, international economics, the European Union, and cost-benefit analysis.

Dr Chris Rumford is reader at the Department of Politics and International Relations at Royal Holloway, University of London, UK and is also Co-Director of the Centre for Global and Transnational Politics. His fields of study are EU integration, globalisation, cosmopolitanism, Europeanisation, and postwesternisation.

Dr. Nathalie Tocci is senior fellow at Istituto Affari Internazionali, Rome, associate fellow at the Centre for European Policy Studies, Brussels, and associate editor of *The International Spectator*. Her research interests include European foreign policy, conflict resolution, European neighbourhood with a particular focus on Turkey, Cyprus, the Middle East and the South Caucasus.

Hasan Turunç is a PhD candidate at the Department of Politics and International Relations at Royal Holloway, University of London, UK. His areas of research include Turkish societal developments, Islamist transformation, secularism, human rights, democracy theories, civil society in global context, Europeanisation, enlargement of the EU.

Preface

A significant research corpus exists on the relations between the EU and Turkey in retrospect. However, these relations extend over such a large span of time and they are so multi-faceted that there still is much to explore. Since Turkey's application for associate membership in 1959 which meant the official inception, these relations have gone through the tensest days of the Cold War, seen the collapse of communism and experienced the obscure period following the 9/11 attacks. They were influenced by the interests of many actors, from the Caribbean countries to the USA, equated with the relations between the East and the West or Christianity and Islam, and identified with heresy or treason. They sometimes became a proxy for the ongoing friction between Turkey and Greece, and sometimes served as a coordinate system whereon the definition of Europeanness was projected. Together with all the conspiracies, accusations, adversities and frustrations involved, there is enough material in the EU–Turkey relations to pen a tragedy. This book was not intended to be a literary work, but readability was a major concern in the writing of it.

A second concern was to provide an exhaustive coverage of the fifty-year period examined in the book. Nevertheless, instead of containing a little bit of everything, the book draws more on some fields of study and emphasises certain themes more than others. That such important fields as environment or agriculture, or such key dimensions as democracy or human rights remain outside the scope of the book should be ascribed to practical reasons rather than negligence or omission.

Attributing equal importance to early and later years of the period in question was another concern. However, in some cases, focusing on certain parts of this period was inevitable due mainly to data availability. For example, no dependable and uniform information is available on European public opinion on Turkey for the first few decades of this period. It is also difficult to talk of a significant security dimension of EU–Turkey relations for the same early years.

Remaining fair and neutral was also a concern in the formulation of the book. Yet, the first feedbacks we received on the drafts of the book indicated that there still was a hint of pro-Turkish bias in the text. At this point, the contributors to this book concluded that trying to eliminate further the passages that may be seen in Turkey's favour would mean distorting their opinions. This should not lead the reader to infer that the contributors are a team of like-minded scholars; there do exist considerable differences of opinion among them. For instance, while for Nas the side-benefits of the EU–Turkey relations are of central importance, Diez contends that Turkey could have enjoyed most of these benefits anyway without the EU.

It is the collective conviction of the authors that even after Turkey's accession to the EU, the history of relations between the EU and Turkey will not lose its appeal. They hope that this volume will be a modest contribution to this literature and stimulate new questions and debates.

Armağan Emre Çakır
Washington, DC, May 2010

Acknowledgements

The contributors of this volume deserve all the credit not only for their diligence, care and creativity in preparing their respective chapters but mainly for their tolerance of and responsiveness to my whims; the late A.H. Weiler, editor and critic for *The New York Times* for half-a-century, once said 'nothing is impossible for the man who does not have to do it himself'. Heidi Bagtazo (Senior Editor) and Harriet Frammingham (Editorial Assistant) from Routledge were the guardian angels who watched over this project and touched it with their wands whenever I appealed to them for help. I am grateful to Dr Gökçen Yavaş for her comments on the draft of this volume. I would also like to express my warm appreciation to Todd V. Crosby and Stephanie A. Cryer, who provided me with the warmth of a family during the preparation of this volume.

Abbreviations

ACP	African, Caribbean and Pacific
AKP	see JDP
Art.	Article
BSEC	Organization of the Black Sea Economic Cooperation
CAP	Common Agricultural Policy
CDU/CSU	Christian Democratic Union of Germany and the Christian Social Union of Bavaria
CEECs	Central and Eastern European Countries
CHP	see RPP
CI	Confidence intervals
EB	Eurobarometer
EC	European Community
EC6	European Community of six Member States (1957–1972)
EC9	European Community of nine Member States (1973–1980)
EC10	European Community of ten Member States (1981–1985)
ECO	Economic Cooperation Organization
ECSC	European Coal and Steel Community
ECU	European Currency Unit
EDF	European Development Fund
EEC	European Economic Community
EFTA	European Free Trade Association
EMU	European Economic and Monetary Union
EPP-ED	The Group of the European People's Party (Christian Democrats) and European Democrats
ESI	European Stability Initiative
EU	European Union
EU12	European Union of twelve Member States (1986–1994)
EU15	European Union of fifteen Member States (1995–2003)
EU25	European Union of twenty-five Member States (2004–2006)
EU27	European Union of twenty-seven Member States (since 2007)
EUR	Euro
FDI	Foreign direct investment

FNSEA	National Federation of Farmers' Unions [Fédération nationale des syndicats d'exploitants agricoles] (of France)
FPÖ	Freedom Party of Austria [Freiheitliche Partei Österreichs]
FYROM	Former Yugoslav Republic of Macedonia
GDP	Gross domestic product
GNP	Gross national product
ICC	International Criminal Court
ICTY	International Criminal Tribunal for the Former Yugoslavia
IMF	International Monetary Fund
ISPA	Instrument for Structural Policies for Pre-Accession
JDP	Justice and Development Party [Adalet ve Kalkınma Partisi] (of Turkey)
LAOS	The Popular Orthodox Rally [Laïkós Orthódoxos Synagermós] (political party of Greece)
MEDA	Mediterranean Economic Development Area
MHP	see NMP
NAFTA	North American Free Trade Agreement
NATO	North Atlantic Treaty Organisation
NFD	Negotiating Framework Document
NMP	Nationalist Movement Party [Milliyetçi Hareket Partisi] (of Turkey)
OECD	Organisation for Economic Co-operation and Development
OEEC	Organisation for European Economic Co-operation
OPEC	Organization of Petroleum Exporting Countries
PHARE	Poland and Hungary: Assistance for Restructuring their Economies (programme)
PKK	Kurdistan Workers' Party [Partiya Karkeren Kurdistan] (terrorist organisation)
RPP	Republican Peoples' Party [Cumhuriyet Halk Partisi] (of Turkey)
SAPARD	Special Accession Programme for Agricultural and Rural Development
SPO	State Planning Organization
TRNC	Turkish Republic of Northern Cyprus
TRT	Turkish Radio and Television Corporation [Türkiye Radyo ve Televizyon Kurumu]
TÜSİAD	Turkish Industrialists' and Businessmen's Association [Türk Sanayicileri ve İşadamları Derneği]
US/USA	United States / United States of America
USD	United States dollar
USSR	Union of Soviet Socialist Republics

1 Introduction

Armağan Emre Çakır

It has been fifty years since Turkey applied for associate membership of the European Economic Community (EEC) on 31 July 1959.[1] As of 2009, Turkey is still not a member of the – now – European Union (EU), and by even the most optimistic estimates, it cannot become a member before 2014.[2] Being the next applicant after Greece – who lodged its application to the EEC only a few weeks before Turkey, but who became a member in 1981 – Turkey's long stay in the waiting room deserves closer examination. It is true that decades are like days in the lives of countries. It is also true that admission to a family of states may take a long time. For instance, among the states of the United States it took 40 years for Arizona, and 62 years for New Mexico to achieve their statehood status.[3] In the case of the EU, the 'average waiting time' is around 9 or 10 years, whilst Turkey will have waited 55 or 27 years if it manages to become a full member in 2014[4] (see Table 1.1.)

This considerably long waiting time of Turkey has a few important connotations:

**It is not good enough for things to be planned – they still
have to be done; for the intention to become a reality, energy
has to be launched into operation.**
Walt Kelly (American cartoonist, 1913–1973)

Since the coming into force of the Ankara Agreement in 1964, Turkey–EU relations have followed a certain schedule: the schedule that was put forward by the Agreement itself. Accordingly, the relations would go through three stages (Art. 2 of the Agreement): (i) a preparatory stage, (ii) a transitory stage, and (iii) a final stage. The final stage would possibly culminate with Turkey's full membership (Art. 28).

This schedule has been duly followed to this day. Having established a customs union with the EU, Turkey is now in the final stage, engaged in accession negotiations with the EU. Thus, *prima facie* it may seem that there has been no delay in Turkey–EU relations. However, in reality a series of delays stretched out each of these stages to its limits. Together with the delay between the application in 1959 and the coming into force of the Ankara Agreement in 1964, the completion of Turkey's membership process is taking much longer than

Table 1.1 Waiting times of the EU members and applicants

	Date of Application	Date of Admission	Waiting Time
Greece	1959 or 1975	1981	22 or 6
Cyprus	1990	2004	14
Malta	1990	2004	14
United Kingdom	1961	1973	12
Ireland	1961	1973	12
Denmark	1961	1973	12
Bulgaria	1995	2007	12
Romania	1995	2007	12
Hungary	1994	2004	10
Poland	1994	2004	10
Portugal	1977	1986	9
Spain	1977	1986	9
Estonia	1995	2004	9
Latvia	1995	2004	9
Lithuania	1995	2004	9
Slovakia	1995	2004	9
Czech Republic	1996	2004	8
Slovenia	1996	2004	8
Austria	1989	1995	6
Sweden	1991	1995	4
Finland	1992	1995	3
Croatia	2003	Negotiating	–
FYROM	2004	Negotiating	–
Montenegro	2008	Negotiating	–
			Average: 10 or 9
Turkey	1959 or 1987	2014 or later	At least 55 or 27

expected. A comparison between the membership chronology of Greece and that of Turkey may give a better idea about the prolongation in the case of the latter (see Table 1.2).

The delay in each of these stages had its own reasons; sometimes it was Turkey that dragged its feet, or actually asked for time extensions, and sometimes it was the Union or some of the Member States that insisted on procrastination. As partners in crime, Turkey, the EU and the Member States did not put enough energy into the plan, and pushed it into oblivion.

The contributors to this volume help us understand the reasons behind this fifty-year delay.

Table 1.2 A comparison between the duration of the stages of the membership processes of Greece and Turkey

MEMBERSHIP PROCESS OF GREECE		MEMBERSHIP PROCESS OF TURKEY	
Application for associate membership	1959	Application for associate membership	1959
Signing of the Association Agreement	1961	Signing of the Association Agreement	1963
Coming into force of the Association Agreement	1962	Coming into force of the Association Agreement	1964
Stages of the association process — Preparatory stage	No preparatory stage was needed for Greece	**Stages of the association process** — Preparatory stage	1964–1973
Transitory stage	1962–1984 (Lodged its application for full membership in the transitory stage)	Transitory stage	1974–1994 (Lodged its application for full membership in the transitory stage)
Final Stage	Accession occurred before the start of the start of the final stage	Final stage	1995–?
Application for full membership	1975	Application for full membership	1987
Community's response	1976 (favourable)	Community's response	1989 (negative) (candidacy approved in 1999)
Start of the accession negotiations	1976 (Commission suggests a pre-accession period. EC Council rejects the idea and begins accession negotiations).	Start of the accession negotiations	2005
Completion of the accession negotiations	1979	Completion of the accession negotiations	?
Signing of the Treaty of Accession	1979	Signing of the Treaty of Accession	?
Date of full membership	1981	Date of full membership	?

Delay always breeds danger, and to protract a great design is often to ruin it.
Miguel de Cervantes Saavedra (Spanish novelist, poet and playwright, 1547–1616)

The prospect of Turkey's admission to the European Union bears greater importance than the accession processes of many other European states. If Turkey becomes a member of the Union, for both Turks and Europeans this will be the realisation of an age-old idea first contemplated by William Penn.[5] This membership will mean the inclusion of a country with a 99 per cent Muslim population in Europe, heralding the peaceful coexistence or rather the blending of Christianity and Islam, of Europe and Asia as well as of the East and the West. It was with this vision and enthusiasm that Walter Hallstein, a Christian Democrat and the then President of the Commission of the EEC, uttered the following words on the occasion of the signing of the Ankara Agreement on 12 September 1963:

> Today we are witnessing an event of great political importance. Turkey belongs to Europe. This is the deepest meaning of this process. This process is conceivable, in the most contemporary form, as the confirmation of a truth which is more than an abbreviated expression of a geographical statement or a historical observation that has been valid for several centuries. Turkey belongs to Europe.
> [...]
> So, we find ourselves at the beginning of an era of close cooperation between Turkey and the Community. The two sides will meet in the Association Council and as equal partners discuss their concerns and, in this new spirit, resolve the emerging problems of such an endeavor. [...] And one day, the last step should be realized: Turkey should be a full member of the Community.[6]

However, at the 27 September 2006 debates of the European Parliament, Hartmut Nassauer another Christian Democrat and the then vice chairman of the Group of the European People's Party (Christian Democrats) and European Democrats (EPP-ED)[7] claimed that '[i]t [was] inconceivable that Turkey should become a Member State of the EU without facing up to the facts of history'.[8]

The change of attitude from September 1963 to September 2006 is an indicator of a deterioration that has evolved over a long period of time. This deterioration is becoming established in the minds of the European public and the number of EU citizens who are against Turkish membership of the EU is steadily increasing (see Figure 1.1).

This fifty-year period has had its negative influence on the minds of Turks as well, and now 'Turkey seems to have every reason to turn its back on the West';[9] Turkish public-support for EU membership has declined drastically (see Figure 1.2). In a similar vein, Turkish people's trust in the EU is also in decline (see Figure 1.3).

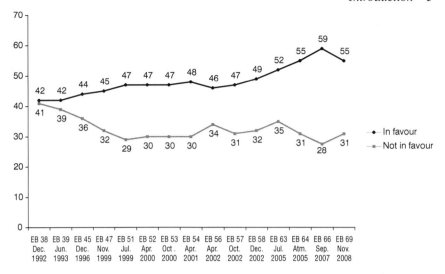

Figure 1.1 Percentage of the EU citizens who support Turkish membership to the EU

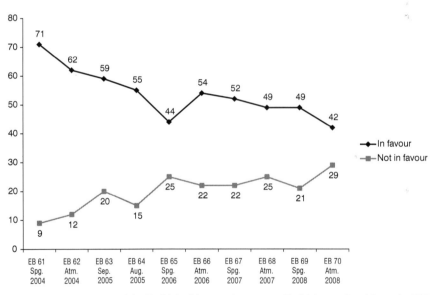

Figure 1.2 Percentage of the Turkish citizens who support Turkish membership to the EU

This is a delay that has bred the danger of deterioration of the relations between Turkey and the EU, and imperilled the great design of anchoring Turkey to Europe. The peoples of both parties have been aloof from each other for some time.

Having this decline in mind, the contributors to this volume help us understand the costs of this fifty-year delay for Turkey, for the European Union as well as for intercivilisational dialogue.

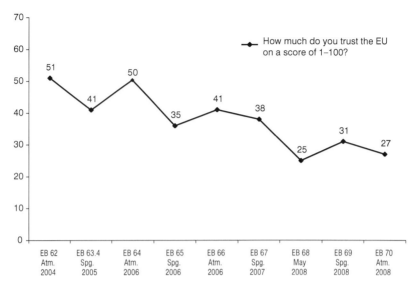

Figure 1.3 Trust of Turkish people in the EU on a score of 0–100

Delay is the deadliest form of denial.
Cyril Northcote Parkinson (British naval historian and author, 1909–1993)

Since the second half of the nineteenth century, Turkey has turned its face towards the West. With the Kemalist revolution, many parameters of Turkish society, from the alphabet to clothing, were changed in a dramatic and almost irreversible way. Politically, Turkey allied with the West by becoming a NATO member and a candidate for membership of the EU, and thus alienated itself from its Eastern neighbours and especially from Islamic countries. However, Turkey's expectations went unfulfilled.

> Although the secular Turkey (officially, at least) that emerged out of the Ottoman Empire's ashes nine decades ago politically distanced itself from Islam and Muslims to an extent, the EU-led 'Christian World' has not seemed to become satisfied by Turkey's sacrifices to the 'Christian World', most notably, Europe, and the USA.[10]

Turkey's relations with the other countries of the region are far from constituting an alternative to Turkey–EU relations: the Hamas leader Khaled Meshal's visit to Turkey in 2006 and Prime Minister Erdoğan's harsh condemnation of Israel's campaign during the 2008–2009 Israel–Gaza conflict strained the relations between Turkey and Israel. The performance of the Economic Cooperation Organisation (ECO) (whose members are Afghanistan, Azerbaijan, Iran, Kazakhstan, Kyrgyzstan, Pakistan, Tajikistan, Turkey, Turkmenistan and Uzbekistan) and the

Organisation of the Black Sea Economic Cooperation (BSEC) (whose members are Albania, Armenia, Azerbaijan, Bulgaria, Georgia, Greece, Moldova, Romania, Russia, Serbia, Turkey and Ukraine), both created to emulate some mechanisms and functions of the EU, remain unsatisfactory.

Every single year that Turkey's membership of the EU is further delayed increases its grievances arising from denial by the West and the East alike. As the former Chancellor of Austria Wolfgang Schüssel once said 'without any alternative, Turkey would be left "in a black hole" if negotiations were to fail'.[11]

Keeping in mind this position of Turkey in between the East and the West, the contributors to this book analyse the meaning of accession to the European Union in the context of the identity and foreign policy of Turkey.

I am extraordinarily patient, provided I get my own way in the end.
Margaret Thatcher (British politician, 1925–)

Art. 28 of the Ankara Agreement gave Turkey a hope of accession to the EU:

> [a]s soon as the operation of this Agreement has advanced far enough to justify envisaging full acceptance by Turkey of the obligations arising out of the Treaty establishing the Community, the Contracting Parties shall examine the possibility of the accession of Turkey to the Community.

However, from time to time some prominent figures in the EU have tried to devise ways to circumvent this prospect.

First, they claimed that Turkey's association relationship did not necessarily have to end up with membership of the EU:

> The commitments entered into in the 60s were in a different context. They were about the possible entry of Turkey into the Common Market, which had an exclusively economic dimension then. It can be said that these commitments have been honoured, since the EU signed with Turkey in 1995 a customs union treaty that gives her access to this market.[12]

Turkey insistently denied this approach, and claimed it was eligible for full membership.

Secondly, they devised some options that were alternative to Turkey's full membership. One of these options was the 'privileged partnership' concept launched by Angela Merkel's CDU/CSU block in Germany in 2004. Privileged partnesrship would be a status that was more than associate membership and less than full membership, but the concept was never formalised nor was its substance clarified, although it gained the support of former French president and head of the European Convention Valéry Giscard d'Estaing, the French President Nicolas Sarkozy and the former Chancellor of Austria Wolfgang Schüssel. Turkey rejected this option categorically.

Another option offered to Turkey was its inclusion in the 'Union for the Mediterranean' project voiced by Sarkozy in 2007. Initially, this option was planned to be an alternative to Turkey's full membership, but when Turkey refused this alternative as well, the plan was modified in 2008 in such a way that membership of the Union for the Mediterranean was no longer an alternative to membership of the European Union but rather a stepping stone into the EU. It was only then that Turkey accepted the invitation to join the Union for the Mediterranean.

The contributors to this volume trace this zigzagging trajectory of Turkey whose target in fact has always been full membership. They approach this fifty-year period from various intriguing and unconventional perspectives.

Armağan E. Çakır claims that Turkey's rivals have had an important impact on EU–Turkey relations; although not commonly invoked in the literature, the actions of these countries have been among the major factors behind the fifty-year protraction.

Tevfik F. Nas reverses the familiar causal logic of Turkey's economic performance affecting its chances of accession to the EU, and asserts that the prospects of Turkey's membership of the EU has had a positive effect on Turkey's economic development in the last fifty years.

Pınar Bilgin traces the construction of the respective security cultures of the EU and Turkey over the years. She maintains that whereas the EU has constructed a 'security community' through the adoption of broader conceptions and non-military practices, Turkey's security culture has remained dependent on military means.

Nathalie Tocci sheds light on the missing link between Turkey's accession process and European debates on Turkey. She contends that European elites turned their gazes to EU–Turkey relations only recently, and that their vision is still blurry since in fact these relations are actually out of their focus.

Ebru S. Canan-Sokullu and Çiğdem Kentmen analyse the transformation of European public opinion on Turkey, and explain key determinants of variation in popular support for Turkey's possible membership of the EU.

Chris Rumford and Hasan Turunç challenge the prevalent belief that equates Turkey's accession to the EU with Westernisation. They maintain that both the EU and Turkey, each in its own terms, are in an era of Postwesternisation.

Thomas Diez applies international ethics to EU–Turkey relations and concludes that established routines, rules and procedures of enlargement processes should be the only guide for the negotiations between the EU and Turkey, and the only source of rights and obligations of the parties.

Notes

1 Although this application of Turkey was for associate membership, Turkey's full membership of the EEC was in prospect (see Art. 28 of the Ankara Agreement). Turkey lodged another application in 1987, this time directly for full membership.

2 The year 2014 was first mentioned in the Negotiating Framework document adopted by the Council on 3 October 2005, the date which officially marked the start of

the negotiations between Turkey and the EU: 'as Turkey's accession could have substantial financial consequences, the negotiations can only be concluded after the establishment of the Financial Framework for the period from 2014'. Online. Available http://ec.europa.eu/enlargement/pdf/st20002_05_tr_framedoc_en.pdf (accessed 20 December 2009).

3 The idea of establishing a connection between Turkey's case and those of Arizona and New Mexico belongs to Scherpereel. See: John Scherpereel, 'The dynamics of EU enlargement in American Perspective,' in N. Jabko and C. Parsons (eds.) (2004) *The State of the European Union: With US or Against US – European Trends in American Perspective.* Oxford: Oxford University Press, p. 358.

4 The UK, Ireland and Denmark made three applications, the first two of which were vetoed by France. Here, the date of their first application is taken into consideration. Morocco whose application was rejected by the EEC, and Norway and Switzerland whose memberships were rejected by their domestic public vote are not included in the table. Since Turkey and Greece first applied for associate membership status with a membership perspective, but each made a later application this time for membership, there are two options for their 'waiting time'. This also leads to two average waiting times for the EU-total.

5 In the seventeenth century William Penn imagined a kind of European parliament which he called the *Diet*. European states would have certain number of seats in the *Diet*, that would be determined in accordance with their wealth. The problems that could not be solved via intergovernmental negotiations could be brought to the *Diet* and determined by three-quarter majority. According to Penn, Russia and the Ottoman Empire could also take place in the *Diet* if they wished to do so. See Gladwyn Jebb (1967) *The European Idea*, London: New English Library.

6 European Navigator, 'Rede von Walter Hallstein anlässlich der Unterzeichnung des Assoziationsabkommens zwischen der EWG und der Türkei (Ankara, 12. September 1963)'. Online. Available http://www.ena.lu/?doc=17464&lang=03 (accessed 17 December 2008), my translation.

7 The EPP-ED Group reverted to its original name (EPP) in 2009.

8 European Parliament, 'Debates, Wednesday, 27 September 2006, Strasbourg'. Online. Available http://www.europarl.europa.eu/sides/getDoc.do?pubRef=-//EP//TEXT+CRE+20060927+ITEM-006+DOC+XML+V0//EN (accessed 10 December 2008).

9 S. Özel (2007) 'Turkey faces West,' *The Wilson Quarterly*, 2007, Winter. Online. Available http://www.aicgs.org/documents/oezel0107.pdf (accessed 18 February 2009).

10 A. Al-Hail (2006) 'Whose Accession to Whom: Turkey to EU? Or Vice Versa', *Today's Zaman*, 6 December.

11 P. Kieffer 'Germany's new chancellor discusses EU admission for Turkey'. Online Available http://www.ucg.org/commentary/euturkey.htm (accessed 12 March 2009).

12 V. Giscard d'Estaing (2004) 'Turquie: Pour le retour à la raison,' *Le Figaro*, 25 November, my translation.

2 Political dimension

Always in the list of 'also-rans': Turkey's rivals in EU–Turkey relations

Armağan Emre Çakır

Introduction

Turkey has always had rivals in its relations with the EU. It competed with some of them for membership of the Union, and with the others for whom membership was not possible technically, in achieving other benefits the Union could provide. Although Turkey had been one of the first two countries (the other being Greece) who established a contractual relationship with the EEC by means of an association agreement offering an outlook for full membership, all those in the membership race breasted the tape before Turkey, while Turkey is still running. Similarly, the rivals in non-membership benefits got more than Turkey did in most cases.

'Turkey's rivals' is not a frequently examined topic in the European studies literature. Such an examination could have been based on quantitative data.[1] However, the present analysis assumes a qualitative perspective by trying to answer the following questions: How were Turkey's rivals perceived by Turkey, by the Union and by the Member States? What were Turkey's strategies towards its rivals? How were these strategies formulated and perceived by different circles within Turkey? Were Turkey's perception of and approach towards its rivals in harmony with its approach towards European integration?

Since its inception, European integration has undergone five waves of enlargement. The following is a list of the countries that joined the Union in each of these enlargement waves:

- First Enlargement (1973): Denmark, the UK and Ireland
- Second Enlargement (1981): Greece
- Third Enlargement (1986): Spain and Portugal
- Fourth Enlargement (1995): Austria, Finland and Sweden
- Fifth Enlargement (First Group) (2004): Cyprus, Czech Republic, Estonia, Hungary, Latvia, Lithuania, Malta, Poland, Slovakia, and Slovenia
- Fifth Enlargement (Second Group) (2007): Bulgaria and Romania.

The countries in the first wave of enlargement were in a different league to Turkey and would never be rivals for it. The rest of the enlargement waves, on the other hand, all included countries Turkey regarded as rivals. Thus, the analysis of this chapter will start with the second wave of enlargement which included Greece, and will continue with the subsequent enlargements. Some countries that have not been included in any of the enlargement processes but had a clash of interests with Turkey will also be examined in the text.

Greece

Almost every detail in the accession process of Greece to the EEC has had a substantial influence on Turkey's relations with the EEC. Probably the first question to ask in this framework should be whether Turkey's application was indeed lodged to follow in the footsteps of Greece. It is a prevailing rumour that Turkey did not have a vision, strategy or preparation for the EEC at that time. For example, Birand[2] dramatises the atmosphere in the Turkish Foreign Ministry on 15 July 1959: the news about the Greek application for associate membership of the EEC on 8 June has just been received, and the Foreign Minister Zorlu is scolding the diplomats for their negligence in going after Greece. The phrase allegedly uttered by Zorlu that day, 'you should never leave Greece alone even if it jumps into a dry pool; you should jump after it without hesitation' has since been used to imply how shallow and extemporaneous Turkey's approach towards the EEC and Greece was.[3] Zorlu may have indeed pronounced these words; Oğuz Gökmen who was one of Zorlu's attendants attests that he too received the same warning from Zorlu.[4] Zorlu was a steadfast advocate of Turkey's membership of the EEC, and he was also taking Greece as an important parameter in Turkey's foreign policy. For him 'Turkey's chances to be accepted by such an [...] [an organisation of Western countries was] [...] to a great extent dependent on Greece, the golden child of Europe, the cradle of western civilisation. When Greeks begin to move, [Turks] should run alongside them, without considering anything else.'[5]

However, Turkey was not acting unilaterally or following Greece blindly. In his visit to Ankara in March 1959, the Greek Prime Minister Karamanlis had agreed with his counterpart Menderes to follow a common course of action towards the EEC.[6] When Greece submitted its application four months later, it honoured this gentlemen's agreement by sending a telegram and informing Ankara of the application. Since the two parties were of the opinion that their strategies towards the EEC were not coordinated enough, they met once again on 7–9 January 1960, this time in Athens. In this meeting they discussed the issues that had arisen and were likely to arise in the context of their association with the EEC, and agreed to share the arguments that they would put forward in their negotiations with the EEC as well as the responses of the EEC with each other in a most expeditious and convenient way.[7]

In Turkey, even ordinary citizens had the opportunity to be informed about the EEC and Turkish–Greek engagement. Despite the limited facilities of the time, EEC news would garner significant media coverage. For instance, Hikmet Saim, a journalist specially sent to Athens by a Turkish daily *Zafer*, reported that he and other Turkish journalists had been received by the Greek Foreign Minister Averoff. Saim quoted Averoff saying that Greece was in agreement with Turkey in every issue including the EEC matters. The same news included a declaration by J. F. Cahan, the Deputy Secretary-General of the Organisation for European Economic Co-operation (OEEC) who visited Ankara and Athens. Cahan's words were encouraging for Turkey and Greece towards EEC membership. This news was published on 2 July 1959, and was longer than half a page.[8] Other newspapers of the week contained news about declarations of Turkish chambers of commerce and industry that supported Turkey's approach to the EEC.

Turkey had already been conducting reconnaissance flights around the EEC. After the Rome Treaty was signed, the OEEC aimed at bringing together the Six, and the other seven members of the OEEC by setting up a European Free Trade Area.[9] An intergovernmental ministerial committee was set up to pursue the negotiations. This Committee met a few times in October 1958. Turkey announced its conditions to join the project,[10] but the Free Trade Area could not be realised due to differences of opinion. When the Seven decided to establish the European Free Trade Association (EFTA) among themselves, Turkey observed the preparatory work that continued during 1959. The Turkish daily *Akşam* published a column indicating that Turkey was 'undecided between the Six and the Seven'.[11] Saraçoğlu claims that before making its final decision in the direction of the EEC, due to its hesitation over agricultural matters and the common customs tariff in the EEC, Turkey made an unanswered application to EFTA, and that, however, this application is not documented.[12]

Turkey lodged its application to the EEC on 31 July 1959, fifty-three days after the application of Greece, and this was the beginning of a long and arduous road.

The ECC had not proved itself yet, and was very happy with the applications of Turkey and Greece. Sir Christopher Soames was quoted as saying that 'the EEC was not a worldwide player in the 1960s. When ministers came together, they would try to solve their own problems. It was the Ankara and Athens Agreements[13] that first imparted a foreign policy dimension to the Community'.[14] The USA was also happy with the concord between Turkey and Greece. A US National Security Council Report from 5 October 1960 contained the following sentence:

> Greco-Turkish relations have steadily improved and the two countries are cooperating in such areas as their approach to the EEC.[15]

The Community tried to follow an equality strategy between Turkey and Greece. At the Council of Ministers meeting on 11 September 1959, both the Commission President Hallstein and the German representative van Scherpenberg declared that the relations with Turkey and Greece had to be managed in parallel, and the Community sent missions to Turkey and Greece. However, in a few weeks' time, the work of these missions brought the Community to the conclusion that Turkey's size and its economic problems[16] were obstacles for it to proceed at the same speed as that of Greece. At the Council of Ministers meeting on 24 November 1959, Jean Rey, the Commissioner responsible for external relations, declared that the negotiations for the association agreement with Turkey were advancing slowly in comparison with the negotiations with Greece. The Community even considered the option of slowing down the negotiations with Greece until Turkey made up its mind and clarified its potentialities, terms and conditions. However, this option was fervently opposed by the Greek Premier Karamanlis.

From December 1959 onwards, the Community started pursuing different strategies for Turkey and Greece. Jean Rey's words at the Council of Ministers meeting in March 1960 were indicative of the Commission's attitude towards Turkey: 'Tell the Turkish representatives clearly that the agreement [to be concluded] with Greece can on no account constitute an example for them'.[17] The Community officials were now saying that they had been relatively inexperienced when the text of the agreement with Greece was formulated, and that such an agreement would never be made again with any other country including Turkey. Nevertheless, in May 1960, the Council of Ministers requested the Commission to prepare an agreement for Turkey that would lead to customs union. During the negotiation process of this agreement, Turkey did not want to undertake as many responsibilities as Greece had done. While negotiations were going on a coup d'état occurred in Turkey on 27 May, and relations with the Community were cut off.[18]

In the meantime, Greece signed its association agreement known as the Athens Agreement on 9 July 1961.[19] Around this date some radical changes were observed in the strategies of the main players, as discussed below.

First, Greece, which had concealed its rivalry until then, started putting pressure on Brussels for Turkey not to be given more agricultural concessions compared with those awarded to itself. Greece also requested to be informed of the negotiations between the EEC and Turkey.

Secondly, as the text of the Turkish association agreement also became gradually clear, domestic opposition to the EEC became more outspoken in Turkey. In the cabinet, 'not entering into the EEC' was clearly voiced as an option. However, due to a series of reasons including the possibility that if Turkey did not accede to the EEC, it may lose its competitive power against Greece in agriculture, the government decided to sign the agreement.

Thirdly, differences of opinion emerged among the Six on the nature of the agreement to be concluded with, the policy to be pursued towards, and the concessions to be given to Turkey. For example, for Italy, Turkey was a rival in the agricultural sector. France[20] and Belgium argued for fewer favours to Turkey compared with Greece. Germany, on its part, supported Turkey unconditionally.

Fourthly, the USA started showing signs of discomfort that the tobacco quotas the EEC could extend to Turkey would adversely affect the tobacco exports of the USA, and that Turkey's preferences in foreign policy would shift from the USA to Europe.

Fifthly, as the Cold War intensified towards 1961, the Community started favouring Turkey and Greece not only for economic reasons but also for political reasons. Together with Greece, Turkey had been a NATO member since 1952, and was a bulwark against the USSR.

Finally, for Turkey which had not known what exactly to request from the Community until then, there was now a concrete example. The agreement Greece had signed became a reference text for Turkey against the Community who was offering Turkey less. Saraçoğlu who was in the Turkish delegation in the negotiations recounts Turkey's struggle:

> [t]he Community's offer that did not go beyond an extended trade agreement was not in line with Turkey's expectations. What Turkey had in mind was a duplication of the agreement signed with Greece.[21]

According to him, Sicco Mansholt, the European Commissioner for Agriculture at that time said that the concessions given to Greece were exceptions, and that these concessions would not constitute a basis for the association agreements with 'other countries'.[22] Turkey was the only other country at that time engaged in association negotiations with the Community. The Commission's Director-General for Agriculture Louis Rabot was also very much concerned, and declared that if the concessions that had been given to Greece were to be extended to Turkey as well, this would paralyse the Common Agricultural Policy (CAP). The head of the Greek team that negotiated the Athens Agreement, Ioannis Pesmazoglou held a press conference in February 1961 and claimed that while concluding agreements with other countries, the Community had to protect the concessions extended to Greece.[23]

After ten meetings that spread over 45 months and occupied 77 actual negotiation days,[24] the association agreement of Turkey was concluded. This Agreement, informally known as the Ankara Agreement, was signed on 12 September 1963.[25]

In most parts, the Ankara Agreement was indeed a duplication of the Athens Agreement. Both were contractual documents aiming at establishing a customs union between the respective country and the EEC. The Ankara Agreement mostly incorporated the provisions of the Treaty of Rome and especially of the Athens Agreement either exactly or with small amendments. The majority of the differences between the two agreements were in such areas as free movement of workers which could be considered relatively minor, technical points.[26] However, the Ankara Agreement also had two substantial dissimilarities to the Athens Agreement:

1   Whilst the Athens Agreement immediately initiated the gradual establishment process of a customs union between Greece and the EEC, the Ankara Agreement included a preparatory stage before this process. In this stage, Turkey was not supposed to undertake any obligations, but 'with aid from the Community, strengthen its economy so as to enable it to fulfil the obligations which [would] devolve upon it during the transitional and final stages'.[27]
2   In the preparatory stage, Turkey would receive 175 million USD, whereas Greece received 125 million USD without a preparatory stage.

When the Ankara Agreement was signed, Greece's attitude against Turkey's associate membership became more manifest. The Greek Union of Exporters protested to their government and demanded the Ankara Agreement be annulled.

The Greek Foreign Minister summoned the ambassadors of the Member States of the EEC to his office, and registered a complaint about the Agreement. The Greek government could only be convinced at the last minute not to file an official protest to the EEC, and the Greek newspapers bombarded the government with criticisms.[28]

Due to a coup d'état in Greece on 21 April 1967, the EEC partly suspended its relations with the country on paper, and the association relationship was frozen[29] except for daily trade relations engendered by mutual obligations. However, in practice gradual reduction of customs duties and measures having equivalent effect as well as harmonisation of the agricultural policy of Greece with that of the Community continued as planned.[30] Soon after the Community's decision, Turkey decided to end its Preparatory Stage two years earlier than scheduled, and pass to the Transitory Stage. This demand of Turkey was declared at the Association Council meeting on 16 May 1967.[31] A Turkish official who had played an important role in the EEC–Turkey relations claimed that one of the reasons for Turkey deciding to proceed to the Transitory Stage was Greece. This was a great opportunity to catch up with Athens.[32] On 13 December 1968, Greece also left the Council of Europe.

In Turkey's case, passage from the Preparatory Stage to the Transitory Stage would be with an Additional Protocol to be concluded between the parties. Between 17 and 29 January 1968, a series of meetings were held between the officials from the Commission of the EEC and Turkish representatives for the Additional Protocol to be formulated. In these meetings, determination of mutual concessions or obligations was left either to bargaining process or to trial and error, and Greece's gains were important points of reference for Turkey.[33] Turkey considered itself as having the chance of being granted the same rights as Greece did especially for agricultural products. It also requested the Community to contribute to the vocational training programmes of Turkish workers, because Greece was receiving assistance of this kind.[34] However, towards the end of the negotiation process Turkey realised that its expectations were unrealistic. The Community's intention was to insert some important restrictive clauses into the Additional Protocol. Among these restrictions were national production quotas, especially in the textile sector which was one of the trump cards of Turkey. However, Greece had been given 'guarantee of purchase' in tobacco.[35] The defence of the Community for this discrimination was – once again – that the mistakes made in the Athens Agreement were not going to be repeated.[36]

In those days, chambers of commerce and industry in Turkey were curious about the relative competitive power of Greece as well as its relations with the EEC. A study commissioned by the Chamber of Commerce of Eskişehir, one of the major cities of Turkey, concluded that the Greek economy was not as sound as it looked, and it had reached the break-even point due to the customs tariff reductions Greece had been implementing. It was the claim of the study that further tariff reductions would lead to a net loss in Greek economy.[37] The Union of Chambers of Turkey commissioned another study to examine the competitive position of Turkish tobacco against Greek tobacco which had a privileged status in the EEC.[38]

Turkey's Additional Protocol was finally signed on 23 November 1970. One of the main targets of Turkey in signing the Protocol was to complete the Customs Union within 22 years and attain the privileges Greece had had and would have had in agriculture and industry. However, the Protocol excluded unprocessed agricultural goods. In 1972, an official visit of a crowded group was organised to the capital cities of the EEC member states. The outcome of this venture was not satisfactory since it had been organised in a rather haphazard way and without adequate preparation. Until the entering into force of the Protocol on 1 January 1973, domestic discussions in Turkey focused on Turkey's gains in the Protocol in comparison to those of Greece. For some, this was a text that did not provide Turkey with concessions comparable to those given to Greece, whereas for some others, although concessions given to Turkey for industrial products were relatively satisfactory, in general Greece had got more than Turkey did.[39] There also was a third group who believed that Turkey's gains were more than those of Greece.[40] The following news from a prominent Turkish daily evidences that in its relations with the EEC in the transitory period Turkey sometimes wasted time and effort with petty calculations which, it hoped, would make it triumphant over Greece:

> It is a fact that Greek canned food is exported to the Community without being subject to customs duty, and there is huge demand for this food among Turkish immigrants as it emulates the Turkish cuisine. While the sales of the Greek canned food are increasing even among Turkish workers, because of a high customs wall comparable Turkish products have to either be sold at high prices or remain outside the EEC market.
>
> To Turkey, the Common Market has only made the concession of abolishing the customs duty on import of canned peas and carrots, and reducing the customs duty by fifty per cent on import of canned okra, horse beans, and stuffed eggplants. Turkey has been insisting on having the same customs duty concessions for other varieties of canned vegetables.[41]

On 12 March 1971, the Chief of the General Staff in Turkey handed the Prime Minister a memorandum that amounted to an ultimatum by the armed forces. The reaction of the EEC to this event was rather mild and by any measure less than its reaction to the coup in Greece in 1967. On the other hand, after Turkey's intervention in Cyprus in 1974 the EEC's position was:

> difficult if one considers that the Community was also aiming to keep both Greece and Turkey inside NATO by adopting, on the one hand, a positive attitude to Greece's application for EC membership, while on the other hand, permitting some of its member states to provide Turkey with an alternative source of arms to replace those denied by the United States embargo.[42] After the EC responded favourably to a Greek application for membership in 1975, Turkish suspicion that the Community was favouring Greece prevented any

real diplomatic influence. In fact, the Community, at that point attempted to keep out of the Cyprus conflict.[43]

Combined with the global economic crisis, the effects of the US embargo were severe for Turkey until it was lifted in October 1978. Greece, on the other hand, was doing relatively well: democracy had been restored, and its association mechanisms with the Community were functioning without a problem (90 per cent of the customs duties on imports from the Community had been abolished). At the request of Greece, US President Ford decided to support Greece in its quest for full membership of the EEC: he contacted German Chancellor Schmidt who had been one of the staunchest opponents of the membership of Greece of the EEC, and convinced him in favour of Greek membership. Under these conditions, Turkey chose to develop closer relations with Greece, hoping that this would change the anti-Turkish attitude of the Greek lobby in the US Congress, and would lead to lifting of the embargo. However, the Congress voted for the maintenance of the embargo. Turkey declared that all the US bases on its soil would be closed. Meanwhile, Greece made its application for full membership of the Community on 12 June 1975, earlier than expected, and its accession negotiations started on 27 July 1976. Greece was aware of the fact that Turkey was well behind it in the race, so much so that only one day after their application to the EEC, the permanent representative of Greece to the EEC held a press meeting and announced that they would be happy if Turkey would also apply for full membership.[44]

When the accession talks of Greece started, there was a difference of opinion among the Member States. Whereas France believed that there was no need to maintain a balance between Greece and Turkey, the other Members were saying that some concessions had to be given to Turkey.[45] It could have been a wise move for Turkey if it had lodged its application just after Greece; it would have probably been difficult for the Community to accept one of these countries and refuse the other one. Maybe for this very reason, the Community implied to Turkey that the time was not ripe for Turkey's application. There was another difference of opinion in the internal politics in Turkey. For Necmettin Erbakan, the leader of one of the coalition parties, the EEC was a 'Christian club'. Bureaucracy, media, public and even Turkish ambassadors were also hotly debating Turkey's application.[46] Finally, Turkey decided not to apply.

The Greek application encouraged Spain and Portugal, the other major rivals of Turkey. Spain lodged its application on 28 March 1977 and Portugal on 28 July 1977.

Until the coming to power of the Ecevit government in Turkey in 1978, no substantial change was observed in Turkish–Greek relations with reference to the EEC. It had been expected that this government would bring about radical changes to EEC–Turkey relations, and restore Turkey's determination for full membership. However, these expectations did not materialise. On the contrary, Ecevit requested the Commission to give a guarantee to prevent a probable Greek veto on Turkey's membership after Greece itself became a full member. Naturally, the Commission could not give such a guarantee.[47] A prevailing rumour holds that in 1978 Leo Tindemans came to Ankara and tried to convince the Turkish prime minister of the coalition government Ecevit to follow Greece and lodge Turkey's application for full membership of the EEC.[48] Some other sources claim that no such visit took place at all.[49] However, a first-hand account[50] states that it was in fact Émile Noël who came to Turkey, not just once but twice. Ecevit's answer was negative since he was of the opinion that in the case of its membership, Turkey would become no more than a 'market' for the EEC, and that the Turkish economy would not be able to withstand the competitive pressures from the EEC. As indicated above, the deputy Prime Minister Erbakan was also against Turkish membership of the EEC for political reasons.

On 14 July 1978, the Ecevit government demanded that Turkey's obligations specified in the Additional Protocol be postponed for five years. At first, the Community was hesitant about Turkey's request, fearing that this may encourage Greece to raise similar demands. However, Turkey was given a positive reply in return for freezing the Community's obligations for agricultural products and free movement of labour for five years.[51] Meanwhile Greece was very much focused on its accession negotiations. Karamanlis had sensed that if Greece were to linger, the membership process of Greece could be combined with those of Spain and Portugal, and thus slowed down. He instructed his negotiators not to raise any problems against the demands of the EEC. The leader of the main opposition party, the Centre Union, Papandreou criticised this attitude of Karamanlis, and declared that if he himself came to power, he would withdraw Greece from the EEC. However, when he did come to power, he did not find enough support for his views. The accession treaty of Greece[52] was signed on 28 May 1979, and approved by the Greek Parliament. In February 1980, the Foreign Minister of Turkey Hayrettin Erkmen made a public announcement that Turkey would lodge its application for full membership of the EEC. His main aim was to guarantee Turkey's membership before Greece became a member and gained veto power. However, a motion of censure was immediately brought against Erkmen on the ground of incompatibility of his action with national interests, and he was removed from office on 5 September 1980.[53] A week later, on 12 September 1980 a coup took place in Turkey. Although relations between Turkey and the EEC were not frozen, the EEC assumed a negative attitude towards Turkey which was evident especially in the decisions of the European Parliament. Only a few months after the coup in Turkey, and three years earlier than the date stipulated in the Athens Agreement, Greece became a full member on 1 January 1981. One of the first actions of Greece against Turkey would be to veto the implementation of the Fourth Financial Protocol which foresaw financial aid to Turkey amounting to 600 million ECU. Years later, retired ambassador Gökmen would still regret that Turkey did not prevent the accession of Greece, claiming that both the Athens and Ankara Agreements contain provisions entitling either of the two countries to be consulted about and interfere in the relations of the other with the EEC. In his opinion, Turkey could have objected to the accession of Greece on the ground that Turkey had disputes with this country.[54]

Commentary

Greece was the main competitor of Turkey in the latter's quest for membership of the EEC; the rivalry that had always been present in the relations between the two countries was transposed to the EEC context. Turkey's application for associate membership, its decision to proceed from the Preparatory Stage to the Transitory Stage, its decision in 1980 to lodge its application for full membership and many other developments in its relations with the EEC had connections with Greece.

As preferred by the two countries as well as the EEC initially, the relations between the EEC and Turkey and those between Greece and the EEC were parallel and coordinated. However, this situation changed in a matter of a few months, and disconnectedness and competition prevailed between the two processes. Greece went ahead of Turkey and finished the race in as early as 1981 whereas Turkey is still struggling for membership as of 2009. In this process, the preferences of the EEC quickly shifted towards Greece.

There is no doubt that Greece deserved its achievement. With its relatively small and manageable economy that had better indicators, it could adapt itself to the conditions required by the EEC and was able to carry out the necessary reductions in customs tariffs. Instead of following protectionist policies and favouring short-term interests for its industry, it did not hesitate to make sacrifices for the long-term target of membership. The determination symbolised in Karamanlis's personality, the consensus among Greek bureaucrats and technocrats, continued with Papandreou who at first was against Greek membership of the EEC. This resolution and coherence, together with well-prepared files submitted to the EEC, created a positive impression on the EEC.

Turkey, on the other hand, showed a fairly good performance in the beginning. It pondered the option of EFTA before deciding on the EEC, and also came to an agreement with Greece whereby they decided to act together in their relations with the EEC. However, Turkey's momentum quickly lost steam, mainly due to the structural problems of its economy as well as the size of the country. Yet, instead of continuously demanding concessions from the EEC, Turkey could have been willing to undertake some more obligations. Emulating the moves of Greece was a wise strategy as long as the EEC tried to treat Turkey and Greece equally, but the EEC soon changed its attitude, and Greece proceeded so quickly that it was not possible for Turkey to catch up with it. The impression Turkey left on the EEC must have been that of an ambivalent, unprepared and reluctant country.

Differences of opinion between successive governments in Turkey also affected the process negatively. Whereas Papandreou had to change his anti-EEC attitude when he came to power, in Turkey parties or individuals who were openly or tacitly against the EEC did make it to the government, initiated a motion of censure against a foreign minister on the ground that he had decided to lodge Turkey's application for full membership, and together with the two coups they slowed down the process of accession of Turkey to the EEC.

The attitude of Turkish interest groups was favourable towards the EEC, but was not based on wise strategies or elaborate studies. The study commissioned by the Eskişehir Chamber of Industry, for example, was aimed at trying to comfort the industrialists by saying that the Greek economy would not be able to cope with the pressures coming from the reductions in customs tariffs; which was rather wishful thinking or even self-deception.

Discord within – such as disputes between ambassadors – or between – such as the Foreign Ministry and State Planning Organisation (SPO) – state institutions was another negative factor.

The Community on its part soon abandoned the strategy of maintaining equality and balance between Turkey and Greece. From then on, it continued to guide, support and inform Turkey, but was rather cautious towards Turkey's full membership. It established close relations with Turkey by giving concessions and economic aid, and by showing tolerance. For example, it was more understanding towards the military coups in Turkey, and while relations were frozen – at least on paper – with Greece during the Colonels' Junta, the EEC's relations with Turkey continued during the 1971 and 1980 coups. The economic gains of Turkey were less than those of Greece in most cases. For example, despite the fact that Turkey enjoyed a Preparatory Stage, the 175 million USD Turkey received in this stage was not a large amount in relative terms, taking into consideration the size and population of Greece which received 125 million USD without a preparatory stage. The Community explained this by saying that it did not want to repeat the mistakes it had made in the case of Greece.

Germany, France and the USA were the countries that were individually involved in the process. Germany refrained from favouring Turkey over Greece explicitly, but supported Turkey's accession, tried to slow down that of Greece, and exerted efforts to ensure that the Community would maintain its relations with Turkey during the 1980 coup. France's attitude towards Turkey was negative especially in de Gaulle's time as well as when the accession negotiations with Greece started. The USA was rather against Turkish membership at the beginning, but quickly changed its attitude to support Turkey both in the EEC matters and in the Cyprus issue, sometimes to the extent of annoying Greece.

Spain and Portugal

In his column[55] penned on New Year's Eve of 2004, Sedat Ergin, a prominent Turkish journalist, gave an inventory of the factors that contributed to the delay of Turkey's accession to the EU. What was interesting in this column was that the backbone of the text was the opportunities seized by Greece, Spain and Portugal in the EU. A week later, Hasan Cemal, another well-known journalist, wrote a similar column[56] which made reference to Ergin's text, and which also focused on Greece, Spain and Portugal. Hasan Cemal dedicated another of his columns[57] published on an important national holiday to evidence that Spain and Turkey had similar problems related to terrorism and institutionalisation of democracy, but that Spain had gone a long way to solving its problems thanks to the EU. These were not among the usual 'holiday themes' seen in newspaper columns. Besides, shortly before these columns were published, on 1 May 2004 ten countries had become members of the EU (the First Eastern Enlargement). Also Austria, Finland and Sweden had become members in 1995. Even so, Ergin and Cemal were still referring to Greece, Spain and Portugal who became members in the 1980s. Because these last three countries were seen – at least by Turks – as in the same league as Turkey, and no matter how many other rival countries came and went, these three were the focus of Turkey.

Due to the fierce and emotional competition with Greece, sometimes amounting to animosity, Turkey's pride may have made it difficult for it to follow Greece's footsteps leading to the EU. In the case of Spain and Portugal, however, Turkey seems to have felt less discomfort. The Spanish Minister of Industry and Energy Joan Majó i Cruzate visited Turkey only days after the official accession of Spain to the EEC on 1 January 1986. The aim of this visit was to share Spain's experience in the framework of accession to the EEC, to express Spain's political support to Turkey's accession, and to offer co-operation to Turkey in the fields of aeronautics and energy.[58] Since then, several circles from within Turkey have proposed that Turkey should follow Spain's practices in such fields as combating terrorism,[59] tourism,[60] municipal administration,[61] sale of property to foreigners,[62] agricultural co-operatives,[63] individual retirement schemes,[64] Olympic Games[65] and even political traditions,[66] constitutional structure[67] or foreign policy moves.[68] Some also claimed that the 'Spanish trajectory' that culminated in EEC membership could be 'a source of inspiration for Turkey'.[69]

In the case of Portugal, the similarities between this country and Turkey are frequently emphasised, but there are only a few instances where Portugal is presented as an exemplary for Turkey.[70] Yıldırım Keskin, who was the Turkish Ambassador in Portugal between 1989 and 1991 emphasised the cultural and economic similarities between Turkey and Portugal, but even in his memoir it is impossible not to notice the disconnect between the two countries: in Keskin's term of office, the Turkish Foreign Minister made an official visit to Spain, and instead of visiting Portugal from there, he summoned the ambassador Keskin to Madrid.[71] In most cases, Portugal constitutes a negative example in evaluating Turkey's position vis-à-vis the EU. For instance, two years after Portugal's accession to the EEC, the chairman of the employers' federation in France was saying that Turkey's economy was not in a worse situation than that of Portugal.[72] In a documentary[73] broadcast on the national television of Turkey, Portugal was presented as a country whose situation got worse after EU membership, whose agricultural sector was having difficulties, and whose people were not happy with the EU. The documentary implied that the plight of Portugal had to be a lesson for Turkey.[74]

Spain and Portugal were among the arch-rivals for Turkey until they became full members. Compared with Turkey, Spain and Portugal were integrated into the political structures of Europe at a later date. These two countries did not participate in the Second World War, but since Spain established close relations with the Axis States, it was excluded from the European family in the post-War period. This exclusion, together with the after-effects of the internal war Spain had gone through just before the World War, brought about political and economic difficulties for Spain. Portugal was relatively luckier. It had not experienced an internal war, and established closer relations with the UK and USA to the extent to let them make use of some military bases on its soil.

While Turkey was among the countries that founded the Organisation for Economic Co-Operation and Development (OECD) in 1948, Spain was admitted to this organisation as late as 1959. Spain was the only major European country kept outside of the Marshall Plan and received some American aid only after 1951. It made its application to the EEC in 1962, three years after Turkey. This application was refused on the ground that the Franco regime in the country was not democratic enough. Portugal, on the other hand, acted together with its historical ally the UK, and became an EFTA member in 1959.

Nevertheless, Spain and Portugal quickly improved their relations with the EEC. Following Franco's death in 1975, the two countries made their applications to the EEC in 1977. The following year, the Commission issued a favourable report for them both, and in 1986 they became members of the EEC.

Turkey watched closely the accession process of Spain and Portugal because these two countries were competitors for Turkish agricultural products, and would share the funds Turkey was hoping to get from the EEC. Spain and Portugal had always been aware of this situation and tried to protect their interests. Towards the end of 1969, well before lodging its second application to the EEC, Spain tried to make use of its close relations with some major Member States, and prevent some rival Turkish products from being given privileged status in the negotiations of the Additional Protocol to the Ankara Agreement.[75]

In the 1970s, the Community started to conclude preferential trade agreements with Mediterranean countries. The agreement with Spain was signed in 1970[76] and with Portugal in 1972.[77] Turkey expressed its discomfort at the Association Council meetings, and claimed that being an associate member, it deserved higher reductions in customs duties than Spain had been granted for some agricultural products with the 1970 agreement.[78] The concessions Spain received increased until its application for full membership. At the March 1976 meeting of the Association Council, it was clearly stated to Turkey that its associate membership did not entail any priorities for it, and that it would not be given a general concession.[79]

In 1978, the Commission prepared a proposal which included a scheme for gradual realisation of free movement of goods for Turkish agricultural products. It was hoped that this would appease Turkey. However, this proposal was not accepted.[80] One of the reasons behind the failure of this proposal was the objection of the USA to granting commercial privileges to and conclusion of preferential trade agreements with Turkey. In the trade negotiations between the EEC and the USA, the head of the US mission said that the EEC was harming US interests by agreements concluded with such countries as Turkey, and that the EEC should not narrow down the opportunities of the American market while trying to expand into new markets.[81]

While Turkey was denied of some of the privileges already granted to Spain and Portugal, some other privileges it demanded were also refused by the EEC on the ground that Spain and Portugal may demand the same. For example, in the harmonisation negotiations between the EEC and Turkey held on 21 January 1981, the concessions Turkey demanded for its agricultural products were denied by the EEC who claimed that this may constitute a precedent to be followed by Spain and Portugal in the future when they become full members.[82]

Another parallel between these two countries and Turkey exists between the attempted coup d'etat[83] in Spain on 23 February 1981 and the one[84] that took place in Turkey on 12 September 1980. Before the coup attempt in Spain, the EEC was rather sympathetic to the military regime in Turkey. However, probably thinking that this would be a double standard, the Community changed its attitude and assumed a negative stance against both of the coups.[85] Spain and Portugal themselves were also critical of the military regime in Turkey:

> [t]he behaviour of the governments and parliaments of Spain and Portugal who had just been liberated from military regimes, and who, therefore, esteem it a national duty to be against any military regime no matter where or why it had been established also created serious difficulties in Turkey's relations with the EEC. Spain and Portugal always voted against Turkey, thinking that if 'the Turkish type of military democracy' would succeed they themselves would encounter the biggest difficulty.[86]

When Spain and Portugal became members of the Community on 1 January 1986, Turkey thought that this development would soon seal the end of the enlargement process of the EEC; it had to lodge its application for full membership as soon as possible. This perception was an important factor for Turkey to take the decision of making its own application.[87] Indeed, the Commission, in its Opinion[88] issued in 1989 in response to Turkey's application for full membership lodged in 1987, among other reasons indicated that '[s]ince its third enlargement and the entry into force of the Single Act, the Community ha[d] been in a state of flux. It ha[d] entered into a new stage in its development which, on account of the importance of the objectives at stake, require[d] all its energy' and that the answer to Turkey's application was negative.

Commentary

Turkey started its race with Spain and Portugal, having the advantage of being emancipated politically by the West. It was considered a pivotal country in the Containment Policy. Spain, on the other hand, had been excluded from the post-War political organisation of Europe and the Spanish economy was devastated. Portugal was in only a slightly better position. Yet, Spain and Portugal improved their situation quickly, with the help of some European countries they were soon accepted to the 'democratic European family', and became members of the EEC.

Of these two countries, Spain was the one Turkey focused on. Producing and exporting similar products, Spain was a major trade competitor for Turkey. Both countries went through coups, and the EEC's attitude towards military regimes was shaped by its experiences with these two countries. From Turkey's perspective, the EEC would have problems in terms of absorption capacity in the case of Spanish membership, and this would delay Turkish membership further – a fear that later proved justified. In connection to the Spanish accession process, the Community openly expressed that Turkey's associate membership status did not entail any priorities.

Portugal acted together first with the UK, and then with Spain. It made its application three months prior that of Spain. Turkey did not concentrate on this country much, and saw it as a country which, despite all its problems, managed to become a member of the EEC, and which is still uncomfortable with its EEC membership.

The accession of Spain and Portugal also lead to an enlargement fatigue in the Community, which caused a further delay in Turkey's accession.

Austria, Finland and Sweden

The Turkish Directorate General of Press and Information functioning under the Office of the Prime Minister publishes a detailed chronicle called *Ayın Tarihi* [89] [History of the Month] that goes back to the year 1947. This comprehensive archive does not even mention the accession of Austria, Finland and Sweden to the EU on 1 January 1995. Turkey's interest in the relations of these countries with the EEC/ EU was not comparable to that in Greece, Spain or Portugal. Among these three countries, the Turkish media was more focused on Austria, and the accession of this country was most often mentioned in only one sentence in major Turkish daily newspapers.[90] On 18 July 1989, columnist Metin Toker entitled his column 'A Turkey ignorant of the World, and a Prime Minister ignorant of Turkey'[91] where he wrote '[t]hey talk about a new European house which will extend from the Atlantic to the Urals. Finland, and Norway, Bulgaria and Greece will all be inside that. What about Turkey?' Ironically, even in this column there was no mention of the full membership application of Austria to the EEC lodged only a day prior to its publication. One exception to this ignorance was Sami Kohen's column[92] entitled 'Our rival, Austria' that analysed Austria's application in detail. He pointed to the fact that in Turkey various circles including the government were of the opinion that this application would not have a substantial influence on Turkey's relations with the EEC. However, in his own opinion, such claims[93] as that Turkey lodged its application before Austria, that as a NATO member Turkey was advantageous compared to Austria who was a neutral country, or that Turkey had geostrategic advantages, were irrelevant.

With its economic, social, political and religious characteristics Austria was much closer to the EEC than Turkey was, and once Austria acceded to the EEC, it would become one of the biggest opponents of Turkey at both political and public levels.

Turkey submitted its membership application on 14 April 1987, and the Avis of the Commission as a negative response came on 20 December 1989.[94] Austria lodged its application on 17 July 1989. In 1990, the Foreign Minister of Italy, which held the Presidency of the Council, declared that Austria would be admitted to the Community. The co-chairman of the Turkey–EEC Joint Parliamentary Committee, Bülent Akarcalı reacted fervently to this, and claimed that the content of this declaration was in contradiction with the Avis on Turkey's application.[95] He went on to say that if this commitment was not kept, either the Community was lying to Turkey, or the behaviour of the Italian Foreign Minister was opportunistic. The Turkish government as well as some civilian society organisations also reacted. Soon it became clear that the declaration of the Italian Foreign Minister was not his own formulation but reflected the policy of the Community towards Turkey. When he visited Turkey shortly after his declaration, he noted that Turkey did not have any priority or a vested right, and that Austria was ahead of Turkey for political and economic reasons. He also added that if other EFTA members were to apply for full membership, the EEC would also evaluate their applications.[96] Indeed, Sweden made its application on 1 July 1991, and Finland on 18 March 1992. These two countries, together with Austria became members of the EEC on 1 January 1995.

Commentary

The period between Austria's application for full membership of the EEC in 1989 and its admission in 1995 was short but important for Turkey. Turkey thought it had priority over Austria. The response of the Community to the Turkish application could be negative; Turkey was prepared to hear that, but it was expecting to hear a negative answer to Austria's application too. The developments occurred contrary to this expectation. Austria, together with Sweden and Finland became members in 1995. Austria proved to be one of the Member States that was the most antagonistic towards Turkey's membership.

It seems that neither the government nor the media in Turkey attributed enough importance to the application of Austria to the Community, or followed the events closely. Turkey's efforts did not go beyond reacting to Austria's accession.

The Community, on its part, repeated once again – as it did at the 1976 meeting of the Association Council, in the context of the Spanish application – that Turkey did not have any privileged status emanating from its associate membership, and this time did not even bother with giving any 'consolatory prize' to Turkey as it attempted to do with the Commission's failed proposal in 1978.

The African, Caribbean and Pacific countries

Articles 131 and 136 of the Treaty of Rome foresaw technical and financial aid to some countries that were colonies of some of the Member States at the time of the signing of the Treaty. Accordingly, the European Development Fund (EDF) was established. This fund has since been released at five-year intervals, the first being in 1959, the year Turkey applied for associate membership. Between the years 1959 and 1995, the countries known as the African, Caribbean and Pacific (ACP) countries received 28.437 million EUR with seven regular EDFs.[97] Turkey, on the other hand, received 1.005 million EUR between 1964 and 1995[98] with one financial protocol being vetoed. After 1995, eighth, ninth and tenth EDFs were also concluded regularly,[99] whereas the EU dishonoured some of its commitments in its financial assistance to Turkey in the 1996–1999 period.[100]

Parallel to the Development Fund, the Community concluded a series of agreements with these states: the Yaoundé Convention (1963) signed with 18 African countries was followed by Yaoundé II (1969), Lomé I–IV (1975–1989) and Cotonou (2000). The number of the non-EU parties increased to 79 with the addition of other African, Caribbean and Pacific countries. The content of this scheme improved in time: while at the beginning the main idea was to conclude preferential trade agreements which would ease the access of some African goods to the Community market, with the Cotonou Convention a conditionality dimension was added that aimed at developing such fundamental values as democracy or human rights. In this process, the ACP countries enjoyed favourable terms: between 1975 and 2008 the ACP countries enjoyed non-reciprocal trade preferences awarded by the EU. They also received fixed allocations in the context of EU aid. It is only recently that trade preferences between the ACP countries and the EU have become reciprocal and EU aid has been made provisional on assessment and performance.

Until the end of the 1990s, the relations of the ACP countries with the EU were not followed closely by Turkey. A search in the archives of the three best-selling newspapers in Turkey for the 1993–2003 period does not yield a reference to the Yaoundé, Lomé or Cotonou conventions; one would expect at least a comparison between the rights granted to the ACP countries and to Turkey. This comparison could have demonstrated how similar these two baskets of rights are except for the fact that Turkey has been given a membership perspective. In 1995, a report[101] prepared by a special subcommission within the institutional structure of the SPO allocated only twenty lines to the relations of the EC with the ACP countries. Within these twenty lines there was no mention of the effects of these relations on Turkey. Even Onur Öymen, a retired ambassador and an active MP who is otherwise knowledgeable in Turkey's foreign policy issues, was not very well-versed on the ACP countries at that time. In one of his speeches in the Turkish Parliament in 2003 he said 'the European Union itself lifted or minimised the preconditions over the aid it renders to the so-called Lomé countries of Africa and of some underdeveloped regions. This being so, why is the European Union trying to change this grant aid that has been extended to Turkey without any precondition for so many years to a conditional grant?'[102] However, as indicated above it was not the Lomé but the Cotonou Convention that was in force in 2003, and Article 9 of this convention stipulated that the support of the EU for these countries was conditional on their respect for all human rights and fundamental freedoms, including respect for fundamental social rights, democracy based on the rule of law and transparent and accountable governance.

In the framework of the policy documents 'Opening up to Africa Policy' [sic] and the 'Strategy for Developing Economic Relations with the African Countries' it adopted in 1998 and 2003 respectively, Turkey turned its face to Africa. The year 2005 was a milestone in Turkey's relations with – at least some of – the ACP countries. The Turkish government declared this year 'the Africa Year'. Between 28 February and 7 March that year an official visit was organised to Africa. Ethiopia was at the centre of this visit. The Turkish press criticised this visit, claiming that nothing would be gained from this new opening of the government except the cost of an expensive safari tour and having become closer with an Ethiopia whose total volume of exports is barely 2 billion USD.[103] However, this visit did have an indirect but important effect on Turkey's relations with the EU: immediately after this visit, Turkey secured observer status at the 53-member African Union,[104] and upgraded its status in the context of EU–Turkey relations:

> [w]hen Prime Minister Erdoğan was delivering his speech at the summit of the African Union in Addis Ababa, his Italian counterpart Prodi was in the position of a member of the audience. I believe that the following words of a [Turkish] diplomat who took part in the summit of the African Union are important: 'During the Lebanon talks of the Prime Minister Erdoğan, some European Foreign Ministers approached us and requested information about Lebanon. We replied: "Wait a minute; have not you told us that you would not talk about the foreign policy issues with us in the negotiations?" They, in turn, said that we had misunderstood them.'[105]

Along the same line, with the participation of representatives from fifty African countries a Turkey–Africa Cooperation Summit was held in Istanbul between 18 and 21 August 2008.

Commentary

Since 1959 until recently, the EU has granted several benefits to some ACP countries that are comparable in relative terms to those granted to Turkey. Neither Turkish governments nor the Turkish media has shown a substantial reaction to this situation. Since the end of the 1990s, however, Turkey has been trying to establish closer ties with especially the African group of these countries. This move may have two possible effects on Turkey–EU relations: first, in its relations with African countries the EU may resort to Turkey's mediation and intervention, and secondly Turkey may benefit from the support of the African countries in its relations with the EU and in its actions in various international fora such as the UN.

Morocco, Tunisia, Algeria and Israel

Under present conditions, these four countries of the Mediterranean basin cannot join the EU. On 20 July 1987 – only three months after the Turkish application – Morocco made a landmark application to the EEC that was rejected by the Community on the ground that the country was not located on the European continent. This decision of the Community constituted a precedent for the other three. However, these countries had established close contacts with the EU well before this date, and attained important privileges, especially when compared with Turkey.

The 'Declaration of Intent on the Association of the Independent Countries of the Franc Area with the European Economic Community' which was included in the Final Act of the Treaty of Rome (1957), aspired to maintain and intensify 'the traditional trade flows between the Member States of the EEC and [the independent countries of the Franc Area (Morocco and Tunisia)] and to contribute to the economic and social development of the latter'. In the same Declaration, the Member States expressed 'their real readiness, as soon as this Treaty enter[ed] into force, to propose to these countries the opening of negotiations with a view to concluding conventions for economic association with the Community'. In addition, the 'Protocol on Certain Provisions Relating to France' annexed to the Treaty of Rome allowed France to maintain 'the system of aid to exports and special charges on imports in force in the franc area' which included Morocco and Tunisia (Algeria was not independent then).[106]

Whilst the importance of Turkey started to deteriorate in the eyes of the Community towards the end of the 1960s, thanks to the provisions in the Treaty of Rome, Morocco and Tunisia retained their duty-free access to the French market for most of their exports. At the 10 November 1967 meeting of the Association Council, Turkish Counsel Semih Akbil demurred saying that the EEC treated such countries as Morocco or Tunisia better than it did Turkey, although these countries were not bound to the EEC with an association relationship.[107] At the Association Council meeting held on 13 May 1969, Turkey once again reacted to the favourable status these countries enjoyed.[108] Morocco, Tunisia and Algeria, the so-called Maghreb countries, signed preferential trade agreements with the Community in July 1969 for a period of five years.[109] The same issue came to the table at the 9 December 1969 meeting of the Association Council. At this meeting, Tunisia and Algeria's interests were protected against Turkey, and the Community refused to apply to Turkey the same regime that was being applied to Tunisian and Algerian olive oil, as well as to reduce the customs duties to Turkish citrus exports.[110]

In a study conducted for the SPO in 1970, it was stated that the 3 per cent customs duty on figs exported from Turkey to the EEC that was applied following the request of France had to be abolished, and that Turkish exports of citrus products had to enjoy total exemption since Tunisian citrus exports benefit from an 80 per cent reduction.[111]

The trade agreement the Community signed with Israel dates back to 1964. Turkey was once again unhappy with the fear of losing its relative competitive power. At the 25 May 1970 meeting of the Association Council, the head of the Turkish mission Semih Akbil insisted on a reduction in customs duties the EEC applied to Turkish citrus products that was supposed to be higher than the 40 per cent Israel enjoyed at that time. After intense discussions, Turkey was given a 50 per cent reduction.[112] At the Association Committee and Association Council meetings held in 1969 and 1970, the Netherlands was seen protecting Israel's interests in tobacco.[113]

In 1972, the Community initiated the Global Mediterranean Policy. The first agreement within the framework of this policy was signed with Israel in 1975. This was followed by agreements signed with the Maghreb countries.[114] Turkey was also covered by this policy. However, with these agreements, the concession given to Turkey in 1970 remained below those given to the four countries covered by the present title. Israel was given concessions on 50 extra products.[115] This situation was brought to the negotiation table of the Association Council on 1 March 1976. Depending on a formula that had been previously accepted by the Community itself,[116] Turkey requested that this difference be eliminated. However, the Community refrained from taking a decisive step, and declared that Turkey was not a privileged country any more and the principle of automatic elimination of differences was no longer valid.[117] The claim that the privileges given to the agricultural products of the Mediterranean countries weakened the competitive power of Turkish agricultural products was evidenced by a report prepared by a joint committee of experts from the EEC and Turkey.[118] A similar discussion occurred at the 20 December meeting of the Association Council, and Turkey was given the same rate of customs reduction conceded to Israel.[119] This meant the end of the 10 per cent advantage Turkey had attained at the 25 May 1970 meeting. Despite the 15 meetings focusing on this point, Turkey could not get a favourable result.[120] In this period, Algeria received 65–75 per cent tariff cuts in the agriculture and textile sectors.[121]

In 1981 and 1986, the cooperation agreements and financial protocols with the Maghreb countries were renewed for another period of five years, with a net increase in the Commission grants and loans. In the following years, further initiatives favourable to the Maghreb countries and Israel were taken. In 1982, the Commission proposed that a new Mediterranean Policy be determined so that the relations with the Mediterranean countries could develop, excess production of olive oil, wine and citrus products in these countries could be prevented, and product variety could be increased. The Mediterranean Policy of 1990 brought new support mechanisms in several fields extending from environment to small and medium enterprises. At the Barcelona Conference held in November 1995, a decision was taken to establish a Euro-Mediterranean Free Trade Area by 2010. Tunisia and Morocco signed their association agreements in 1995. Algeria's association agreement was signed in 2002.

As mentioned above, Turkey received 1.005 million EUR with three financial protocols between the years 1964 and 1995. In this period, Morocco received 1091 million EUR, Tunisia 742 million EUR, Algeria 854 million EUR, and Israel 215 million EUR.[122]

Israel has always maintained close relations with the EU. The Cooperation Agreement it signed with the EEC in 1975 was replaced by an association agreement. Because of its relatively high national income per capita, Israel does not qualify for MEDA funds. However, it benefits from the youth and culture programmes under the MEDA project. On the road to establishment of the Euro-Mediterranean Free Trade Area, the EU and Israel made important mutual reductions in customs tariffs.[123] Israel declared its intention to become member of such European institutions as the European Space Agency, European Environment Agency and Europol. Although Israel is frequently criticised by the EU due to continuing settlement-building and the blockade of the Gaza Strip, there do exist high-ranking politicians in the EU who favour a higher status for Israel than association. The President of the European Parliament Hans-Gert Poettering called for Israel to be given a 'privileged partnership' status by the European Union. Gert Weisskirchen, foreign affairs spokesman for the Social Democrats, said that he would very much like Israel to be a full member of the EU.[124] Considering the fact that Nicolas Sarkozy and Angela Merkel have been trying to downgrade Turkey's EU bid to privileged partnership status,[125] it would not be an exaggeration to say that Israel's position and chances towards the EU are not much less favourable than those of Turkey except for the fact that Turkey has had a candidacy status since 1999. Besides the fact that Israel is not located in Europe, the place of religion in the governance of the state, and the continuous regional political turmoil Israel is involved in seem to be obstacles to its membership of the Union. Future developments in all these three issues may have curious references to Turkey's case since a large portion of Turkey is also not located in Europe, a substantial majority of its population is Muslim, and terrorism afflicts the south eastern part of the country, besides its neighbourhood with war-torn Iraq.

Commentary

The close relations of the EU with Morocco, Tunisia, Algeria and Israel are thanks to the patronising of these countries by certain EU members. These four countries have acquired most of the gains given to Turkey (such as customs tariff reductions) except an official full membership perspective. The financial assistance they have received is comparable to that of Turkey. While these countries attained several concessions effortlessly, in some cases Turkey struggled to get comparable benefits during 15 meetings and still faced a rebuff. It would not be surprising if Israel comes very close to full membership status in the future.

The fifth enlargement

With a lengthy title, an 'Act Concerning the Conditions of Accession of the Czech Republic, the Republic of Estonia, the Republic of Cyprus, the Republic of Latvia, the Republic of Lithuania, the Republic of Hungary, the Republic of Malta, the Republic of Poland, the Republic of Slovenia and the Slovak Republic and the Adjustments to the Treaties on which the European Union is Founded'[126] was signed on 16 April 2003 and came into force on 1 May 2004. The acts of accession of Bulgaria and Romania,[127] on the other hand, were signed on 25 April 2005 and came into force on 1 January 2007. These twelve countries had made their applications for full membership between the years 1990 and 1996.

Central and Eastern European countries

The countries of the fifth enlargement wave, with the exception of Cyprus and Malta, were Central and Eastern European Countries (CEECs). The accession of these countries to the EU increased the total population of the Union by one third whereas the gross domestic product of the Union increased only by 4 per cent. Thus, it may be worthwhile to examine the intentions of the Union in admitting these countries.

After the collapse of the Eastern bloc, the Union focused on of Central and Eastern Europe. The probable reason behind this was to ensure stability, security and wealth in this region that had always been regarded as a part of European family. The importance the Member States attributed to each of the CEECs would vary in accordance with the intensity of the relations they had with these countries. The Member States who had close relations with certain CEECs were Finland, Germany, Austria, Greece and to some extent Italy.[128]

The Community was relatively late in formulating an elaborate strategy towards the CEECs. At the June 1993 Copenhagen Summit, membership of the CEECs was set as a target and the so-called Copenhagen criteria were determined for their admission. At the Essen Summit of December 1994, a pre-accession strategy for the CEECs was formulated. This strategy would be based on four initiatives: first, with the bilateral Europe agreements political and economic cooperation would be improved between these countries and the EU. Secondly, by publishing a list of the legal instruments regulating the internal market of the EU as well as a White Paper on the Single Market aspects of enlargement, the EU would provide guidance to these states. Thirdly, with the PHARE programme set up in 1990 these countries would receive financial and technical aid.[129] Fourthly, with the so-called Structured Dialogue a multilateral negotiation platform would be provided to these countries, which was believed to produce better results than bilateral negotiations. This strategy remained at work until the year 2000, but was criticised for being of rather technical nature and based on ad hoc solutions.[130] To counter these criticisms, the so-called Agenda 2000 document was prepared by the Commission in 1997, and accepted at the Berlin Summit in March 1999. With this document, a new strategy aiming at more substantial and longer term outcomes was formulated, and to support the PHARE programme ISPA and SAPARD programmes were initiated. These programmes included aids for environment, agriculture and transportation. Further agricultural assistance and structural funds were also extended to these countries.

With this strong support and determination of the Union, the Central and Eastern European Countries completed their accession process quickly. As early as 1997, in the Agenda 2000 document, the Commission advocated opening negotiations with some of the CEECs. The accession process of a group of CEECs actually began in 1998, and that of the others in 2000. Finally, the Czech Republic, Estonia, Hungary, Latvia, Lithuania, Malta, Poland, Slovakia and Slovenia became members in 2004, and Romania and Bulgaria in 2007.

Turkey, on the other hand, was pushed aside. By not including Turkey in the list of candidate countries in the Presidency Conclusions of the 1997 Luxembourg Council and not mentioning Turkey's candidacy in the Agenda 2000 document, the Union created a contrast between its attitude towards the CEECs and Turkey. Upon a request formulated at the Luxembourg Summit, the Commission prepared a document called 'A European Strategy for Turkey'.[131] The document contained some recommendations for Turkey on the way towards membership without giving any prospect of financial assistance. This generated profound mass indignation in Turkey and the Turkish government declared that Turkey maintained the aim of full membership of the EU and that continuation of the relations with the EU would be conditional on the EU's change of mentality. It was also announced that Turkey would not attend the European Conference to be held on 12 March 1998.

Among the Turkish public, the dominant impression was that the enlargement of the EU to the CEECs was based on an element of 'kinship-based duty'[132] which was absent in the case of Turkey. Upon this exclusion and rebuff, the Turkish government turned its attention towards Central Asia. In May 1998, an official visit was organised to this region. In China, Deputy Prime Minister Ecevit said '[f]or Turkey, the world does not consist only of Europe. Turkey has entered into a process of rediscovering its roots in Asia'.[133] When Ecevit became the Prime Minister, he resumed the close contacts with China. In April 2002, the Chinese Prime Minister came to Turkey and four agreements were concluded between the two countries, on agricultural co-operation, customs co-operation, international information technologies and automotive technologies. However, this opening, seen as perfect and promising by the Turkish media[134] in those days, could not provide a substantial and permanent alternative to the EU.

Turkey's candidacy status was finally approved at the December 1999 Helsinki Summit. Turkey took part at the December 2000 Nice Summit. In appearance, Turkey's invitation to this Summit meant that Turkey was not discriminated from the other candidates. However, at the Summit the institutional restructuring schemes were prepared for a 27-member Union, again ignoring Turkey.

Turkey ran into a similar situation at the December 2001 Laeken Summit. At this Summit the Union divided the candidate countries into two groups. The first group consisted of ten countries with which the Union was planning to conclude accession negotiations by the end of the year 2002. The second group contained two countries which would start their accession talks in 2002. Turkey was in neither of these groups. The Presidency Conclusions of the Summit mentioned Turkey in a small paragraph indicating that Turkey had made progress and that there was hope for the start of accession negotiations. However, there was no timetable. From then on, the EU's double standards became a frequently pronounced issue,[135] and Turkey based its strategy upon getting a date for the start of accession negotiations. The Turkish Prime Minister and the Foreign Minister had bilateral talks with the heads of state and of government of several EU Members from Greece to France as well as with the President of the European Parliament.[136] However, these talks did not lead to any concrete results. When it became obvious at the Copenhagen Summit of 12 December 2002 that Turkey would not be given a date, Turkish President Sezer decided not to go to Copenhagen. Prime Minister Erdoğan said that the Turkish people would rethink about the EU, and the EU would have to bear the results. He recalled the fact that the twelve countries in question were admitted to the EU although they had not fulfilled the Copenhagen criteria in full, whereas Turkey was the only country that was not given a date. He drew attention to one million Russians living in Lithuania and six million Roma living in the CEECs, and added that although these groups experience difficulties in their respective countries, Turkey was the only country that was criticised on the ground of minorities.[137]

Turkey was able to get a date for the start of the accession negotiations only at the Brussels Summit held on 16–17 December 2004: the negotiations would start on 3 October 2005. Meanwhile, the last two of the twelve countries, Bulgaria and Romania acceded to the EU on 25 April 2005.

Commentary

The EU seems to have done its best to make the membership of the CEECs possible. With the necessary financial, political and technical support of the Union, these countries became EU members relatively quickly and easily. The Turks thought that the CEECs were favoured by the EU as kin. Yet, it is also likely that thanks to this fifth enlargement, the discrimination Turkey had been subjected to became more pronounced than ever, which in turn mobilised Turkish politicians and the public to react and which contributed to the EU's approval of Turkey's candidacy in 1999 as a means of redress. In this process, Turkey on its part saw that it did not have many options other than the EU.

Cyprus

The history of Cyprus and its accession process to the EU have always been of interest to Turkey and a part of the rivalry between Greece and Turkey. The Republic of Cyprus was established in 1960, Turkey, Greece and the UK being its guarantor states. Government posts and public offices were allocated by ethnic quotas. As Cypriot Turks were in a minority they were given 30 per cent of the seats in the parliament and administration, as well as a permanent veto right. In 1963, inter-communal violence broke out on the island. Although the first ten years of the Republic were turbulent, neither the Cypriot government nor the guarantor states carried these initial problems to the EEC context. It would have especially been to the benefit of Turkey to bring this turmoil to the attention of the EEC in the 1960s, when Greece was in a relatively disadvantaged position with the coming into power of the Colonels' Junta in 1967 or with the country's withdrawal from the Council of Europe in 1968.

In 1971, on behalf of the Republic of Cyprus, the Greek Cypriots lodged an application to the EEC for associate membership. It was only then that Turkey brought the Cyprus issue to the EEC's agenda: with the advice and support of Turkey, Turkish Cypriots prepared a letter protesting the application, and this letter was transmitted to the Commission by the Permanent Representation of Turkey to the EEC. The main theme of the letter was that the application of Cyprus had been made without the consent of the Turkish Cypriots. Yet, the association agreement between Cyprus and the EEC was signed on 19 December 1972 and entered into force on 1 June 1973. To placate the fears of Turkish Cypriots and Turkey, a provision was included in the Agreement that stipulated that there would be no discrimination in practice, and the European Commissioner for External Relations and Trade Dahrendorf had a calming talk with the leader of the Turkish Cypriots Denktaş over the issue.[138]

In 1974, the Cypriot President and Archbishop Makarios III was deposed by a military coup which was led by Greek officers of the Cyprus National Guard and backed by the Junta in Greece. Taking this event and the ethnic violence into consideration, Turkey staged two consecutive military interventions in the same year. The EEC did not show any reaction to the first intervention started on 20 July 1974, whereas for the second one started on 13 August 1974 a condemnation came from the EEC on 22 November 1974, mainly due to the return of Greece to democracy between the two interventions and its success in arguing its case at the EU. Turkey has retained a permanent military presence in Cyprus since then, which has attracted international criticism.

The 1972 association agreement of Cyprus foresaw two stages. The first stage would be based on reduction of import duties by the Community for Cypriot industrial products and a number of agricultural products. The Community would also abolish the quotas on certain Cypriot products. Cyprus, on the other hand, would progressively reduce the duties on a number of EEC imports and could prefer to retain – but not increase – existing quantitative restrictions. This first stage was supposed to be completed on 30 June 1977. However, especially due to the turbulence on the island, this stage was prolonged with successive extensions and a protocol regarding the transition to the second stage could only be signed on 19 October 1987. The second stage would aim at completion of a customs union and itself would be composed of two phases. The first phase would cover the 1988–1997 period. The second phase would end in 2002 or 2003 depending on the decision of the EC–Cyprus Association Council. On 4 July 1990, the Republic of Cyprus submitted an application for membership of the EEC. The European Commission issued a favourable opinion, and the accession negotiations started on 31 March 1998. With the start of the negotiations, the second phase of the customs union was considered unnecessary. Meanwhile, in 1983 Turkish Cypriots established an independent republic they called the Turkish Republic of Northern Cyprus (TRNC) which received diplomatic recognition only by Turkey.

The Republic of Cyprus received considerable financial support from the Community. Between 1978 and 1999, Cyprus and the EEC signed four protocols on financial and technical cooperation providing for financial aid amounting to 210 million EUR. This aid included loans, grants, special loans and contributions to risk capital formation. On the other hand, Turkey – which is 86 times larger and 67 times more populated[139] than Cyprus – received only 1.005 million EUR between 1964 and 1995 mainly via three financial protocols. As indicated above, a fourth financial protocol that envisaged an aid package of 600 million EUR was initialled between Turkey and the EEC in 1981, but was not concluded because of the coup in Turkey as well as the veto of Greece.

The Turkish application for full membership of the EEC on 14 April 1987 gave Greece a chance to bring the Cyprus issue to the EU's agenda. Until the announcement of the Opinion of the Commission on 20 December 1989[140] on Turkey's application, on several occasions Greece declared that Turkey's accession to the EEC would be subject to the approval of Greece and this approval was conditional on the solution of the Cyprus problem.[141] The Opinion itself contained the following paragraph:

> [e]xamination of the political aspects of the accession of Turkey would be incomplete if it did not consider the negative effects of the dispute between Turkey and one Member State of the Community [Greece], and also the situation in Cyprus, on which the European Council has just expressed its concern once again. At issue are the unity, independence, sovereignty and territorial integrity of Cyprus, in accordance with the relevant resolutions of the United Nations.

The Presidency Conclusions of the 25–26 June 1990 Dublin Summit included a 'Declaration on Cyprus' which stated that the issue of Cyprus affected EC–Turkey relations. Turkey reacted to this and declared that this declaration meant that the EC had left its constructive role in the Cyprus problem and become a party to it by sharing the responsibility of the sustenance of it together with Greece and Greek Cypriots.[142] It is meaningful that the Greek Cypriot Community lodged its application for full membership on 4 July 1990, only a few days after the Dublin Summit.

In 1994, Greece succeeded in carrying the case of the TRNC to the European Court of Justice. With the Anastasiou decision,[143] the Court stated that only goods bearing certificates of origin from the Government of Cyprus could be recognised for trade by EU member countries. Mainly due to this decision, TRNC exports to the EU decreased from 36.4 million USD (or 66.7 per cent of total Turkish Cypriot exports) in 1993 to 24.7 million USD (or 35 per cent of total exports) in 1996.[144]

In the meantime, the USA made a historical move inspired by the aspirations of Turkey and Cyprus for EU membership in an attempt to please these two countries and at the same time to solve the Cyprus problem. Mainly with the efforts of the Assistant Secretary of State for European and Canadian Affairs Richard Holbrooke, Greece agreed to lift its veto before the signing of the Customs Union decision between Turkey in return for a promise made by the EU: on 6 March 1995, the General Affairs Council declared that the accession negotiations of Cyprus would start six months after the upcoming intergovernmental conference (launched at the Turin European Council in 1996 and ending with the Treaty of Amsterdam in 1997). It is striking that the EC–Turkey Association Council met in Brussels again on 6 March 1995 and agreed on the completion of the Customs

Union.[145] Thereby, the advantageous position of Cyprus over Turkey was once again confirmed when, unlike Turkey, it was invited to the 1997 Luxembourg Summit. The accession negotiations of Cyprus commenced in March 1998. At the December 2002 Copenhagen Summit, while the Union confirmed that the Cyprus Republic would become member of the EU, Turkey was not even given a date for the start of accession negotiations. A month before the Summit, the UN offered the so-called Annan Plan for the solution of the Cyprus problem. The Plan was based the idea of a unified Republic of Cyprus. Had the Plan been accepted, the island would have acceded to the EU as a whole. However, with the two referenda held separately in the Turkish Cypriot and Greek Cypriot communities of the island on 24 April 2004, the Plan was accepted by the Turks but rejected by the Greeks. In the interim, the EU did not even wait for the referenda, and the treaty of accession of Cyprus to the European Union was signed on 16 April 2003.

Commentary

Rather than being a rival on its own for Turkey, Cyprus has been an integral element of Greece's policy towards Turkey. By using its de facto and de jure dominance over the island, Greece used Cyprus against Turkey, and made Cyprus's membership of the EU possible. Several times, Greece declared that Turkey's accession to the EEC would be conditional on the solution of the Cyprus problem.

The EU became involved in the Cyprus issue in 1971 when Cyprus applied for associate membership. Despite the reluctance of the Cypriot Turks and Turkey, the EU–Cyprus association agreement was signed the following year. Notwithstanding its diminutive size and population, the island received substantial financial support from the EEC comparable to the amount that Turkey received in the same period. At the 1997 Luxembourg and 2002 Copenhagen Summits, Cyprus proceeded towards full membership step by step while Turkey was kept aside. With the Anastasiou decision the EU market was closed off to Turkish Cypriot exports.

Turkey, on its part, missed the opportunity to bring the conflict on the island to the attention of the EEC at the end of the 1960s when the Colonels' Junta came to power and Greece left the Council of Europe. The two military interventions of Turkey in 1974, Turkey's subsequent military presence and the declaration of independence by the TRNC were moves that weakened Turkey's position. The positive attitude of Turkish Cypriots in the referendum held for the Annan Plan did not bring concrete results as treaty of accession of Cyprus to the EU had already been signed.

Future enlargements

The countries to be included in the future enlargement waves have been divided into two groups by the EU. Those in the 'Candidate Countries' group are Croatia, Former Yugoslav Republic of Macedonia (FYROM) and Turkey, whereas the group of 'Potential Countries' includes Albania, Bosnia and Herzegovina, Montenegro, Serbia, Kosovo and Iceland.[146]

Among these countries Croatia gradually closed the gap between itself and Turkey on the way to EU membership. It applied for full membership in 2003, sixteen years after Turkey did so. Yet, its candidacy status was approved in 2004, only five years after Turkey's. Paragraph 23 of the Presidency Conclusions of the Brussels European Council (16–17 December 2004)[147] stipulated that 'accession negotiations with individual candidate States [would] be based on a framework for negotiations' and that each framework would address certain elements according to 'the specific situations and characteristics of each candidate state'. This paragraph was a token of the – official and overt – ending of the EU's equal treatment of the candidate states during negotiations, and, as such, was important; the 'rivalry' between candidates would now be traceable in the official texts of the EU. The Negotiating Framework Documents (NFDs) of Croatia[148] and Turkey[149] were the first ones prepared. Croatia's negotiations started in October 2005, at the same time as those of Turkey. Croatia has not only caught up Turkey, but is likely to go ahead of it: '[n]egotiations with Croatia may be concluded within a few years; those with Turkey are expected to take considerably longer'.[150] Germany as a Member State and the Christian Democrats in the European Parliament show strong support for Croatia:

> Bernd Posselt MEP, Shadow Rapporteur on Croatia for the EPP-ED Group [indicated that] 'the Parliament should take the final decision on Croatia before the next European Parliament Elections of June 2009, so that the ratification process in the Member States can start as soon as possible'.[151]

Turkey has always followed Croatia's relations with the EU, and established connections between them and its own relations with the Union. It claimed that its own NFD included heavier terms compared with those of Croatia. In response, Turkey was reminded of Paragraph 23. The accession negotiations of Croatia were supposed to start in March 2005 on the condition that Croatia continued to cooperate fully with the International Criminal Tribunal for the Former Yugoslavia (ICTY). In March, the EU postponed the start of negotiations because the ICTY prosecution assessed the Croatian efforts to capture the fugitive general Ante Gotovina as being neither timely nor sufficient. Only when the Spanish Police finally arrested Gotovina with the help of the Spanish and Croatian government in December 2005 could the negotiations start. This postponement in March 'created shock waves in Turkey, with media comments saying it was a message that accession talks with Turkey could also face the same fate later [that] year if EU criteria [were] not fully met'.[152] However, the head of the Commission's delegation to Turkey, Hansjoerg Kretschmer reassured Turkey that the cases of Turkey and Croatia were not linked and Ankara's accession talks would commence as scheduled.[153]

On 9 July 2009, the EU justice commissioner declared that the European Commission proposed to allow citizens of Montenegro, Serbia and FYROM to travel to the EU without visas from 1 January 2010.[154] Later on, the EU's permanent representatives to the EU Council proposed that the visa regime be abolished as of 19 December 2009 instead of 1 January 2010.[155] This led to reactions in the Turkish media. One of the dependable news agencies in Turkey claimed[156] that the EU favoured these countries against Turkey, and drew attention to the fact that Romanian and Bulgarian citizens had been enjoying visa-free travel to the EU since 2000, long before their accession in 2007. However, there was a small error in the commentary: in fact Bulgaria had been removed from the EU visa list in April 2001 and Romania in January 2002. The commentary went on to draw attention to the fact that while keeping Turkey in the visa list, the Union was in breach of the decisions[157] of the European Court of Justice which entail abolition of the visa requirement for Turkish citizens.

Commentary

The present focus of the EU seems to be on the Western Balkans. The creation of the NFD system just before the commencement of the negotiations of Croatia and Turkey makes it possible for us now to see the different treatment of Turkey and its rivals.

It is very probable that Croatia will accede to the EU well before Turkey does. The other countries of the Western Balkans have been given a membership perspective and some of them have already been promised such benefits as visa-free travel in the EU. Turkey reacted to this process with over-sensitivity. In this emotional state, the Turkish media developed the delusion that the problems in the accession process of Croatia would have a negative effect on that of Turkey, and some respectable news agencies misrepresented some historical facts such as the date of the removal of Romania and Bulgaria from the EU's visa regime. This reaction of the Turkish media may be attributed to the continuous frustration of having been discriminated against in every enlargement wave so far, and the 'here we go again' feeling.

Conclusion

Turkey's rivals have had a substantial impact on EU–Turkey relations. In many historic cases, Turkey made its moves by taking its rivals very much into consideration. For instance, in Turkey's application for associate membership in 1959, Greece played an important role, whereas for the full membership application in 1987, the accessions of Spain and Portuguese were among triggering factors. Sometimes Turkey focused too much on its rivals (as was the situation with Greece) and this distracted its attention from the EU. Turkey thought that the early date of its application for associate membership would give it seniority over the others and thus it would have some privileges. However, in the cases of Morocco, Spain and Austria for instance, Turkey was explicitly told that it did not have any such privileges. After the December 2001 Laeken Summit, Turkey adopted a strategy of getting a date for the start of negotiations, emphasising that the EU was applying double standards to Turkey and to the twelve candidate countries of the time. Turkish politicians and the Turkish media closely followed the accession of Greece, Spain and Portugal. However, they were relatively ignorant, negligent, erroneous or alarmist especially in the case of later rivals of Turkey; major news agencies, newspapers or authors skipped the accession of Austria, Finland and Sweden, exaggerated the EU's sanctions to Croatia, misrepresented Turkey's concerted actions with Greece, or gave wrong dates for the free trade agreements of the EEC with Morocco and Tunisia, whereas even some prominent politicians were not proficient in such details as the Yaoundé, Lomé or Cotonou conventions.

The EU initially pursued an equality strategy for Turkey and its principal rival Greece. It even considered the option of slowing down the negotiations with Greece until Turkey caught up with Greece. However, this strategy lasted only a few months, and since then, it has prioritised Turkey's rivals over Turkey in most cases. Sometimes the EU bluntly refused to keep its promises to Turkey. For example, in 1976 it said that its promise of automatic elimination of the differences between the customs duties applied to products originating from Turkey and those coming from the 77 countries covered by the Generalised Preference System was no longer valid. While the ACP countries benefited from the regular series of EDFs, in the 1996–1999 period the EU reduced the amount of financial assistance to Turkey, which it had unilaterally promised to make available. On several occasions, Turkey was also told that it did not have a special status emanating from its associate membership. Sometimes, the EU's different treatments of Turkey and Turkey's rivals gave rise to accusations of double standards. The present transparency brought about by NFDs may prevent allegations of inequality if not unfairness.

Within the EU, some Member States have favoured Turkey's rivals. For example, for France, Maghreb countries were important, whereas the Netherlands patronised Israel. Certain circles like the Christian Democrats also protected the interests of such countries as Croatia.

Finally, Turkey's rivals in most cases regarded their competition with Turkey as a zero-sum game. The only exception to this has been the short honeymoon period with Greece at the end of the 1950s. The present course of events with African countries may also lead to a concerted action with them and Turkey. After its accession to the EU, Spain has become a role model and also a supporter of Turkey.

All these details evidence that during the past 50 years, Turkey–EU relations have not occurred in a vacuum where the performances of Turkey and the EU were the only determinants; among many other factors outlined in this volume, the protracted nature of Turkey–EU relations is due also partly to the issues related to Turkey's rivals. Unfortunately, most of the time the developments related to its rivals had a negative impact on Turkey's relations with the EU, due to its own mistakes, to its rivals' deleterious moves, as well as to the EU's predilection for Turkey's rivals.

Notes

1 See for example Z. Öniş, 'An awkward partnership: Turkey's relations with the European Union in comparative-historical perspective', *Journal of European Integration History*, 2001, vol. 7, no. 1, pp. 105–120.

2 M. A. Birand, *Türkiye'nin Ortak Pazar Macerası*, İstanbul: Milliyet Yayınları, 1990, p. 71.

3 See for instance G. Cıvaoğlu, 'Boş havuz söylemi', *Milliyet*, 22 September 2005. This hearsay is still travelling through the grapevine and evolving: '... if it jumps into a pool filled with serpents ...'. See: E. Yaşar, 'Kömür Birliği'nden Avrupa devletine (2)', *Akşam*, 15 December 1999.

4 İ. Ertuğrul, 'Yazarımız Oğuz Gökmen, tarihi bir gerçeği açıklıyor: Avrupa macerasını...', *Türkiye,* 24 October 2004.

5 Ş. Çalış, 'Formative years: A key for understanding Turkey's membership policy towards the EU', *Perceptions: Journal of International Affairs*, 2004, vol. IX, no. 3, p. 80. For a discussion on Turkey's Westernisation see also the chapter by C. Rumford and H. Turunç in this volume.

6 İ. Tekeli and S. İlkin, *Türkiye ve Avrupa Topluluğu: Ulus Devleti Aşma Çabasındaki Avrupa'ya Türkiye'nin Yaklaşımı – Vol. I*, Ankara: Ümit Yayıncılık, 1993, p. 125.

7 Ö. Çınar, 'Altılarla Müşareket Mevzuunda Tevellut Etmiş ve Edebilecek Meseleler Üzerine Yunan Hükümetiyle Atina'da Yapılmış Olan Görüşmeler Hakkında Rapor' cit. in Tekeli and İlkin, op. cit., pp. 140–142.

8 H. Saim, 'Türkiye ile her mevzuda mutabakata varılmıştır', *Zafer*, 2 July 1959. For Cahan's visit see also 'Organization for European Economic Cooperation', *International Organization*, vol. 12, No. 3 Summer, 1958, 408–415, p. 414.

9 Not to be confused with the European Free Trade Association (EFTA) to be established in 1960. For details, see J. Ellison, *Threatening Europe: Britain and the Creation of the European Community, 1955–1958*, Basingstoke: Palgrave Macmillan, 2000, pp. 151–198.

10 Tekeli and İlkin, op. cit., p. 125.

11 'Müşterek Pazar için NATO'ya başvurduk', *Akşam*, 20 July 1959. See also 'Avrupa Pazarı – Henüz müracaat etmediğimiz Pazar hakkında yayımlanan asılsız haber', *Zafer*, 31 July 1959.

12 T. Saraçoğlu, *Türkiye-Avrupa Ekonomik Topluluğu Ortaklığı*, İstanbul: Akbank Yayınları, 1992, p. 4. Thirty years later in 1990, Turkey would follow the footsteps of Spain this time, and approach EFTA once again. Since a merger between EEC and EFTA was seen as likely in those days, EFTA was thought to be a stepping-stone for Turkey to the EEC. Turkey signed a free trade agreement with EFTA countries in 1991. N. Akad, 'AT'ye EFTA üzerinden yürümek', *Güneş*, 7 February 1990. For the text of the agreement, see: EFTA 'Agreement between the EFTA states and Turkey'. Online. Available http://www.efta.int/~/media/Documents/legal-texts/free-trade-relations/turkey/Free%20Trade%20Agreement%20EFTA-Turkey.ashx (accessed 5 December 2009).

13 The association agreements of Turkey and Greece respectively.

14 Birand, op. cit. p. 111, my translation.

15 NSC 6015/1. Source: United States Department of State / Foreign relations of the United States, 1958–1960. Eastern Europe; Finland; Greece; Turkey, vol. X, Part 2 (1958–1960), p. 891.

16 For an overview of Turkey's economy in the context of EU–Turkey relations, see the chapter by T. F. Nas in this volume.

17 My translation.

18 Birand, pp. 97–102. For an evaluation of the place of the army in Turkish politics see the chapter by P. Bilgin in this volume.

19 OJ (1963) L 293/63.

20 For de Gaulle, Greece was a small country under the imminent threat of Communism, whereas Turkey did not need support. De Gaulle also believed that because of its pro-American policies, Turkey did not deserve Europe's assistance. Besides, he would see Turkey as a rival for France in some agricultural products such as tobacco and figs (Birand, op. cit., pp. 149–152).

21 Z. Atikkan, 'Saraçoğlu', *Hürriyet*, 25 March 1999, my translation.

22 Several member states shared this opinion of Mansholt. See P. Coffey, *The External Economic Relations of the EEC*, London: Macmillan, 1976, p.18.

23 Saraçoğlu, op. cit., p. 16.

24 Ibid., p. 51.

25 OJ (1973) C 113/2.

26 For a detailed comparison of the two agreements, see ibid. pp. 55–125.

27 Art. 3.

28 Birand, pp. 193–194.

29 This situation continued until 1974. For details, see European Commission, 'Opinion on Greek application for full membership', COM (76) 30 final, 5.

30 R. Clogg, *A Short History of Modern Greece*, London: Cambridge University Press, 1985, p. 193.

31 R. Karluk, *Avrupa Birliği ve Türkiye*, İstanbul: İstanbul Menkul Kıymetler Borsası, 1996, p. 407.

32 Birand, op. cit. p. 210.

33 İ. Tekeli and S. İlkin, *Türkiye ve Avrupa Topluluğu: Ulus Devleti Aşma Çabasındaki Avrupa'ya Türkiye'nin Yaklaşımı – Vol. II*, Ankara: Ümit Yayıncılık, 1993b, p. 48, also see pp. 66 and 73.

34 Ibid., p. 76.

35 Ibid., p. 88.

36 Ibid., p. 91.

37 Ibid., p. 104.

38 Ibid., p. 26.

39 Birand, op. cit., pp. 306–307.

40 Tekeli and İlkin, 1993b, p. 121. Also see pp. 122–123.

41 M. A. Birand, 'AET'den konserve için kolaylık istedik', *Milliyet*, 1 March 1973, my translation.

42 Turkey encountered a mild and tolerant attitude from the USA at first. Turkish forces took control of almost 40 per cent of the island. After Greece left the military wing of NATO as a protest, the USA changed its approach to the Cyprus crisis, and imposed an embargo on military aid and the supply of arms to Turkey in February 1975.

43 C. Tsardanidis 'The European Community and the Cyprus problem since 1974', *Journal of Political and Military Sociology*, 1988, vol. 16, pp. 155–171 and 167.

44 Tekeli and İlkin, 1993b, p. 239.

45 Tekeli and İlkin, 1993b, p. 202.

46 For a summary of the discussions in the media in that period see Tekeli and İlkin, 1993b, p. 243.

47 Uluengin claims that in 1975 and 1979 Turkey was promised that Greece would not use its veto power. H. Uluengin 'AET ile yeni sorun', *Cumhuriyet*, 29 January 1986.

48 For example Y. Doğan, 'Geceyarısı muhteşem teklif' *Hürriyet*, 3 January 2004.

49 For example H. Uyar 'Ecevit'in 1978'de AET Üyeliğini Reddettiği İddiası, Avrupa Yolunda Kaçırılan Fırsatlar', *Toplumsal Tarih*, no. 132, December 2004.

50 EurActiv (2007) 'AB çelişkili uygulamaları gidermeli'. Online. Available http://www.euractiv.com.tr/yazici-sayfasi/interview/ab-celiskili-uygulamalari-gidermeli (accessed 7 June 2009). See also H. Uluengin, 'Hangi fırsat kaçmadı ki?', *Hürriyet*, 4 June 2002.

51 Tekeli and İlkin, 1993b, pp. 221–234.

52 OJ (1979) L 291, pp. 179–191.

53 Birand, op. cit., pp. 403–404.
54 İ. Ertuğrul, op. cit. Interestingly, Art. 21 of the Ankara Agreement and Art. 64 of the Athens Agreement indeed seem to include such provisions that could have been referred to the effect Gökmen had in mind.
55 S. Ergin, 'Şimdi bana kaybolan yıllarımı verseler', *Hürriyet*, 31 December 2004.
56 H. Cemal, 'Kayıp yıllar ve AB farkı', *Milliyet*, 6 January 2005.
57 H. Cemal, 'Cumhuriyet ile AB', *Milliyet*, 29 October 2005.
58 'İspanya Türkiye'nin AET'ye tam üyeliğini destekleyecek', *Cumhuriyet*, 29 January 1986.
59 S. Kohen, 'Terörden barışa geçiş', *Milliyet*, 24 March 2006; E. Şafak, 'Sahi hazır mısınız?', 25 March 2006; and A. Özçer 'Eve dönüşe İspanya modeli', *Yeni Şafak*, 19 August 2009.
60 G. Benmayor, 'Nuh Çimento'nun Tarragona ortaklığı neler getirecek?', *Hürriyet*, 9 November 2004.
61 'Kar Avrupa'yı gördü, 'yaya kalmışız' dedi', *Milliyet-Ege*, 7 May 2006.
62 D. Sipahi, 'İspanya almış başını gitmiş, bizde ise siyasi bir argüman', *Milliyet*, 9 August 2006.
63 D. Sipahi, 'Tarımsal kooperatifçilikte İspanya modeli bize de örnek', *Milliyet-Ege*, 21 August 2009.
64 A. Yıldız, 'KOBİ'ler çalışanlarını bireysel üyesi yapıyor', *Hürriyet*, 16 July 2005.
65 E. Demirtaş, 'Barselona'da mucizeyi gördük', *Milliyet-Ege*, 16 February 2006.
66 M. Yılmaz, 'Türkler için İspanya dersleri', *Milliyet*, 16 March 2004 and S. İdiz, 'Yahudi vatansever, niçin Genelkurmay Başkanı olmasın?', *Milliyet*, 7 August 2006.
67 A. Özçer, 'Anayasa'ya İspanya modeli', *Yeni Şafak*, 20 December 2007.
68 For instance, Turkey followed the example of Spain who approached EFTA before the EU. See footnote 12.
69 Open Society Institute AF – Turkey, *Spanish Trajectory: A Source of Inspiration for Turkey*, İstanbul, 2008.
70 For an example see S. Kohen, 'Sabır ve sebat', *Milliyet*, 18 September 2003.
71 Y. Keskin, *Avrupa Yollarında Türkiye*, Ankara: Bilgi Yayınevi, 2001, p. 344.
72 M. Soysal, 'AT'nin arpası', *Milliyet*, 27 December 1988.
73 B. Avar, Sınırlar arasında: Portekiz'in AB serüveni [TV Documentary], *TRT-1*, 26 February 2007.
74 Although Portugal is a similar to Turkey in many respects, this coverage of this country in Turkish press is minimal except in the context of football.
75 Tekeli and İlkin, 1993b, p. 86.
76 OJ No L 182, 16.8.1970.
77 OJ No L 301, 31.12.1972.
78 Tekeli and İlkin, 1993b, p. 91.
79 Birand, 1990, p. 362.
80 Tekeli and İlkin, 1993b, p. 230.
81 Tekeli and İlkin, 1993b, p. 154.
82 Tekeli and İlkin, 2000, p. 42.
83 This failed coup, also known as '23-F', was attempted with 200 soldiers. The soldiers held the Parliament and cabinet hostage for 18 hours, but surrendered the next morning.
84 This was the third coup in Turkey. The Turkish armed forces would rule the country for the next three years.
85 Tekeli and İlkin, 2000, pp. 50–51.
86 Birand, 1990, p. 442. Also see, p. 452, my translation.
87 Birand, 1990, p. 468.
88 European Commission, 1989.
89 The Turkish Directorate General of Press and Information, Ayın Tarihi. Online. Available http://www.byegm.gov.tr

90 For example, see 'Avusturya AT'a başvurdu', *Milliyet*, 18 July 1989.
91 M. Toker 'Dünyadan habersiz bir Türkiye ve Türkiye'den habersiz bir Başbakan', *Milliyet*, 18 July 1989, my translation.
92 S. Kohen, 'Rakibimiz Avusturya', *Milliyet*, 19 July 1989.
93 Here, Kohen probably refers to the arguments put forward by Ali Bozer who was the Deputy Prime Minister at that time. See Tekeli and İlkin, 2000, p. 138.
94 European Commission 'Commission's Opinion on Turkey's Request for Accession to the Community' SEC(89) 22/90 final/2, 20 December 1989.
95 Tekeli and İlkin, 2000, pp. 216–217. Article 4 of the Avis contained the following passage: '[I]t would be unwise, with regard both to the candidate countries and to the Member States, to envisage the Community becoming involved in new accession negotiations before 1993 at the earliest, except in exceptional circumstances.' European Commission, 1989.
96 Tekeli and İlkin, 2000, p. 217.
97 European Commission, *Report on arrangements and possibilities for budgetizing the European Development Fund, 6 June 1994, Brussels SEC(94) Final*, p. 20.
98 Dış Ticaret Müsteşarlığı (2010) 'Turkey–EU Financial Co-operation'. Online. Available http://www.dtm.gov.tr/dtmweb/yaziciDostu.cfm?dokuman=pdf&action=d etayrk&yayinid=456&icerikid=560 (accessed 10 February 2010).
99 European Commission 'European Development Fund'. Online. Available http://europa.eu/legislation_summaries/development/overseas_countries_territories/r12102_en.htm (accessed 24 December 2009).
100 Dış Ticaret Müsteşarlığı, loc. cit.
101 Devlet Planlama Teşkilatı, *Dünyada Küreselleşme ve Bölgesel Entegrasyonlar (AT, NAFTA, Pasifik) ve Türkiye (AT, EFTA, KEİ, Türk Cumhuriyetleri, EKİT (ECO), İslam Ülkeleri) İlişkileri Özel İhtisas Komisyonu: Türkiye ve Avrupa Entegrasyonu Alt Komisyonu Raporu*, 1995, Ankara, p. 48. The name of the subcommission is strange – it can be translated as 'The Turkey and European Integration Subcommittee of the Special Expertise Committee on the Relations of Globalisation in the World and Regional Integrations (EC, NAFTA and Pacific) and Turkey (EC, EFTA, BSEC, Turkish Republics, ECO and Islamic countries)'. Within the text of the report, the grammatical mistake in the title of the twenty-line section on the ACP countries is also an indication of a lack of care.
102 O. Öymen, 'Türkiye Cumhuriyeti Hükümeti ile Avrupa Birliği Komisyonu Arasında Merkezî Finans ve İhale Biriminin Kurulması ile Ulusal Fonun Kurulmasına İlişkin Mutabakat Zabıtlarının Onaylanmasının Uygun Bulunduğu Hakkında Kanun Tasarısı ile Plan ve Bütçe ve Dışişleri Komisyonları raporlarının görüşülmesinde CHP grubu adına yapılan konuşma,' *TBMM Tutanak Dergisi*, vol. 4, no. 29. Session date, 30 January 2003, my translation.
103 'Safarisiz Afrika yılı', *Sabah*, 28 March 2005. For different comments, see: G. Şimşek, 'Afrika için geç kalmayın', *Sabah*, 15 January 2005; and Y. Doğan 'Hatt-ı Üstüva'ya seyahat', *Hürriyet*, 7 April 2005.
104 N. Elibol, 'Afrika'nın merkezine yolculuk', *Türkiye*, 28 January 2007.
105 M. Ocaktan, 'Afrika Birliği Türkiye'nin neyi oluyor?', *Yeni Şafak*, 31 January 2007, my translation.
106 J. Damis, 'Morocco's 1995 Association Agreement with the European Union', *The Journal of North African Studies*, vol. 3, no. 4, 1998, pp. 91–112, 92. Damis' quotations from the Treaty bears minor differences from the official text.
107 Birand, 1990, p. 223.
108 Tekeli and İlkin, 1993b, p. 78.
109 MEDEA 'Euro-Mediterranean Co-operation'. Online. Available http://www.medea.be/index.html?doc=1097 (accessed 23 May 2009).
110 Tekeli and İlkin, op. cit., pp. 85–86.
111 Ibid., p. 89.

44　*Armağan Emre Çakır*

112　Ibid., 1993b, p. 91.
113　Saraçoğlu, op. cit., p. 134.
114　MEDEA, ibid. (accessed 20 May 2008).
115　Tekeli and İlkin, 1993b, p. 192.
116　With the Generalized System of Preferences which the Community put into force on 1 July 1971, customs duties applicable to exports from less developed 77 countries were abolished or reduced. Turkey requested the same concession. However, the Community refused this request. Instead, the differences between the Additional Protocol and this System would be eliminated by individual decisions to be taken every year (Birand, 1990, pp. 308–310).
117　Birand, 1990, pp. 358–365. Tekeli and İlkin (1993b, pp. 199–200) assert that no such event took place.
118　Tekeli and İlkin, 1993b, p. 200.
119　Tekeli and İlkin, 1993b, p. 209.
120　Birand, 1990, p. 342.
121　N. Eren, 'Turkey, NATO and Europe: A deteriorating relationship?' *Atlantic Papers*, no. 34. The Atlantic Institute for International Affairs, 1977.
122　Compiled from European Investment Bank, *Annual Report*, 1978, p. 12; 1988, p. 63; and 1990, p. 44; and Commission of the European Communities, *XXVth General Report on the Activities of the European Communities* 1991, p. 284.
123　European Commission (2007) 'Israel'. Online. Available http://ec.europa.eu/comm/ external_relations/israel/intro/index.htm (accessed 2 May 2009).
124　EUbusiness (2009) 'German politician says Israel could join EU in 15 years'. Online. Available http://www.eubusiness.com/news-EU/1244116022.14/ (accessed 4 October 2009).
125　Ş. Kardaş, 'Merkel and Sarkozy Call for Privileged Partnership Angers Turkey,' *Eurasia Daily Monitor*, 2009, vol: 6, no: 92. Online. Available http://www.jamestown. org/single/?no_cache=1&tx_ttnews%5Btt_news%5D=34983 (accessed 3 January 2010).
126　OJ No L 236, 23.9.2003.
127　OJ No L 157, 21.6.2005.
128　Summarized from H. Grabbe and K. Hughes, *Enlarging the EU Eastwards*, London: The Royal Institute of International Affairs, 1991.
129　Later on Phare was enlarged to include Albania, Bosnia and Herzegovina and the Former Republic of Macedonia (FYROM).
130　Grabbe and Hughes, 1998, pp. 31–40.
131　European Commission, 'European Strategy for Turkey: The Commission's Initial Operational Proposals', Communication from the Commission to the Council, COM (98) 124 final, 4 March 1998.
132　For the concept, see H. Sjursen, 'Why expand? The question of legitimacy and justification in the EU's enlargement policy,' *Journal of Common Market Studies*, vol. 40, no. 3, 2002, pp. 491–513.
133　'Türkiye'ye Türkistan uyarısı', *Radikal*, 2 June 1998, my translation.
134　'Çin'le dört dörtlük temas', *Radikal*, 17 April 2002.
135　See for example, S. A. Düzgit, *Seeking Kant in the EU's relations with Turkey*, İstanbul: TESEV, 2006.
136　'Kopenhag'da soluk kesen diplomasi', *Hürriyet*, 12 December 2002.
137　Ü. Turan and T. Yılmaz, 'AB'ye çifte rest', *Hürriyet*, 10 December 2002.
138　Birand, 1993, pp. 294–295.
139　1975 census figures.
140　European Commission, 1989.
141　Birand, 1993, pp. 459–461.
142　Tekeli and İlkin, 2000, pp. 215–216.

143 C-432/92. In this case, the Greek Cypriots acting on behalf of the Republic of Cyprus complained about the UK who had accepted the certificates of origin issued by the TRNC for the imports from TRNC. For details, see S. Talmon, 'The Cyprus question before the European Court of Justice,' *European Journal of International Law*, 2001, vol. 2, no. 4, pp. 727–750.

144 US Department of State, 'Cyprus'. Online. Available http://www.state.gov/outofdate/ bgn/c/19449.htm (accessed 4 June 2009).

145 The veracity of this rather behind--closed-doors deal is ascertained by E. H. Prodromou ('Reintegrating Cyprus: The Need for a New Approach,' *Survival,* vol. 40. No. 3, 1998, pp. 5–24), R. Holbrooke himself (*To End a War*, New York: The Modern Library, 1999, p. 61) as well as the author's interview on 15 April 2010 with T. Miller (former ambassador to Greece).

146 European Commission 'Enlargement'. Online. Available http://ec.europa.eu/ enlargement/index_en.htm (accessed 10 November 2009).

147 Council of the European Union, *Brussels European Council, 16/17 December 2004, Presidency Conclusions*, Brussels, 1 February 2005, 16238/1/04REV 1.

148 Online. Available http://ec.europa.eu/enlargement/pdf/st20004_05_hr_framedoc_ en.pdf (accessed 20 December 2009).

149 Online. Available http://ec.europa.eu/enlargement/pdf/st20002_05_tr_framedoc_ en.pdf (accessed 20 December 2009).

150 European Commission 'Enlargement'. Online. Available http://europa.eu/pol/enlarg/ index_en.htm (accessed 25 November 2009).

151 European Parliament (2008) 'Strong support for Croatian EU membership'. Online. Available http://www.eppgroup.eu/press/showpr.asp?PRControlDocTypeID=1&PRC ontrolID=7104&PRContentID=12416&PRContentLG=en (accessed 10 September 2009)

152 'No need to panic over Croatia decision', *Turkish Daily News*, 18 March 2005.

153 EurActiv (2005) 'EU reassures Ankara that Croatia and Turkey are not linked'. Online. Available http://www.euractiv.com/en/enlargement/eu-reassures-ankara- croatia-Turkey-linked/article-136936 (accessed 10 September 2009).

154 EurActiv (2009) 'Serbia, Macedonia and Montenegro to break visa barrier'. Online. Available http://www.euractiv.com/en/enlargement/serbia-macedonia-montenegro- break-visa-barrier/article-183950 (accessed 1 August 2009).

155 Barlovac, B. (2009) 'Balkan visa free regime may start earlier'. Online. Available http://www.balkaninsight.com/en/main/news/23471/ (accessed 4 December 2009).

156 Anadolu Ajansı (2009) 'AB'den Balkan Ülkelerine Vize Muafiyeti'. Online. Available http://www.aa.com.tr/tr/abden-balkan-ulkelerine-vize-muafiyeti.html (accessed 8 August 2009).

157 The commentary seems to be referring mainly to the Soysal case (C-228/06) in which the ECJ ruled that it was inadmissible to impose a visa requirement on Turkish nationals entering the territory of a Member State with a view to providing services there on behalf of an undertaking established in Turkey.

3 Economic dimension

The Turkish economy from the 1960s to EU accession[1]

Tevfik F. Nas

Introduction

With its ongoing economic transformation spanning nearly half a century, Turkey has managed to stay on a high-growth path in spite of recurring financial crises and political instability, and in recent years, particularly the period following the 2002 parliamentary elections, its economic growth rate has accelerated, boosted by positive developments with respect to its full membership prospects in the European Union. While challenges remain in view of the global financial crisis and the economic slowdown that started in December 2007, the Turkish economy is still vibrant and poised for new restructuring initiatives to further accelerate the modernisation process. Was the prospect of full integration with the EU the driving force of Turkey's ongoing economic transformation and growth since the early 1960s? Has the gap between the Turkish economy and the economies of the European Union narrowed as envisioned by the Ankara Agreement? Or, more specifically, is the state of the Turkish economy still an issue for the EU in comparison to the time when Turkey had not yet been recognised as a candidate state?

In formulating a response, this chapter begins with a background and a brief summary of the continuing membership negotiations between Turkey and the EU, followed by an examination of the main economic developments since the early 1960s. The first part of the chapter describes the economic imbalances of the 1970s and highlights the primary changes in macro-economic policy making as well as the critical stabilisation and economic restructuring of the 1980s. It was during the 1980s that economic and financial restructuring intensified, and it has continued to date with the introduction of key political and economic reforms in the hope of modernising the Turkish economy. Through privatisation and public-sector reforms, government policies have focused on aligning Turkey to the forces of an open market economy and promoting long-run growth through trade and financial-sector liberalisation and increased efficiency in both public and private sectors. The focus of the chapter then shifts to some of the major economic reforms and financial events of the 1990s and beyond, a period in which Turkey stepped up its post-1980 restructuring, while opening its economy and simultaneously dealing with its internal economic and political complexities. The remainder of the chapter examines the principal aspects and economic impact of the customs union with the EU and highlights the main economic developments and restructuring during the period leading up to and following the 2002 parliamentary elections. And finally, the chapter provides a concluding commentary on Turkey's full membership prospects in the EU.

The path to joining the EU

During the 1960s, the prevailing economic and policy environment in Turkey was typical of predominantly import substitution and inward-looking industrialisation. By fostering infant industries under protectionism and through a series of five-year development plans, the policymakers in those years hoped to be able to attain high economic growth, self-sufficiency in development finance, and the needed capital accumulation to further import-substitution industrialisation. Following a strategy of allowing for the prospect of Turkey joining the European Union, which at the time was called the European Economic Community (EEC), the policy making also aimed at increasing the production capacity of intermediate and capital goods for the purpose of energising industries in which Turkey had a comparative advantage.[2] In the 1960s, economic integration between Turkey and the Community was conceivable and seemed to make sense: Turkey, a semi-industrialised economy that was potentially complementary to the industrialised member nations of the Community, was capable of competing in the production of some industrial goods, such as clothing and textiles, and increasing its market share in several traditional agricultural commodities. The proportion of Turkish trade with Europe was higher than with other trading partners and regions of the world, and moreover, economic integration with the Community was expected to generate dynamic effects that included the impact of a larger common market on efficiency through economies of scale, external economies, and a more competitive market structure.[3]

The process of economic association between the EEC and Turkey began with the Ankara Agreement, signed in 1963.[4] The agreement included clauses to establish 'ever closer bonds' between Turkey and the Community, to ensure improved standards of living through economic progress and expansion of trade, and to narrow the gap between the Turkish economy and the economies of the member states of the Community. To that end, and in compliance with the Additional Protocol, which was signed in 1970, and became effective in 1973, a transitional stage of 22 years was allowed for Turkey to gradually eliminate its tariff protection and enter the customs union with the EEC. During the transitional period, Turkey was also expected to take the necessary steps for the unification of policies in preparation for the prospect of full membership.

Beginning in 1971, the Community abolished tariffs and all quantitative restrictions on Turkey's manufactured goods and granted preferential customs duties on the majority of Turkish agricultural exports to the Community. Turkey, in return, agreed to adopt the common external tariff against third-country imports and gradually reduce trade restrictions on industrial products from the

Community. The removal of trade restrictions by the Community (completed in 1973) excluded textiles and clothing, and the Association Council decided in 1980 to completely remove restrictions on agricultural imports by 1987. There were some rough spots along the way, however. One key provision of the Ankara Agreement, the free movement of workers, which was expected to begin in 1986, did not materialise. After abolishing tariffs on imports from the Community in 1973 and 1978, Turkey also put its forthcoming prescheduled tariff rate reductions on hold. However, the process did resume in 1988, one year after Turkey applied for full membership.[5] Responding unenthusiastically to the full membership application, the Community showed interest in intensifying relations on the basis of existing agreements and accordingly introduced a comprehensive package to improve relations with Turkey, which ultimately led to the formation of a customs union. The formation of the customs union allowed for the adoption of the EU's commercial policy toward third countries, harmonisation of agricultural policy, implementation of intellectual property rights, and elimination of all quantitative, non-quantitative, and technical barriers to trade between Turkey and the Union.[6]

The customs union agreement, which went into effect in 1996, did not slow Turkey's drive for full membership. The government continued to lobby for support among the member states of the EU and managed to secure a confirmation of its eligibility for accession to the EU during the Union's 1997 enlargement summit in Luxembourg, but with a caveat.[7] The summit did confirm Turkey's eligibility but it also spelled out that the political and economic conditions necessary for starting accession negotiations had not been satisfied and noted that Turkey's status with the EU depended on the successful implementation of political and economic reforms.[8]

During the late 1990s, Turkey's prospective membership had become a lesser priority for the EU. With the emphasis of EU enlargement gradually shifting toward Eastern Europe, the EU was prepared to welcome any justification or initiative to put Turkey on hold while keeping its European perspective alive. Turkey had no choice but to stay the course; it determinedly took the necessary steps for the introduction of the needed reforms and began to lobby intensely to improve its status. Subsequently, in the 1999 Helsinki Summit, the EU upgraded Turkey's status from eligibility to candidacy for full membership and this was followed by the 2002 Copenhagen decision that granted a conditional date of December 2004 to start accession negotiations, with the expectation that Turkey would fulfil the Copenhagen criteria.[9]

The Copenhagen decision was an improvement, because it once again reconfirmed Turkey's candidacy for full membership and came somewhat closer to setting a date for the commencement of accession negotiations. In contrast to the Luxembourg Summit, the sentiment of the member states in Copenhagen was also positive and more responsive to Turkish demands for full membership. Thus, motivated by the Helsinki and Copenhagen decisions, Turkey continued to introduce the needed economic and political reforms, and in December 2004 in Brussels, based on the recommendation of the Commission in charge of the enlargement, the EU Council agreed to start the negotiation talks on October 3, 2005.[10]

An important section of the recommendation document was the framework for negotiations. Even though it was noted that the design of the framework took into account the experience of the fifth enlargement, which included three Baltic nations, five Central and Eastern European applicant states, Cyprus, and Malta, it appeared that it was tailored to Turkey's unique position. The framework clearly stated that, given the financial and institutional impact of Turkey's potential accession and the complexity of a negotiation process that would involve all member states, an early Turkish membership was out of the question. It seemed unlikely that the EU would conclude the negotiations before 2014, since the EU was still in the process of negotiating its budget for 2007–2013.[11] Also, in contrast to earlier enlargements, the possibility of including permanent safeguard clauses was stated in the Brussels Presidency Conclusions, specifically because of a high probability of increased migration of Turkish workers. In the case of the last enlargement, there was a transition period of seven years for new member states, during which time free movement of workers was constrained. But given the demographic profile of Turkey, the framework not only allowed for the possibility of permanent safeguards but also provided for a maximum role in the decision-making process 'regarding the eventual establishment of freedom of movement of persons' to individual states that might be most affected.

The framework also highlighted the fact that the negotiations were open-ended, a statement that was not stressed in previous rounds of enlargements. The open-ended nature of the negotiations was specifically included in the framework to allow for possible alternatives to accession, and on the insistence of some member states, if it becomes necessary, the need to fully anchor the Candidate State (the reference is to Turkey) to the European structures was added.

The negotiation framework underwent further revisions during the EU foreign ministers' meeting in Luxembourg in June 2005, when it became clear that some EU member states were yet to abandon the idea of privileged partnership status as an alternative to full admission. Hoping to change the nature of the integration process, they insisted on including a provision in the accession framework that would allow for the prospect of privileged partnership, which Turkey strongly opposed. During the EU foreign ministers' meeting, there was also debate over whether Turkish entry into the EU should be reassessed, not only in terms of the Copenhagen criteria but also on the basis of the EU's absorption capacity, an added condition that was not applied to previous enlargements.

In the final version of the document, drafted after painstaking negotiations and deliberations on alternative scenarios, reference to privileged partnership was dropped, but the condition of absorption capacity remained. The paragraph that was the source of the controversy was ultimately worded as follows: 'As agreed at the European Council in December 2004, these negotiations are based on Article 49 of the Treaty on European Union. The shared objective of the negotiations is accession. These negotiations are an open-ended process, the outcome of which cannot be guaranteed beforehand. While having full regard to all Copenhagen criteria, including the absorption capacity of the Union, if Turkey is not in a position to assume in full all the obligations of membership it must be ensured that Turkey is fully anchored in the European structures through the strongest possible bond.'[12]

Even though the added provisions appeared to be potential setbacks capable of delaying or diminishing the prospect of full membership, the wording of the document excluded those possibilities at least in the intermediate term. The final draft was unusually restrictive, but acceptable. Leaving behind the uncertainty surrounding its membership status, Turkey was anxious to move forward, with heightened confidence and determination in an environment where it could continue to institutionalise its reforms and deepen its legal, political, and economic restructuring.

Economic change and restructuring

Inward-looking industrialisation, which started during the protectionist years of the 1930s and evolved through the planning decades of the 1960s and the 1970s, had become the driving force of Turkish economic growth. During this period, the Turkish state advocated heavy industrialisation and strategically increased its presence in the domestic economy through the formation of state economic enterprises, producing a wide range of production and consumption goods, both public and private. The state also reaffirmed itself as the driving force of industrialisation, encouraging and supporting the formation of private capital in key sectors and at the same time securing domestic markets for the emerging infant industries. This form of industrialisation, which was also embraced by a large number of newly independent nations, continued throughout the 1970s, and despite occasional shortages of imported inputs and moderate foreign-exchange availability, it enabled Turkey to remain on a high-growth path and perform exceptionally well (see Figure 3.1). However, towards the end of the 1970s, increased dependence on imported inputs created foreign-exchange shortages; that, combined with serious imbalances resulting from the external shocks, led to a significant decline in the growth rate of output, an increase in inflation, and the debt crisis of the late 1970s. Consequently, in view of changing economic and financial conditions both at home and abroad, Turkey's 40-year-old, state-led industrialisation was no longer sustainable. Major revisions in Turkey's development and growth strategy had to be made, and that led to the dramatic change in macro-economic policy making as well as the stabilisation and economic restructuring of the 1980s.

The new macro-economic policy making consisted of both short- and long-term objectives that would stabilise the economy and build the foundation of an outward-looking free-market economy. As an immediate measure, a sharp devaluation of the Turkish lira accompanied by steep price adjustments for state enterprise products was enacted to lessen the widespread shortages of essential goods. To lower inflation, tight monetary and fiscal policies were implemented and in addition to these urgent measures, which were intended to have a shock effect on the economy, foreign-exchange restrictions were also gradually relaxed. As a result of all of these critical stabilisation policies – plus several direct and

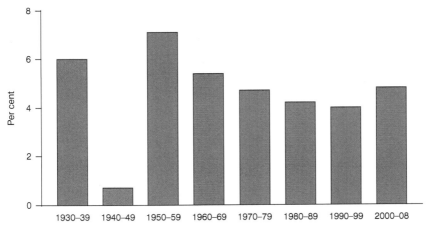

Figure 3.1 GDP growth rates, 1930–2008, Turkey
(Data from Nas, *Tracing the Economic Transformation of Turkey*; IMF, World Economic Outlook Database, April 2009)

indirect incentives for export promotion and gradual liberalisation of import and export regimes – external balance goals were achieved and the economy settled on a sustainable growth path that was mainly fuelled by improved export performance. Exports were significantly higher than in the pre-1980 years, having been helped by successive devaluations, and most importantly, the normalisation of Turkey's creditworthiness eased some of the financial restraints.

The outcome of this decade-long stabilisation and liberalisation period was not entirely favourable, however: unemployment and inflation continued, and the level of private-sector investment remained far below expectations despite signs of a substantial increase in industrial production toward the end of the 1980s. Opening the economy to capital account movements in 1989 also led to increased capital flows, in and out of the economy, that at times became disruptive and were accompanied by costly adjustments, prompted by defaults, bank failures, and speculative attacks. The inflow of external capital depended on the expected value of the domestic currency and real interest rates, and attempts to lower interest rates during the early 1990s triggered speculative attacks on the domestic currency and contributed to the unfavourable financial environment that led to the crisis of 1994.[13]

The destabilising effects of the 1994 financial crisis, which erupted after several failed stabilisation attempts, were extensive. By the end of 1994, the growth rate of real GDP turned negative with a substantial drop of 5.5 per cent, and the year-end inflation rate surged to 119.2 per cent (see Table 3.1). Although the growth rate improved in the next year, reaching an impressive 7.2 per cent, reducing the inflation rate remained the top priority despite the anticipated drop that was sought in the austerity plan that was introduced in April 1994.

In the years that followed, the economy grew more vulnerable to future crises; exposure to the volatility of the financial markets continued, and twice during that period the financial system in Turkey proved it was not immune to such speculative

Table 3.1 Selected macroeconomic indicators, 1990–2008

	GDP growth rate	Inflation rate	Percentage of GDP			
			Budget deficit	Domestic debt	Current account	External debt
1990	9.3	50.0	−2.5	10.8	−1.3	26.1
1991	0.9	73.3	−4.0	11.5	−0.1	26.7
1992	6.0	65.4	−3.2	13.2	−0.5	27.8
1993	8.0	69.8	−5.0	13.4	−3.2	29.6
1994	−5.5	119.2	−2.9	15.4	0.3	38.8
1995	7.2	76.2	−3.0	13.0	−2.4	33.6
1996	7.0	80.1	−6.3	15.9	−1.0	32.6
1997	7.5	99.0	−5.8	16.2	−1.0	33.2
1998	3.1	69.6	−5.4	16.5	0.8	35.6
1999	−3.4	68.8	−8.7	21.9	−0.4	41.7
2000	6.8	39.0	−8.0	21.9	−3.7	44.7
2001	−5.7	68.5	−12.1	50.9	1.9	57.7
2002	6.2	29.7	−11.4	42.8	−0.3	56.2
2003	5.3	18.4	−8.8	42.7	−2.5	47.3
2004	9.4	9.3	−5.4	40.2	−3.7	41.2
2005	8.4	7.7	−1.3	37.7	−4.6	35.3
2006	6.9	9.6	−0.8	33.2	−6.0	39.4
2007	4.7	8.4	−1.7	30.3	−5.8	38.4
2008	0.9	10.1	−1.9	28.9	−5.7	37.4

Sources: IMF, World Economic Outlook Database, April 2009; Undersecreteriat of Treasury, *Treasury Statistical Yearbook.*

attacks. One of these occurrences was the November 2000 liquidity crisis that emerged while the 1999 disinflation programme was being implemented. This specific programme, supported by the December 1999 standby agreement with the International Monetary Fund (IMF), emphasised the structural reforms needed to make the fiscal adjustment sustainable, improve economic efficiency, and accelerate the privatisation of state economic enterprises. Both the restructuring efforts and the exchange-rate-based monetary policy that were proposed in the programme were expected to lower interest rates and reduce inflationary expectations. But due to external factors, such as higher oil prices and rising interest rates on emerging market debt, and internal factors, such as delays in privatisation and restructuring, as well as increased domestic aggregate demand resulting from rapidly declining interest rates, the economy's vital indicators deteriorated. An ongoing corruption investigation in the banking sector and an overvalued Turkish lira also led to heightened speculation of devaluation, and thus short covering of foreign currency positions.[14]

The liquidity crisis that ensued was quickly contained through Central Bank intervention. Financial markets also responded favourably to the news of improved Turkish–EU relations and additional financial support from the IMF.[15] However, as the economy was set to recover from the distress of the November 2000 crisis, a second financial crisis and a major revision of the 1999 disinflation programme followed two months later.[16] Turkey unexpectedly abandoned the crawling peg exchange-rate system in favour of a floating exchange-rate system, and with a strengthened new version of the 1999 disinflation programme, the role of monetary policy was changed to pursuing disinflation by relying on the monetary base rather than the exchange rate as an anchor. The programme also re-emphasised restructuring and adopting tight fiscal policy to restore stability in goods and financial markets and thus achieve sustainable growth. Within a few months the vital statistics improved significantly. And with renewed interest in furthering the full membership bid with the EU, the Turkish government, both before and after the 2002 parliamentary elections, switched focus and stepped up the restructuring efforts and reform process.

Some of the various reforms that were front-loaded during that period included legislative acts to phase out state-supported purchase programmes and price-support mechanisms, increase the pace of the privatisation programme, and reduce monopolistic practices.[17] Among other legislative acts, the public procurement law was introduced in order to set technical and financial criteria for contractors in line with EU standards and to establish an independent agency to enforce the new standards. The new law on public finance and debt mandated that the Treasury, as the single borrowing authority, was to be endowed with the responsibilities of formulating public debt strategy, assessing risk, and coordinating the management of domestic and foreign-debt portfolios.[18]

Most of these expeditiously introduced measures were old initiatives, but because of political constraints, complications stemming from the political fragmentation, and the resulting coalition governments that dominated the 1990s, they were not finalised. But after being hit by a series of economic and financial crises, many of these structural reforms had to be implemented in response to conditions set by the IMF as part of standby agreements. So they were hastily introduced and approved by the Turkish Parliament before the November 2002 parliamentary elections. With these important legislative acts, Turkey took an important step in not only modernising its economy and bringing it closer to its European contemporaries but also paving the way to an economic and policy environment where the state gradually began to withdraw from basic industries that should have traditionally been attended to by the private sector and it took the necessary steps to return to its primary public functions.[19]

During the post-2002 election period, measures to further strengthen the private sector, and at the same time enhance efficiency and facilitate the effective functioning of the public sector through administrative reforms, also took priority. In addition to specific legislation and regulations in the areas of information and communication technologies, energy, and transportation, various further reforms were introduced to decentralise the economy, attain a public- and private-sector output mix that was congruent with a contemporary market economy, and achieve overall efficiency in resource allocation. Most of these measures were specifically introduced to eventually downsize the state sector, make the Turkish economy less vulnerable to internal and external shocks, and improve the internal dynamics of the economy to make Turkey more compatible with the EU nations that it hoped to join in the future.

The administrative reforms involved far-reaching measures to increase the effectiveness of the public sector. These included (a) a constitutional amendment to ensure conformance with the Public Financial Management and Control Law that was amended and had gone into effect in 2006, (b) a budget accounting and reporting system to comply with international standards and strengthen fiscal transparency, (c) local administrative reforms to improve financial and managerial efficiency, and (d) the creation of an ombudsman who represents the interests of the public in the inspection and investigation of complaints against the administration.[20]

To comply with EU regulations and international standards, numerous steps were also taken in the banking and insurance sectors. An insurance bill was introduced to develop an insurance market and to establish provisions to facilitate an effectively functioning insurance sector. With the Banks Law that went into effect in 2005, additional guidelines and standards were introduced to enhance the legal and institutional framework to increase supervision and auditing in the sector. The main objective of the law was 'to regulate the principles and procedures of ensuring confidence and stability in financial markets, the efficient functioning of the credit system and the protection of the rights and interests of depositors'.[21] Another priority of the law, in addition to making the sector more reliable, transparent, and stable, was to ensure its compliance with EU banking standards and facilitate its integration with the international financial system. Thus, as a result of extensive restructuring during the period 2001–2003, the banking system in Turkey has become more 'resilient and sound'. Most of the requirements to align Turkey's banking system to the EU were fulfilled and a significant percentage of the costs that would have resulted from the convergence to the EU banking system have already been incurred.[22]

By the end of 2006, Turkey appeared to have made significant progress in its reforms.[23] As noted by the European Commission, '[a]s regards economic criteria, Turkey can be regarded as a functioning market economy, as long as it firmly maintains its recent stabilisation and reform achievements. Turkey should also be able to cope with competitive pressure and market forces within the Union in the medium term, provided that it firmly maintains its stabilisation policy and takes further decisive steps towards structural reforms'.[24] The report from the IMF, however, was much more upbeat on Turkey's accomplishments. As the IMF March 9, 2007 mission statement concluded: 'Opportunities for the Turkish economy are enormous. The goal should be to build on the economic success of the last five years to firmly entrench high growth, secure low inflation, and make the economy more flexible and resilient to external shocks. Continued disciplined fiscal and monetary policies complemented by bold structural reforms are essential to lift

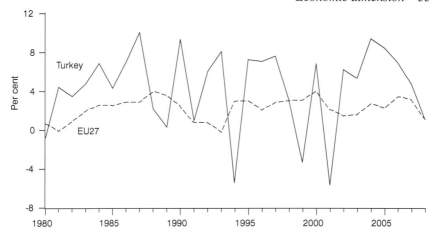

Figure 3.2 Real GDP growth rates, 1980–2008, Turkey and EU 27
(Data from IMF, World Economic Outlook Database, April 2009)

Turkey onto a significantly higher growth trajectory. The agenda is large and some reforms could face resistance, but the rewards in terms of sustained improvements in living standards would make the effort well worthwhile.'[25]

At the time of writing, Turkey's economic transformation appears to be on track and irreversible, despite concerns with respect to external balances, rising unemployment, and the negative impact of the ongoing worldwide recession on economic growth. Excluding the 2007–2009 period, economic growth, specifically during the post-2001 crisis (with an annual average growth rate of 7.2 per cent in 2002–2006), has been robust and unmatched by any sub-period during the post-1980s (see Figure 3.2). The only comparable sub-period is the 1983–1986 politically stable period, when the Turkish economy grew by an annual average of 5.7 per cent. The average annual rate of economic growth during the post-1994 crisis, including the years 1995–1999, was 4.3 per cent. Obviously, an economy is likely to exhibit improved performance in a politically stable environment, as was the case during the post-2002 general election period. High economic growth was attained and far-reaching reforms that dramatically changed Turkey's economic structure were implemented. But even some of the most overdue reforms that set the tone for further restructuring and developed the foundation of an economic renovation were initiated, with important legislation passing through the parliamentary process before the 2002 general election. Thereafter, the restructuring efforts took a much more dynamic and definite turn, not only to comply with the IMF conditions but also to bring Turkey closer to its EU destination.[26]

Factors underlying Turkey's economic transformation

Would Turkey have experienced the latest growth cycle that began after the 2001 crisis had EU membership not been a possibility? In responding to this question, one should acknowledge that Turkey's drive for modernisation had its roots in the early years of the Republic, building Turkey's industrial base with a unique partnership between the state and the private sector upon which an industrialised outward-looking economic structure developed. In retrospect, despite the limited supply of productive resources, particularly during the early years of the Republic, and the shock waves of the worldwide depression that followed, the outcome of both the relatively liberal period of the 1920s and the protectionist years of the 1930s was impressive. The value of GDP nearly tripled in two decades, labour productivity increased significantly, and the structure of the economy changed slightly in favour of industry.[27]

The adoption of protectionist measures, induced by the worldwide depression of 1929–1933, and the state-led inward-looking strategy that followed were also well timed. The strategy not only provided the needed capital accumulation to further the import-substitution industrialisation, which was the driving force behind the growth strategy, but it also promoted a unique state–private sector partnership that lasted more than four decades. And it is from that foundation that today's internationally competitive, highly productive private sector emerged.

The impact of the neoliberal policies of the 1980s should also be recognised. When state-led industrialisation was no longer sustainable, in the late 1970s and at a time when policies were being redesigned for increased liberalisation and privatisation across the developed and emerging economies, Turkey also chose to undo its state-dominated economic structure by implementing the neoliberal growth and development policies. With this 'stabilise, liberalise, and privatise' agenda Turkey was able to recover from the debt crisis of the late 1970s with improved statistics, garnering the support of international financial institutions. Even though there currently seems to be agreement among theoreticians and practitioners that in most cases the neoliberal framework failed to produce its intended results, in retrospect it was one factor that changed Turkey's economic profile, but it did so at a substantial cost: frequent financial crises, chronic inflation, and deteriorating income distribution.[28] What is remarkable, however, is that the Turkish economy, after two decades of experimentation with neoliberal policies, reached a level of development that could at least withstand the rigorous EU reconditioning.

Turkey's more than five-decade-old drive for modernisation, the unique state–private sector partnership that was behind it, and the restructuring process that followed the neoliberal policies of the 1980s clearly offer some explanation for Turkey's economic transformation. Yet, the impact of the EU, particularly of the customs union, on the Turkish economy, and the accelerated pace at which recent reforms were introduced as a result of an improved prospect of future EU membership are also significant and should be noted.

The customs union had already deepened the economic integration with the EU, positively impacting Turkey's economic growth. Based on the recent international trade data, it appears that the customs union with Europe had a positive impact on Turkey's trade volume and broadened its diversification, both in exports and imports. During the three-year period before and after 1996, total exports as a

Table 3.2 Annual total exports and imports, 1993–2008

	Total exports			Total imports		
	Billion $	*% of GDP*	*EU share*	*Billion $*	*% of GDP*	*EU share*
1993	15.4	6.4	49.5	29.4	12.3	47.1
1994	18.1	10.2	47.7	23.3	13.2	46.9
1995	21.6	9.6	51.2	35.7	15.8	47.2
1996	23.2	9.5	49.7	43.6	17.9	53.0
1997	26.3	10.3	46.6	48.6	19.1	51.2
1998	27.0	10.0	50.0	45.9	16.9	52.4
1999	26.6	10.7	54.0	40.7	16.4	52.6
2000	27.8	10.5	52.2	54.5	20.5	48.8
2001	31.3	15.9	51.4	41.4	21.0	44.2
2002	36.1	15.6	51.2	51.5	22.4	45.2
2003	47.2	15.5	51.8	69.3	22.7	45.7
2004	63.2	16.2	54.5	97.5	25.0	46.6
2005	73.5	15.3	52.3	116.8	24.3	42.1
2006	85.5	16.2	51.6	139.6	26.5	39.3
2007	107.3	16.5	56.3	170.1	26.2	40.3
2008	132.0	17.8	48.0	202.0	27.2	37.1

Sources: Undersecreteriat of Foreign Trade, *Foreign Trade Statistics*; Undersecreteriat of Treasury, *Treasury Statistical Yearbook*; Turkish Statistical Institute, *Foreign Trade* Statistics.

Note: Entries for 2004–2006 and 2007–2008 are for EU 25 and EU 27, respectively.

percentage of GDP averaged 8.7 per cent and 10.3 per cent, respectively (see Table 3.2). For the same period, the volume of imports as a percentage of GDP increased from 13.8 to 17.5 per cent. The EU's share in total exports inched up slightly from 49.5 to 50.2 per cent, and imports also rose from 47.1 to 52.1 per cent. Over time, however, both total exports and imports as a percentage of GDP increased significantly from 9.5 and 17.9 per cent in 1996 to 16.5 and 26.2 per cent in 2007, respectively (see Figure 3.3). Clearly, the Turkish–EU customs union affected Turkey's trade volume, with a major impact on imports rather than exports. The share of EU-destined exports continued to increase, rising from 49.7 per cent in 1996 to 56.3 per cent in 2007, and during the same period the share of imports from the EU declined from 53 per cent to 40.3 per cent[29] (see Figure 3.4).

In addition to increasing the trade volume, the customs union may have also caused alterations in both production techniques and production costs, leading to a more competitive market structure in the manufacturing sector.[30] Such dynamic effects, which include the impact of a larger common market on productivity through economies of scale, external economies, more competitive

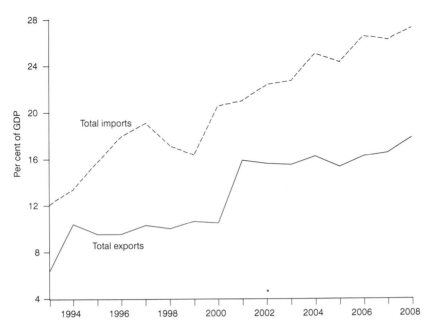

Figure 3.3 Total exports and imports, 1993–2008
(Data from, Undersecreteriat of Foreign Trade, *Foreign Trade Statistics*; Undersecreteriat of Treasury, *Treasury Statistical Yearbook*; Turkish Statistical Institute, *Foreign Trade Statistics*)

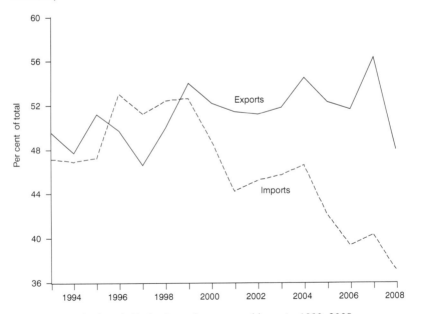

Figure 3.4 EU's share in Turkey's total exports and imports, 1993–2008.
(Data from, Undersecreteriat of Foreign Trade, *Foreign Trade Statistics*; Turkish Statistical Institute, *Foreign Trade Statistics*.)

market structure, and improved investment, are difficult to quantify. There are some qualitative assessments indicating that the customs union has been welfare enhancing, prompted by trade creation, and the dynamic effects have been relatively more significant than the static effects.[31] But a complete assessment of the dynamics effect would require years of experimentation and data.

Will Turkey eventually join the EU?

From the preceding discussion it is clear that during the last decade, the state of the Turkish economy continued to improve, helped by an ongoing economic transformation redirected toward the EU accession, and became less of an issue for the EU in comparison to the time when Turkey had not yet been recognised as a candidate state. Yet, strong opposition to Turkish full membership of the EU remains and will likely continue unabated, even during the long process of the ongoing accession negotiations. Member states that oppose the full membership point out the size of the Turkish economy and its potential burden on EU institutions and markets. They caution that with the lowest per capita income and largest agricultural sector, Turkey may become the largest recipient of financial support from the EU budget, which is estimated to be around 4 per cent of its GDP.[32] Assuming that Turkey becomes a full member in 2015 or beyond, they also argue that by then it will probably be one of the most populated states in the EU.

Such opposition, particularly from those who are yet to view Turkey's admission to the Union with the demeanour of accepting rather than rejecting, does not seem to waver to projections that assuming the economic growth differential between the EU and Turkey remains unchanged, Turkey's contribution to EU total output by 2015 is likely to be about 3.2 per cent.[33] And that the cost to the EU measured in terms of what Turkey will receive under the Common Agricultural Policy and the Structural Funds is not expected to be in excess of an amount in the range of 0.15 to 0.2 per cent of the EU's GDP.[34] Yet, despite these projections, for the sceptics the size and comparatively high growth rate of Turkey's population, the state of the labour market, the poverty level, and income distribution, continue to remain a concern. As highlighted in the 2006 World Bank labour market study, Turkey's employed-to-adult-population ratio, at 43.7 per cent in 2006, is much lower than the EU average, which is around 65 per cent, and significantly below the EU member state employment target of 70 per cent set for 2010. The labour force participation rate is also lower than the EU average, for a number of reasons, such as population growth outpacing employment growth, a high ratio of older workers and low female participation in the labour force, and a tight job market and moderate job creation, largely because of the inability of the industrial sector to absorb the larger outflow of labour from the agricultural sector, creating long-term frictional unemployment.[35]

A close examination of labour data also reveals that despite a remarkable rise in labour productivity since 2000, real wages have been declining during the same period.[36] However, despite the deterioration in real wages, GNP per capita has been increasing: After dropping to its lowest level in 1994, it began to steadily increase during the remaining years of the 1990s, and after falling to another low in 2001 it rose more than 100 per cent during the period 2003–2006.

There has also been a slight improvement in income distribution. In 2002, 20 per cent of the population with the lowest income received 5.3 per cent of the disposable income, while 20 per cent of the population with the highest income received 50.1 per cent.[37] In 2003, the share of income received by all income categories (excluding the top quintile) increased slightly, while the share of the top quintile declined. In 2004, there was no change in income distribution in favour of the lowest income group, but the share of the top quintile decreased further to 46.2 per cent, and the income received by the second, third, and fourth quintiles increased. Compared with 1987 data, the changes are not very significant, but the ratio of total income received by the highest income group to that of the lowest income group decreased from 9.6 in 1987 to 7.7 in 2004, still much higher than the EU ratio, though, which was roughly 5 in 2004.

Even though there has been a modest improvement in the poverty rate in recent years, it is still significantly higher than EU levels.[38] In 2003, the percentage of the population at risk of poverty in Turkey was almost 10 percentage points above that in the EU. It should be pointed out, however, that in a hypothetical case of the absence of social transfers, the difference is less dramatic, and in some cases Turkey fares even slightly better than some member nations. In 2003, the percentage of population at risk of poverty before social transfers was 36 per cent in Ireland, 32 per cent in Denmark, and 31 per cent in Poland, and in Turkey it was 31 per cent. After social transfers, the poverty rates are much lower: 21 per cent in Ireland, 12 per cent in Denmark, 17 per cent in Poland, and 26 per cent in Turkey.[39] It should also be noted that in an effort to eradicate poverty, Turkey has recently taken important steps, including improvements in the social insurance system, pilot implementation of family medicine, the establishment of universal health insurance, and combining the social security institutions under a single organisation.[40]

On another related issue, the fear of migration also poses a roadblock during the accession talks, even though it could be argued that by the time Turkey is admitted as a full member Turkey's economic profile will be more conducive to the functioning of a much more efficient labour market that may actually deter migration. In the short run, however, as Turkey begins to implement the new labour law introduced in 2003 and to align its labour market with the EU in accordance with the *acquis*, there could be a decline in employment with probable negative spillover effects on European labour markets. Employment in manufacturing could decrease significantly as employment policies and the wage structure are applied uniformly within the entire manufacturing sector in accordance with the *acquis*.[41] With the adoption and enforcement of such employment policies and wage structure, small informal sector firms will be required to pay taxes and social security benefits and consequently they will lose their cost advantage and thus their market share. The decline in total employment could be much higher when the impact of the EU regulations on the small informal firms in the agriculture and service sectors is also taken into account.[42] However, with a simulated faster GDP growth rate such 'short-term transitory-costs' stemming from the elimination of the informal sector could be reduced.[43]

With increased productivity and economic growth, therefore, it can be argued that in the long run there would likely be little spillover effects on the European labour markets. Assuming a transition period of ten years, estimates of migration potential from Turkey to the EU range from a level below 1 million to 2.9 million.[44] Under the assumption of no restrictions and a GDP per capita growth rate of 5.5 per cent in Turkey, the Turkish immigrant population could increase from 2.2 million in 2000 to 3.5 million in 2030.[45] Simulation results also indicate a net migration of 1–2.1 million, significantly lower than the likely migration of 2.7 million if Turkey does not become a full member.[46] However, these rough estimates may turn out to be different from actual migration that might take place in 2014 and beyond. Both the EU's and Turkey's demographic profiles will probably change; moreover, in view of possible variations in labour markets, what might have seemed to be a concern in 2005 could very well be an advantage for EU member states that may experience a labour shortage by 2014. Even if, in the worst-case scenario as perceived by the EU, increased migration from Turkey becomes a possibility, there will most likely be some set of mutually agreed upon safeguards that would control the direction and the magnitude of migration.

As the negotiation continues uninterrupted, it is also expected that many of the concerns stemming from Turkey's size and the development level of its economy will diminish. Economic growth and development are likely to gain a fresh dynamism that would lead to considerable improvement in major economic indicators, as has been the case for most of the recent entrants into the EU. The size of the economy could potentially become an asset for the Union rather than a liability. The young, dynamic population of Turkey, rather than being a threat for the mature European labour markets, will arguably be more involved in its growing markets. Moreover, as a future EU member with a flourishing private sector and stable economy, it seems that Turkey will be a magnet for direct foreign investment and thus close the gap with member nations, perhaps much sooner than expected.[47] Two bright spots are the human capital that has been accumulating despite Turkey's inadequate investment in that area and the development of an entrepreneurial class that has been gradually pre-empting the state.

In retrospect, when Turkey first applied for associate membership in 1959, a united Europe vision of the six founding nations was the reasoned doctrine behind the formation of the Community and economic progress was clearly the main driving force, but not the only objective. In the preamble to the Treaty of Rome, the six founding nations stated their determination to strengthen and preserve peace and liberty, and called upon other peoples of Europe to join in their efforts. Turkey, already a member of key European institutions at the time, responded; it became an associate member in 1964, and by the time it started the accession negotiations for full membership nearly half a century later, the Community had already expanded to include 27 member states.[48] A nation that lacked key developmental resources and faced numerous financial constraints during this period has made a transition from an emerging market to a maturing economy and has proven its commitment to establishing a functioning market economy. It remained on the EU-track and continued to enjoy strong economic performance and implement far-reaching reforms despite the EU's ongoing uncertainty over how to proceed with the full membership process.

At the time of writing, even though, from the perspective of the majority of political elites and the officials in Brussels, the EU has already committed itself to proceed with accession negotiations with Turkey, there is still ambiguity over the future path that the EU expansion may take and the effect that will have on future Turkish membership. Questions surrounding Turkey's membership prospects are complicated and fairly comprehensive. They range from issues of political and cultural differences that continue to be at the heart of European scepticism to matters relating to budgetary and institutional changes in the EU that may result from Turkish full membership. In the cost and benefit assessment of Turkish–EU integration, the issues of the readiness of the Turkish economy, the robustness of its economic growth, and the geopolitical realities justifying Turkey's future in the EU continue to weigh in, but not to the extent that they would overcome the EU's anxiety over such issues as large-scale migration and institutional incompatibility, the claim that Turkey is not geographically in Europe, it is too large and culturally too different for the EU to absorb, and other concerns that are yet to be disclosed. At this time, however, what still seems to exist as a common ground between Turkey and the EU, and driving the integration process forward at least in the intermediate term, is the understanding that accession as a legal and political process is bound to proceed at its own pace. Eventual EU membership still looks probable at best, and if and when it materialises, it is likely to speed up Turkey's transition into a modern industrial economy and generate considerable external benefits to Europe and beyond.

Notes

1 Content includes revised sections and references from various chapters in T. F. Nas, *Tracing the Economic Transformation of Turkey from the 1920s to EU Accession*, Leiden: Brill/Martinus Nijhoff, 2008.

2 The third development plan (1973–77) in particular followed a strategy that included deepening import substitution into intermediate and capital goods aiming at establishing an economic structure similar to those of the member nations of the European Economic Community. For a detailed analysis of the five-year development plans, see E. Kongar, *21. Yüzyılda Türkiye* [*Turkey in the 21st Century*], İstanbul: Remzi Kitabevi, 1998, pp. 361–411.

3 The empirical work from the early 1970s had some backing for Turkey's entry into the EEC, although the net effect on Turkey's well-being was not as certain. In free trade with the Community, Turkey was modelled to have a comparative advantage in its traditional exports (mainly agricultural) and in some non-traditional exports, which were industrial, such as food processing, clothing, textiles, and knitting industries. See T. Baysan, 'Economic implications of Turkey's entry into the Common Market', PhD diss., University of Minnesota, 1974. Trade diversion among Turkey's suppliers was also predicted to take place with respect to the United States, and estimates based on

changes in market shares favoured the EEC. See O. Aktan, 'Effects of joining the EEC on the Turkish economy', PhD diss., University of Oxford, 1972.

4 See 'Agreement Establishing an Association between the European Economic Community and Turkey', *Official Journal of the European Communities*, 24.12.1973, No C 113/2, pp. 2–8.

5 In 1981, Turkey attempted to begin the application process for full membership, but that was not pursued due to the EEC's decision to freeze relations with Turkey in 1982, a period that lasted more than four years. Consequently, the fourth of the financial aid packages from the Community that were intended to financially support Turkey in its preparation for the customs union in accordance with the Association Agreement, was also tabled.

6 Even though Turkey had completed most of the procedures required by the agreement and had fully aligned its legislation by 2004, there are still a few exemptions and exclusions outstanding in agriculture and in areas related to trade defence measures and safeguards. Moreover, the customs union is yet to evolve into the next phase, which would eventually allow for the adoption of the common agricultural policy, trade liberalisation in services, and the free movement of workers. See S. Ülgen and Y. Zahariadis, *The Future of Turkish–EU Trade Relations, EU–Turkey*, Working Paper 5, Brussels: Center for European Policies, 2004.

7 The Presidency Conclusions of the summit established that '[w]hile the political and economic conditions allowing accession negotiations to be envisaged are not satisfied, the European Council considers that it is nevertheless important for a strategy to be drawn up to prepare Turkey for accession by bringing it closer to the European Union in every field'. The Council of the European Union, *Presidency Conclusions*, Press Release, Nr: SN400/97, 12 December 1997, Luxembourg.

8 These included 'the alignment of human rights standards and practices on those in force in the European Union; respect for and protection of minorities; the establishment of satisfactory and stable relations between Greece and Turkey; the settlement of disputes, in particular by legal process, including the International Court of Justice; and support for negotiations under the aegis of the UN on a political settlement in Cyprus on the basis of the relevant UN Security Council Resolutions'. The Council of the European Union, *Presidency Conclusions*, Press Release, Nr: SN400/97, 12 December 1997, Luxembourg.

9 The official criteria for becoming a full member during the first three enlargements were those based on the Treaty of Rome, and the fourth enlargement adhered to the full-membership conditions laid out in the Maastricht Summit. Subsequently, all membership applications and admissions to the Union had to observe the Copenhagen political criteria that were agreed upon in 1993. To become a candidate for full membership, it was required that the applicant state 'has achieved stability of institutions guaranteeing democracy, the rule of law, human rights and respect for and protection of minorities, the existence of a functioning market economy as well as the capacity to cope with competitive pressure and market forces within the Union'. See The Council of the European Union, *Presidency Conclusions*, June 21–22, 1993, Copenhagen.

10 The Council of the European Union, *Presidency Conclusions*, 16–17 December 2004, Brussels.

11 As stated in the October 2004 Commission's recommendation, 'The budgetary impact of Turkish membership of the EU can only be fully assessed once the parameters for the financial negotiations with Turkey have been defined in the context of the financial perspectives from 2014 onwards'. *Recommendation of the European Commission on Turkey's Progress toward Accession*, October 6, 2004, p. 6.

12 European Commission, *Negotiating Framework (EU–Turkey)*, 3 October 2005, Luxembourg.

13 The primary source of the 1994 crisis was its financial origin, in particular, the effort to administer the interest rate and the adverse effects of the exchange-rate policy used. The failure on the part of policy makers to recognise the urgency of implementing stabilisation policies despite the growing misalignments in the goods and financial markets was also a contributing factor. For more on this, see O. Celasun, *The 1994 Currency Crisis in Turkey*, Policy Research Working Paper 1913, Washington, DC: The World Bank, 1998; Nas, *Tracing the Economic Transformation of Turkey*, Chapter 4; and F. Özatay, 'The lessons from the 1994 crisis in Turkey: Public debt (mis)management and confidence crisis', *Yapı Kredi Economic Review,* 1996, vol. 7, no. 1, pp. 21–37.

14 For the details, see E. Alper, 'The Turkish liquidity crisis of 2000', *Russian and East European Finance and Trade,* 2001, vol. 37, no. 6, pp. 58–80; E. Alper, H. Berüment, and K. Malatyalı, 'The effect of the disinflation program on the structure of the Turkish banking sector', *Russian and East European Finance and Trade,* 2001, vol. 37, no.6, pp. 81–95; A. Ertuğrul and F. Selçuk, 'A brief account of the Turkish economy, 1980–2000', *Russian and East European Finance and Trade,* 2001, vol. 37, no.6, pp. 6–30; and A. Tükel, M. Üçer, and C. Van Rijckeghem, 'The Turkish banking sector: A rough ride from crisis to maturation', in S. Altuğ and A. Filiztekin (eds) *The Turkish Economy: The Real Economy, Corporate Governance and Reform,* New York: Routledge, 2006, pp. 276–303.

15 The financial turmoil appeared to recede at the end of the first week of December 2000, after the news that Turkey and the EU had finally ironed out their differences concerning Turkey's accession to the EU. A compromise was reached by the EU ministers on 4 December 2000, in Brussels to modify the Accession Partnership Accord to include Turkey's sensitivities regarding the Cyprus issue and the territorial disputes with EU member Greece. Financial markets responded positively to the announcement of the new IMF aid package and the soothing words from the US administration and financial organisations.

16 The triggering event of the second crisis, which started on 19 February 2001, was the dispute between the president and the prime minister on the issue of handling corruption charges.

17 Intensive restructuring was intended to demonstrate the strong will of the administration and thus establish credibility. See K. Derviş, *Turkey: Return from the brink, attempt at systematic change and structural reform,* Practitioners of Development Seminar Series, 2 July Washington, DC: The World Bank, 2003.

18 IMF, *Letter of Intent,* 3 April 2002.

19 As of the end of 2004, about 70 per cent of 241 companies had already been privatised through either public-share or asset sales, and there were 39 state economic enterprises, of which 19 were included in the privatisation programme. See SPO, *Pre-Accession Program, 2004,* pp. 64–66.

20 See SPO, *Pre-Accession Economic Program,* November 2006, pp. 79–82.

21 The Banks Association of Turkey, *Banking Law 5411,* publication no: 55, p. 10.

22 See C. Pazarbaşıoğlu, 'Accession to the European Union: Potential impacts on the Turkish banking sector', in B. M. Hoekman and S. Togan (eds) *Turkey: Economic Reform and Accession to the European Union,* Washington, DC: The World Bank and Center for Economic Policy Research, 2005, pp. 161–186.

23 For a detailed impact analyses of the EU accession in agriculture, manufacturing, services, and network sectors, see Hoekman and Togan, *Turkey: Economic Reform and Accession to the European Union.*

24 European Commission, *Enlargement Strategy and Main Challenges 2006–2007,* p. 54.

25 IMF, *Turkey – 2007 Article IV Consultation, Concluding Statement of the IMF Mission,* 9 March 2007.

26 The Erdoğan government worked with a tight timetable to undertake all the necessary measures in the areas that the EU had been insisting on as conditions for starting the membership negotiations. A process that began with the Ecevit government thus continued with added urgency and determination, creating an economic and political environment that helped lead to sustainable improvements.

27 The share of industry in total output increased from 8.5 per cent in 1924 to 15.5 per cent in 1939, a respectable transformation considering the resource constraints that had to be overcome at the time. Also, during the period from 1928 to 1939 there were significant increases of both aggregate labour productivity (the ratio of GDP to total employment) and relative sectoral productivity (the productivity of each sector divided by the aggregate productivity) in sectors such as manufacturing, services, and utilities. See Altuğ and Filiztekin, *The Turkish Economy*, p. 17.

28 For more on the Washington Consensus debate, see Z. Öniş and F. Şenses, 'Rethinking the emerging post-Washington Consensus', *Development and Change,* 2005, vol. 36, no. 2, pp.2 63–290; D. Rodrik, 'Rethinking growth policies in the developing world', Luca d'Agliano Lecture in Development Economics for 2004, Kennedy School of Government, Harvard University, Cambridge, MA, 2004; and D. Rodrik, 'Goodbye Washington consensus, hello Washington confusion? A review of the World Bank's economic growth in the 1990s: Learning from a decade of reform', *Journal of Economic Literature*, 2006, vol. 44, no. 4, pp. 973–987.

29 These statistics find support in recent empirical work on the subject. For evidence positively linking Turkey's trade performance to the customs union agreement, see, for example, B. Neyaptı, F. Taşkın, and M. Üngör, *Has European customs union agreement really affected Turkey's trade?* Ankara: Department of Economics, Bilkent University, 2003. An earlier study by G. W. Harrison, T. F. Rutherford, and D. G. Tarr, 'Economic implications for Turkey of a customs union with the European Union', *European Economic Review*, 1997, vol. 41, pp. 861–870, predicts a gain of 1 to 1.5 per cent of GDP stemming from Turkish access to third markets through the EU's reciprocal preferential access agreements. Also see U. Utkulu and D. Seymen, *Trade and Competitiveness Between Turkey and the EU: Time Series Evidence*, Turkish Economic Association Discussion Paper 8, Ankara: Turkish Economic Association, 2004, suggesting that the increase in trade volume may have been the result of an increase in demand in the EU, in addition to Turkey's trade and exchange-rate liberalisation policies.

30 Cost–profit margins changing inversely with the volume of exports, for example, could lead to a more competitive market structure in the manufacturing sector. See S. Mıhçı and A. Akkoyunlu-Wigley, *The Effect Of Trade Liberalisation on the Concentration and Profitability of the Turkish Manufacturing Industries*, Ankara: Economics Department, Hacettepe University, 2002.

31 See Ülgen and Zahariadis, *The Future of Turkish–EU Trade Relations*.

32 See K. Lammers, 'The EU and Turkey – Economic effects of Turkey's full membership', *Intereconomics,* 2006, (September–October), pp. 282–288.

33 Given the size of its population, Turkey is likely to have limited influence on economic policy matters, but its weight on the Union's foreign policy issues will be considerable, although it will not be the only player determining the future of EU's foreign policy. See Lammers, 'The EU and Turkey' and K. Hughes, *Turkey and the European Union: Just Another Enlargement? Exploring the Implications of Turkish Accession*, A Friends of Europe Working Paper, Brussels: Friends of Europe, 2004.

34 See K. Derviş, D. Gros, F. Öztrak, Y. Işık, and F. Bayar, 'Turkey and the EU budget prospects and issues', in M. Emerson and S. Aydın (eds) *Turkey in Europe Monitor,* Brussels: Centre for European Policy Studies, 2004, pp. 76–81.

35 Existing labour market practices including high severance pay, early retirement age, restrictions on temporary work, a relatively long average workweek, and so on have also been a deterrent in job creation. See World Bank, *Turkey Labor Market Study*,

World Bank Report No. 33254-TR, 14 April 2006; Eurostat, *Europe in Figures – Eurostat Yearbook 2006–07*; and IMF, *Turkey – 2007 Article IV Consultation, Concluding Statement of the IMF Mission*, 9 March 2007.

36 As documented in the World Bank study, in Turkey real wages in manufacturing dropped significantly during periods after the crises of 1994 and 2001. After 1994, the real wage index fluctuated in an upward trend but fell again after 2001, and even though it rebounded quickly from the 2001 level, real wages were still below those of the pre-1994 crisis period.

37 SPO, *Ninth Development Plan 2007–2013*, 51–53; TÜRKSTAT, *2004 Household Budget Survey*, News Bulletin 27 February 2006. For the analysis and the results of income distribution for earlier dates, see Z. Yükseler, *1994, 2002 ve 2003 yılları hane halkı gelir ve tüketim harcamaları anketleri* [*1994, 2002 and 2003 household income and expenditure surveys*], Discussion paper 23, Ankara: Turkish Economic Association, 2004.

38 The poverty rate defined on the basis of food and basic non-food expenditures was 27 per cent in 2002, and after rising to 28 per cent in 2003 it decreased slightly to 25.6 per cent in 2004. See SPO, *Ninth Development Plan 2007–2013*, p. 52.

39 For more, see Eurostat, *Europe in Figures – Eurostat Yearbook 2006–07*, p. 117.

40 The 2006 social security law was annulled by the Constitutional Court, and at the time of writing the social security reform was yet to be reintroduced.

41 See the simulation exercise by E. Taymaz and Ş. Özler, 'Labor market policies and EU accession: Problems and prospects for Turkey', in Hoekman and Togan, *Turkey: Economic Reform and Accession to the European Union*, pp. 223–260.

42 See S. Togan, 'Economic implications of EU accession for Turkey', in Hoekman and Togan, *Turkey: Economic Reform and Accession to the European Union*, pp. 311–330.

43 See Taymaz and Özler, 'Labor market policies and EU accession'.

44 Relying on reported figures in various studies, one study in particular provided a range of 2–3 million and did not consider this to be a significantly high figure given that it will constitute less than 1 per cent of the population of EU-15. See Lammers, 'The EU and Turkey'.

45 See H. Flam, *Turkey and the EU: Politics and Economics of Accession*. Seminar Paper 718, Stockholm: Institute for International Economic Studies, Stockholm University, 2003 and Hughes, 'Turkey and the European Union'.

46 See R. Erzan, U. Kuzubaş, and N. Yıldız, 'Growth and immigration scenarios for Turkey and the EU', in Emerson and Aydın, *Turkey in Europe*, pp. 114–125.

47 See M. Dutz, M. Us, and K. Yılmaz, 'Turkey's foreign direct investment challenges: Competition, the rule of law, and EU accession', in Hoekman and Togan, *Turkey: Economic Reform and Accession to the European Union*, pp. 261–293.

48 As confirmed in the Commission's 6 October 2004, recommendations: 'For major periods of European history, Turkey has been an important factor of European politics. Turkey is a member of all important other European organisations and has since the Second World War played an important role in contributing to the shaping of European policies' (p. 2). One organisation in particular is the Council of Europe, which was founded in 1949 with the aim of achieving the unity of its members, among which were five of the original six members of today's EU and other members, including Turkey, who joined the Council the same year it was founded. Some of the current EU members were not among the nations that established the Council; it took more than six years before even Austria, for example, became a member.

4 Security dimension

A clash of security cultures? Differences between Turkey and the European Union revisited[1]

Pınar Bilgin

Introduction

The relationship between Turkey and the European Union[2] has had its ups and downs since 1963. Although Turkey and EU member states have always had their differences, a lid was kept on them during most of the Cold War thereby allowing for closer relations under the NATO umbrella. Following the dissipation of the 'Soviet threat', the dismantlement of the Warsaw Pact and the dissolution of the Soviet Union, these differences re-surfaced. Indeed, in the aftermath of the Cold War, EU politicians began referring to Turkey having become a 'burden' for building security in 'Europe'. Such words came as a shock to Turkish policy-makers and analysts alike who, since Turkey's NATO membership in 1952, had come to think of the 'security relationship' as the strongest of ties that bound Turkey to Europe (and the United States). Against such background, EU policy-makers' post-1989 representations of Turkey as a source of 'insecurity', when coupled with the EU's post-1980 coup criticisms of Turkey's democratisation and human rights record, led some to conclude that EU policy-makers were oblivious to (if not negligent of) Turkey's 'legitimate' security concerns.

These debates have taken a different turn since 1999 owing to changes in both Turkey and the European Union. On the EU side, there has emerged a relatively stronger resolve to have a military dimension to policy-making. In 1999 the European Union decided to develop a capacity for autonomous action backed up by credible military force. Accordingly, some EU policy-makers came to see Turkey in the way NATO does – a strategic asset by virtue of its military strength and geographical location. On Turkey's side, critical changes followed the European Union's 1999 decision to grant Turkey candidate country status. In the run-up to and aftermath of this decision, Turkey's Europeanisation gained pace. The 2001 economic crisis created an opening not only for the financial and economic reforms demanded by the International Monetary Fund but also for the political reforms demanded by the EU. During this period, Turkey amended its constitution several times to improve the human rights situation, strengthen the rule of law, and restructure democratic institutions. Although problems with implementation remain, the prevailing view is that Turkey has come a long way toward meeting EU standards.

In tandem with these changes on both sides of the relationship, the tone of the debates on Turkey and the European Union took a different turn. Both sides have the need for closer relations – some called for full membership, others a special relationship. The scholarly literature has invariably viewed this change of tone in debates as indicative of a closing of the gap between the security concerns of Turkey and the European Union due to either an increasing emphasis on military security on the EU's part, or de-emphasis on military security on Turkey's part, or both.[3]

Contrary to those who see a closing of the gap between Turkey and the European Union's ways of 'thinking about and doing security', the present chapter argues that differences between Turkey and the European Union remain; EU policy-makers continue to be concerned about Turkey as a source of 'insecurity' whereas Turkey's policy-makers are wary of the potential repercussions of meeting the EU's demands. These differences, I argue, are rooted in the respective security cultures of Turkey and the European Union. The two have grown apart from each other throughout the Cold War due to different ways of organising political community and identifying/addressing threats stemming from inside and outside this community. Not only have the two grown apart but also they have remained rather oblivious to each other's security concerns. So much so that in the wake of the Cold War there surfaced a *clash of security cultures* between the two – a clash that manifested itself as debates on Turkey's role in the evolving European security architecture during the 1990s and present-day battles on human rights, values and democracy.[4]

I use the term 'security culture' rather loosely, in reference to prevailing ways of thinking about and doing security in any given environment. As such, different cultures of security may exist and contend with each other at any given time. What I take to be the prevailing security culture is the one that is deduced from the discourses and other deeds of practitioners and other policy elite. Rather than taking for granted pre-existing entities and analysing the 'threats' faced by them, I follow the critical constructivist literature and focus on 'representations of danger'[5] by myriad actors.[6] This approach is in contrast to mainstream approaches to security that assume the subject(s) of security to be pre-given and fixed, and that define security as 'securing those fixed entities against objective and external threats'.[7] It is also in contrast to culturalist approaches to security that imagine a pre-given culture determining notions and policies of security.[8] The critical constructivist perspective offered by Weldes et al. points to the mutually constitutive way in which the state (or any other community) is produced in an attempt to secure its identity and interests. They write:

> in contrast to the received view, which treats the object of insecurity and insecurities themselves as pre-given or natural, and as ontologically separate things, we treat them as mutually constituted cultural and social constructions: insecurity itself is the product of processes of identity construction in which the self and the other, are constituted.[9]

Weldes et al.'s critical constructivist approach, thus, makes a significant contribution by focusing on the mutually constitutive relationship between identity, interests and insecurity and the (re)production of 'cultures of insecurity'. In what follows, the chapter traces the divergent evolution of the European Union's and Turkey's security cultures and points to the persistence of these differences thus far.

Highlighting the differences in security cultures as a source of the difficulties in EU–Turkey relations does not entail taking 'culture' as given, fixed or unchanging. Rather, following critical constructivist theorising in International Relations,[10] the argument here stresses the malleability of security culture and the mutually constitutive relationship between security and culture. As Weldes et al. have argued, 'insecurities, rather than being natural facts, are social and cultural productions'.[11] Security cultures are (re)produced through the representation of insecurities, identities and interests of communities. What is of interest for the purposes of this chapter is the differences in the trajectories taken in the (re) production of security cultures in Turkey and the European Union throughout the Cold War and their persistence so far notwithstanding above-mentioned significant changes in the European Union, Turkey and the broader security environment.

The chapter falls into three sections. Section one traces the trajectory of the evolution of security culture in the European Union during the Cold War. The second section looks at the development of security culture in Turkey. Section three illustrates these differences with reference to the concrete case of human rights in present-day world politics.

The evolution of security culture in the European Union

European integration was a 'security policy in response to a non-specific and non-military security problem', writes Bill McSweeney.[12] This may sound paradoxical to some, particularly at a time when EU policy-makers are frustrated over the slow pace of their progress towards adopting common security and defence policies and acquiring an autonomous military force. Yet, the conception of security that is at the root of McSweeney's argument is not one that is 'reduced to its narrowest military dimension'.[13] Nor does the author take the nation-state as the ultimate referent, or prioritise the military instrument in security provision. Rather, this conception recognises the multiple dimensions of security as well as non-military instruments of security policy.[14] Hence the author's reading of European integration as 'security policy'.[15]

Following critical approaches to security, two inter-related arguments are offered in this section. First, it is argued that European integration is best understood as a process of constructing a 'security community' through the adoption of broader conceptions and non-military practices of security with reference to multiple referents within the European Union and 'Europe'. Second, EU security culture was (re)produced during the Cold War through practices aimed at European integration – thus the construction of 'Europe' as a subject of security. As such, security culture in the European Union has evolved differently from that of non-EU states – including Turkey.

In popular discourse, it is NATO that is referred to as the security institution in Western Europe. The European Union is viewed as having taken care of political and economic integration. What lies beneath such representations is the high/low politics divide that is characteristic of mainstream approaches to security. NATO is viewed as having taken care of 'high politics' (security achieved through the threat and use of military force) whereas 'low politics' (political and economic integration) was delegated to the European Union.

Although it is true that there evolved, during the Cold War, a division of labour between NATO and the EU with the former taking care of 'external defence' and the latter focusing on European integration, representing NATO as *the* security institution would be misleading – unless, that is, one is fully committed to a narrow (military) conception of security. Even then, such an argument will not be entirely accurate given the military security concerns that lie at the heart of the European Union's predecessor: the European Coal and Steel Community (ECSC). The ECSC was founded in 1951 in an attempt to prevent history repeating itself. This was endeavoured through strengthening economic and political integration with the expectation (in true neo-functionalist fashion) that cooperation over low politics issues would spill over into high politics issues. In doing so, economic integration made significant progress and spilled over into politics and culture; the military dimension lagged behind.

With the end of the Cold War, hopes were raised among EU policy-makers for the possibility of an independent foreign and security policy. When such expectations did not come true and as the European Union faced difficulties in adopting common foreign and security policies, the EU's Cold War contributions to security building in Western Europe became obscured in its internal and external representations alike. Increasingly, the European Union was represented as a post-Westphalian project that had very little to do with 'security'.[16]

This was partly EU policy-makers' own doing. For, as Ole Wæver has maintained, during the 1960s and 1970s, EU policy-makers avoided using the language of 'security'. Instead, they framed problems as 'normal' politics so that debates over various issues would not be brought to a deadlock because of Cold War concerns.[17] Most notable among these issues was that of human rights, which was central to dialogue with Eastern Europe under *Ostpolitik*, and was deliberated outside the security framework. Indeed, as Bill McSweeney has noted:

> it was only with the Single European Act in 1987 that we find explicit reference to 'security' in the legal instruments binding the member-states in a Community, and then only in respect of what was termed its 'economic and security aspects'.[18]

The policy of avoiding the language of 'security' in EU policy discourse became so successful that in the 1990s EU policy-makers began to face difficulties explaining to the public in the new member states (such as Britain and Denmark) that 'security was central to the rationale of European integration because it played so little a role at the time of their accession (1972)'.[19]

To recap, viewed from a mainstream perspective that rests on a high/low politics divide, the European Union comes across as part of a division of labour agreed with NATO on stability in Western Europe. Yet, from a critical perspective that is cognisant of the original rationale for the ECSC, the EU could be presented as a 'non-security response to a specific security problem'.[20] As McSweeney has argued, 'the evidence points as plausibly to the need to conceptualise European integration as a security policy in response to a non-specific and non-military security problem'.[21] The problem was non-specific and non-military because there was no identifiable threat such as that posed by the Soviet Union to defend the members against (as was the case with NATO). Although 'promoting the reconciliation of France and Germany, and of anchoring the one-year-old Federal Republic in the Western alliance'[22] were prime (and specific) concerns of the time, there was another broader (non-specific) concern and it remains to date: binding member-states in a network of interdependence so that recourse to military means of resolving disputes would become more difficult.[23] This was, to adopt Karl Deutsch's terminology, an explicit attempt to construct a 'security community' in Western Europe.[24]

Deutsch defined a (pluralistic) security community, as 'one in which there is real assurance that the members of that community will not fight each other physically, but will settle their disputes in some other way'.[25] His conviction was that once the conditions and processes that give rise to security communities were identified, it would be possible to replicate them in different parts of the world so that (preparations for and the idea of) war would not enter into calculations of those states.[26] To date, European integration remains the best attempt to construct a security community.[27]

From these arguments one can discern the emergence, during the Cold War, of an alternative model of security building and a security culture in the European Union. This culture is rooted in a broad conception of security that recognises military and non-military threats to states and other referent objects (note the McSweeney quote in the beginning of this section). Yet, at the same time, this culture puts stress on building security without using the language of 'security' for fear of revoking military responses. In Wæver's words, 'the EU has secured the security community not by upgrading joint security activities but on the contrary by doing other things'.[28] Thirdly, and in a related manner, security is sought without relying on the military instrument. Indeed, EU security culture has put emphasis on soft governance, common security practices and the need for non-military responses. Hence the 1990s debates on the EU's self-proclaimed identity as a 'normative power' that utilises 'soft power' (in contrast to US reliance, especially during the 2000s, on 'hard power').[29]

During the 1990s, EU policy-makers sought to export their model to the candidate countries as well. When the walls came down in 1989, the European Union took up the opportunity to move towards further integration whilst seeking to expand towards the East. However, whilst transforming itself the European

Union produced new insecurities. Writing in 1993, Barry Buzan explained the impact of 1989 as follows:

> Traditional fears of military revival still lie in the background, and savage subregional conflicts already disturb Europe's complacency. But more important than these leftovers from the old security agenda is the exposure, and in part creation, of a new form of insecurity ... The principal focus of the new insecurity is society rather than the state.[30]

The demands made by the European Union as part of its rather 'nation-building'[31] project during the early 1990s, when coupled with migration pressures from the Eastern and Southern peripheries, resulted in some setbacks on the path to further integration (as with the case of the Danish 'no' to the EU vote in 1992). Such developments, in turn, gave rise to a fear of 'fragmentation', that resulted in the securitisation of a range of issues, the foremost of which is migration.[32]

For instance, allowing for a freer movement of EU citizens, which was aimed at (re)producing a 'European' identity to back up the process of political integration, eventually constituted 'migration' as a source of insecurity in the European Union, for:

> as French Interior Minister Philippe Marchand has noted: 'France's external border is more Germany's border with Poland and Italy's with Yugoslavia than the German–French or Italian–French borders.' If the EC is not seen to provide adequate defence, then the Community itself could become politically vulnerable to nationalist disaffection and charges that it was undermining national identities by both encouraging migration and by promoting the homogenising forces of Europeanisation.[33]

Then, by the time the Cold War came to an end, the process of European integration had constituted (and was, in turn, constituted by) a security culture that prioritised issues of 'low' politics and sought to address these issues primarily through non-military instruments. During this period, the EU also constituted its main insecurity: 'fragmentation'. 'Integration', in turn, was made 'an aim in itself' and all those issues that threatened the pace of integration were securitised. Fragmentation thus came to be viewed as an 'existential threat' because the prevailing concern was that 'integration/fragmentation is a question not of how Europe will be, but whether Europe will be'.[34] As will be seen below, Turkey's policy-makers remained rather oblivious to their EU counterparts' concerns and failed to realise how these became 'existential threats' from an EU perspective.

The evolution of security culture in Turkey

By the time the Cold War had come to an end, Turkey's understandings and practices of security had come to shape (and was, in turn, shaped by) a different security culture. This had taken place notwithstanding commonalities shared by

Turkey and the European Union as members of NATO and 'the West'. This was to do with Turkey's character as a developing country in that it had to take care of specific and non-specific threats of military and non-military kind emanating from both inside and outside its national boundaries. Specific threats from outside the national boundaries stemmed from perceived Soviet expansionism and external aid to PKK separatism. Specific threats from inside the boundaries included PKK separatists and Islamic reactionaries. Non-specific and non-military threats to Turkey's security took the form of perceived challenges to its sovereign statehood. Membership of NATO in particular and 'the West' in general addressed most of these insecurities (specifically vis-à-vis the Soviet Union and non-specifically in respect of sovereign statehood vis-à-vis 'the West', see below). Other specific insecurities as with the 'difficult' neighbourhood (Iran, Iraq and Syria to the south and Greece to the west) and the 'low intensity warfare' in the southeast, Turkey had sought to address on its own.

In meeting all three categories of threats Turkey relied on the strength of its military instrument. Turkey's use of the military instrument took the form of threat of force vis-à-vis its neighbours (including the Soviet Union) and use of force against PKK separatists.[35] Turkey's 'symbolic' use of the military instrument took the form of acting together with 'the West' within the NATO framework and contributing a significant part of its manpower. Such symbolic use of NATO membership helped to reaffirm Turkey's 'Westernness'.[36] NATO membership in particular and Turkey's Western-oriented policies in general helped to address specific and non-specific, military and non-military threats to its sovereign statehood. By the early 1990s, Turkey's security culture was one that sought to address issues of both high and low politics through resort to the symbolic or actual use of the military instrument through frequent invocation of the language of 'security'. In what follows, this section clarifies Turkey's security culture by way of tracing its emergence and persistence.

A significant component of Turkey's security culture has been the Republican leaders' answer to the identity question: 'Who are we?' 'Western' was the answer the founders of the Republic offered. During the inter-war period, they sought to write Turkey's 'Westernness' into 'race' and 'language' – tapping then prevalent theories of national identity.[37] Later, during the Cold War, the ideological stance of anti-communism and NATO membership served as the marker of Turkey's 'Western' identity.

Contra those who reduce Turkey's Western-oriented policies to the post-WWII Soviet threat or a life-style choice,[38] I have elsewhere called for understanding the option made for a 'Western' identity as a security policy in and of itself.[39] For, from the perspective of early Republican leadership, Western orientation was *not only* a life-style choice or a part of the Republican project of emancipation (as significant as these aspects were) *but also* a crucial aspect of the strategy of seeking security in the face of a 'Europe' that had, in the past, refused equal treatment to the Ottoman Empire by virtue of its apparent 'deficiencies' in terms of the 'standards of civilisation'. In the early Republican period, the Western orientation helped Turkey to meet the 'standards of civilisation' thereby allowing Turkey's founding leaders to claim the right to be treated equally and with respect.

Being part of the West was also a strategy to avoid being on the margins of the world political and economic system. Such concerns were rooted in a particular memory of the final days of the Ottoman Empire that traumatised Turkey's elite – the memory of Anatolia turned into a backwater of the world economic system and pushed to the brink of dismemberment. These concerns were (and still are) a driving force behind Turkey's Western orientation throughout the Republican era.

As such, Turkey's Western orientation was a response to non-specific non-military insecurities tied up with late Ottoman and early Republican encounters with European/International Society. Turkey's present-day relations with the European Union cannot be understood without paying due attention to early Republican leaders' ambivalence to the 'West'; for, the 'West' for them was a source of inspiration *and* insecurity. The otherwise rich literature on Turkey's policies has emphasised the former but overlooked the latter. Accordingly, it has failed to account for the present-day ambivalence in Turkey's policies toward the European Union, which is partly (but not wholly) rooted in Turkey's past insecurities.

The Western orientation that was adopted from the early days of the Republic onwards remained in the cultural and political realms but did not translate into military cooperation until WWII. Even then, Turkey hesitated to join the War until the very last days, and then in an attempt to become a founding member of the United Nations. Turkey's security policies came to run in parallel with Western Europe as the Cold War descended. An analysis of textual renderings of Turkey's intellectuals of statecraft point to specific and non-specific insecurities on Turkey's agenda.[40] Whereas Soviet expansionism and its support for communist subversions constituted specific insecurities, being recognised as belonging to 'Western civilisation' constituted a non-specific concern. There followed Turkey's enthusiastic support for the Korean War effort, search for NATO membership and interest in acceding to European integration.

Over the years, the roles Turkey played in various European security institutions have served as occasions on which Turkish policy-makers articulated and defined Turkey's 'Western' identity as well as insecurities and interests. Turkey's place in and recognition by European security institutions were viewed as strengthening its commitment to liberalism and democracy as well. In the early years of European integration, the Turkish elite sought membership as the next stage in Turkey's development and Westernisation. At the time the 1963 Ankara Agreement was signed, the European Community was considered the economic wing of NATO. Turkey expected that joining another European institution would bolster its efforts at being/becoming Western. Second, the economic dimension of membership was (and remains) of enormous significance, leading to the signing of a Customs Agreement that went into effect in 1995. Third, supporters of EU membership were keen to replicate in Turkey the process of rapid development that other candidates and EU members went through when preparing for and after joining the Union.

It was not only membership of European security institutions that helped re(inscribe) Turkey's 'Western' identity during this period. Turkey's identity as belonging to 'the West' was also written into space.[41] Through the production of a geopolitical discourse that rested on assumptions of 'geographical givenness', Turkey was located firmly in the West – as a 'fact' of geography.[42] Yet Turkey's policy-makers' discourse not only served to locate Turkey in the West but was also utilised to justify a specific approach to security policy-making *and* reliance on the military instrument in addressing Turkey's insecurities.[43] For instance, a former Minister of Defence said of Turkey was located 'in the virtual epicentre of a "Bermuda Triangle"'.[44] As such he stressed the presumably 'pre-given' and 'unchanging' character of the security challenges facing Turkey throughout its history. It is by no means the traditionalist elite alone who have based their arguments on such geographical assumptions of 'givenness'. An academic observer introduced Turkey as a 'country surrounded with reality', thereby justifying its policies as a struggle for 'survival'.[45] Such representations of Turkey have invariably served to explain Turkey's supposedly restricted security policy options – i.e. dependent on the military instrument.[46] In the immediate aftermath of the Cold War, they were used to justify persistence in the very same options notwithstanding changes in the international security environment. The point being, at a time when European policy-makers were seeking to avoid using the language of 'security' for fear of rendering intra-European problems intractable, Turkey's policy-makers increasingly relied on the language of 'national security' to by-pass democratic mechanisms and thwart alternative policy options.

In particular, such representations of Turkey's geographical location have fed into an understanding of Turkey's international relations as a constant struggle for security against 'external' actors (which often use 'internal' actors for their purposes). Such an understanding is epitomised in former Prime Minister Bülent Ecevit's remark that 'considering its geopolitical position, Turkey can never keep out of trouble'. Such representations of Turkey's geography not only serve to depoliticise the process of going to war but also write them as inevitable 'facts' of international relations – facts that can only be prepared for, not prevented. Also referred to as the 'Sèvres syndrome', this understanding of Turkey's international relations advises the citizens to be always vigilant and on the lookout for international ('Western') conspiracies to carve out portions of Turkey's territory.[47] Such conspiracy-oriented thinking, which is difficult to challenge because of geopolitical assumptions and language, has prevented many people's views about international relations from evolving even in the face of change.[48] Indeed, even the process of globalisation is conceived in inside/outside terms and presented as a direct threat to Turkey's 'national security' and not as the enmeshment of the local and the global, and the blurring of the inside/outside divide that creates dangers as well as opportunities for global security.

One problem with such representations of Turkey's geographical location is that they take geography as pre-given and fixed; accordingly, they fail to account for different representations of the same geographical location.[49] After all, the same geographical location has also been represented as follows:

The new risks and challenges that could affect the whole western world have transformed Turkey from a 'flank' to a 'front state'. Turkey is one of the few Western countries whose importance has increased in the post-Cold War period.[50]

The point here is that the relationship between geographical location and security culture is not one of a fixed geography constituting the pre-givens of security policy. Indeed, whereas some in Turkey have tapped so-called 'geopolitical truths' to call for becoming an EU member, others tapped the same 'truths' to caution against EU membership.

Following critical approaches to Political Geography (or Critical Geopolitics)[51] the relationship between geographical location and security could be better understood as one of mutual constitution. Indeed, what is of interest for the purposes of this chapter is what Simon Dalby has called the 'politics of the geographical specification of politics'.[52] Over the years, representations of Turkey's geographical location have been used by various policy-makers to substantiate a range of security policies adopted to meet state-focused insecurities and interests. What was common to all was a deterministic view of the relationship between Turkey's geography and its security policies. The same discourse has also been utilised to justify reliance on the military instrument in addressing these insecurities.

To summarise, during the Cold War, there evolved a security culture in Turkey that sought to address specific military threats (as with perceived Soviet expansionism and PKK separatism aided and abetted by some of Turkey's neighbours) as well as non-specific non-military threats (as with recognition by the West as its fully sovereign equal). The referent for security has remained the state throughout this period. In addressing these threats, Turkey's policy-makers resorted to actual as well as symbolic use of the military instrument and the language of 'security'. Although the military focus has seemingly began to dilute with the end of the Cold War with the appearance of so-called low politics issues on the NATO security agenda and post-1999 changes in Turkey that have resulted in de-emphasis on security language in domestic discourse, as will be discussed below, differences between the security cultures of Turkey and its EU counterparts remain.

Turkey and the European Union: Different security cultures

The post-Cold War era turned out to be one of turmoil for Turkish policy-makers, who to their dismay found out that their EU counterparts were oblivious to if not negligent of Turkey's security concerns. As a result, Turkey's relations with the European Union became increasingly strained during the 1990s. Statements of Turkish policy-makers of the time suggest that some were quite resentful of these new policies and criticised their EU counterparts for their lack of understanding of Turkey's 'different' and 'unchanging' security concerns.[53] There certainly was an element of truth in their arguments. Since threats to the security of the Turkish state did not stem only from the Soviet Union and its allies, East–West détente did not mean the same thing for Turkey as it did for, say, Finland or (then West) Germany. However, this inertia in security thinking in Turkey during the era of détente eventually meant that Turkey was unprepared for the drastic changes introduced by Gorbachev's new thinking that revolutionised security relations across Europe.

As the process of deepening and broadening of the European Union constituted a security culture that was different from that of non-EU states, this has had two major implications for Turkey–EU relations. First, EU policy-makers have come to view security issues from within their own security culture – a culture that evolved during the Cold War in a relatively stable environment provided by the NATO security umbrella. As a result, EU policy-makers grew less understanding of the security needs and interests of those countries, such as Turkey, that are still faced with military threats stemming from both inside and outside the national boundaries. Second, as European integration constituted its own insecurities in the form of 'new' threats such as migration, Turkey's accession to European integration came to be viewed from the lens of 'cultural difference' but not in an everyday sense of the term. Rather, this was 'a difference of security cultures'.

Indeed, highlighting the differences between Turkey and the European Union's security cultures need not render Turkey any less 'European'. After all 'the core fears of each nation are unique; they relate to its vulnerabilities and historical experience. Security thus *means* different things to different nations'[54] and other communities. What lies beneath these differences is not only geography or 'culture' (in the everyday sense of the term) but also diverse paths taken in organising political community and seeing/meeting threats to the security of that community. The end of the Cold War made only more apparent the different trajectories taken by approaches to security in Turkey and the European Union during the Cold War. Hence, the argument of this chapter that the 'difficult' relationship the European Union and Turkey have had since the late 1980s is rooted in their security cultures that grew increasingly apart during the Cold War. What is ironic is that Turkish policy-makers have always assumed that it was the 'security relationship' that brought them closer to 'Europe'.

The clash over the issue of human rights could be viewed as crystallising the differences between the security cultures of Turkey and the European Union. From an EU perspective, Turkey's human rights problems is a major concern, not only because the EU's security culture is rooted in a comprehensive approach that recognises the individual and societal as well as national dimensions of security. Not only that, the EU cares about human rights breaches in its neighbourhood also because the EU is apprehensive about its own future. EU politicians, already faced with difficulties in distinguishing between political and economic refugees, are worried about a further increase in the number of Turkish citizens seeking better life chances in the European Union. In other words, this is an 'existential threat' in the eyes of EU politicians who worry about the EU public's view of the 'Turks'. When one considers the volatility of the project of European integration it becomes somewhat easier to understand how Turkey's policies could be viewed as presenting a societal threat to the European Union. If Turkey is kept out of the Union, it could be viewed as constituting an external security threat – a 'zone of conflict' bordering the EU's 'zone of peace'. If it remains as a candidate it could be viewed as threat to 'internal' security by way of failing to meet the EU's standards – what has made the EU a security community – because Turkey still considers as 'security' concerns those issues the EU has successfully desecuritised over the years.

This gap between the EU and Turkey's respective security cultures remains notwithstanding changes in the external environment (as with the 9/11 attacks) and domestic environment (the EU putting somewhat more emphasis on the military dimension of security and Turkey somewhat less emphasis). On the one hand, since 9/11 the European Union has increasingly came to rely on security technologies for border management and has been making disquieting trade-offs between liberty and security. In doing so EU policies have come to prioritise European integration as a security referent, and not necessarily individual European citizens or non-citizens.[55] On the other hand, Turkey has made significant changes in its constitution as well as other rules and regulations. The role played by the Military in Turkey's political processes has been de-centralised. In foreign policy, there has been less emphasis on the threat and use of force (symbolic and actual) and more on Turkey's ostensibly 'versatile' identity 'between East and West' and 'Europe and Asia'. Yet, in doing so, Turkey's security culture has remained focused on the security of the state and has not considered other referents. This state-centric focus crystallised in Turkey's reception of Sudan's President Omar al-Bashir who has visited Turkey twice in recent years. Most significantly, these visits took place in the aftermath of the International Criminal Court's (ICC) issuing of an arrest warrant for al-Bashir. Turkey not only allowed al-Bashir's visit but also snubbed EU expressions of displeasure with the visit. On paper, Turkey's policy-makers have a legal escape in that Turkey does not yet recognise the ICC. However, in terms of human rights and humanitarian values – on which Turkey's and the EU's security cultures have come to differ – Turkey's prioritisation of its economic interests over rights and values, especially at such a moment of human suffering, speaks volumes about Turkey's present-day stance vis-à-vis security referents other than the state.

Conclusion

Tracing the evolution of respective security cultures of the European Union and Turkey as such allows one to be somewhat more accepting of EU politicians' representation of Turkey as producing 'insecurity'.[56] For, in the aftermath of the 1980 military coup, Turkey began to export some of its domestic problems to the European Union via the Turkish diaspora in Western Europe consisting of migrant workers and political asylum seekers. EU politicians clearly do not wish to see Turkey's domestic insecurities becoming EU insecurities. Added to this is the problem that successive German governments have faced in integrating over two million Turkish citizens into German society. For, in a European Union that perceives fragmentation as an imminent threat:

the problems of integrating [the Turks] into German society are projected onto the issue of integrating Turkey into the EU: the political, social and cultural cohesion of the EU is seen as being endangered by the inclusion of almost seventy million Muslim Turks.[57]

Such juxtaposition of the evolution of two security cultures also allows one to be more accepting of Turkey's policy-makers' insistence on being/remaining a part of 'Europe' notwithstanding aforementioned failings regarding human rights. In the post-WWII period, a substantive part of Turkey's claim to belong to 'Europe' rested on the role it played in the Western security architecture.[58] Over the years, every time Turkey's valuing of 'Western security' came under challenge (such as the late 1980s), such criticisms died down following a crisis (as with the Iraqi invasion of Kuwait in 1990) that enabled Turkey to reinstate its value as a 'strategic asset'.[59] In other words, during times of crisis, the 'security relationship' served as Turkey's anchor in Europe. For Turkey, acceding to European integration (and being a part of Western institutions in general) is not merely about life-style or economy or ideas and ideals – however important and significant those may be. It is also about security – the security of the Republican project, the project of modernisation and secularisation.

Notes

1 This chapter is a shortened, revised and updated version of P. Bilgin, 'Clash of Cultures? Differences between Turkey and the European Union on Security', in Ali L. Karaosmanoğlu and S. Taşhan (eds) *The Europeanization of Turkey's Security Policy: Prospects and Pitfalls*, Ankara: Foreign Policy Institute, 2004, pp. 25–52.
2 'European Union' and EU will be used throughout the chapter to refer to the organisation of European states (EEC and EC) before the adoption of its current title.
3 See, for example, M. Müftüler-Baç, 'Turkey's Role in the EU's Security and Foreign Policies', *Security Dialogue*, 2000, vol. 31, no. 4, pp. 489–502; A. Eralp, 'Turkey in the Enlargement Process: From Luxembourg to Helsinki', *Perceptions*, June–August 2000, pp. 17–32; A. L. Karaosmanoğlu, 'Avrupa Güvenlik ve Savunma Kimliği Açısından Türkiye-Avrupa Birliği İlişkileri' [Turkey–European Union Relations From the Perspective of European Security and Defence Identity], *Doğu Batı*, 2001, 14, pp. 156–166.
4 There also emerged a debate on Turkey's geopolitical identity – i.e. whether it is 'European', 'Mediterranean', or 'Middle Eastern'. P. Bilgin, 'A Return to "Civilisational Geopolitics" in the Mediterranean? Changing Geopolitical Images of the European Union and Turkey in the Post-Cold War Era', *Geopolitics*, 2004, vol. 9, no. 2, pp 269–291.
5 The phrase is David Campbell's, see D. Campbell, *Writing Security: United States Foreign Policy and the Politics of Identity*, Manchester: Manchester University Press, 1992.
6 J. Weldes, M. Laffey, H. Gusterson, and R. Duvall, 'Introduction: Constructing Insecurity', in J. Weldes *et al.* (eds) *Cultures of Insecurity: States, Communities, and the Production of Danger*, Minneapolis, MN: University of Minnesota Press, 1999, p. 10.
7 Ibid., p. 9.
8 S. P. Huntington, 'Clash of civilizations?', *Foreign Affairs*, 1993, vol. 72 no. 3, pp. 22–49; P. J. Katzenstein (ed.) *The Culture of National Security: Norms and Identity in World Politics*, New York: Columbia University Press, 1996.

9   Weldes, Laffey, Gusterson, and Duvall, 'Introduction: Constructing Insecurity', p. 10.
10 See, for example, M. N. Barnett, *Dialogues in Arab Politics: Negotiations in Regional Order*, New York: Columbia University Press, 1998; D. Campbell, *Writing Security: United States Foreign Policy and the Politics of Identity*, Manchester: Manchester University Press, 1992; F. Kratochwil, *Rules, Norms and Decisions: On the Conditions of Practical and Legal Reasoning in International Relations and Domestic Affairs*, Cambridge: Cambridge University Press, 1989; B. McSweeney, *Security, Identity and Interests: A Sociology of International Relations*, Cambridge: Cambridge University Press, 1999; J. Weldes, 'Constructing national interests', *European Journal of International Relations*, 1996, vol. 2, no. 3, pp. 275–318; J. Weldes, M. Laffey, H. Gusterson and R. Duvall (eds), *Cultures of Insecurity: States, Communities, and the Production of Danger*, Minneapolis, MN: University of Minnesota Press, 1999; A. Wendt, *Social Theory of International Politics*, Cambridge: Cambridge University Press, 1999.
11 Weldes, Laffey, Gusterson, and Duvall, 'Introduction: Constructing Insecurity', p. 10.
12 McSweeney, *Security Identity and Interests*, p. 8.
13 Ibid., p. 7. On security studies cognisant of individual and social groups as referents, see K. Booth, 'Security and emancipation', *Review of International Studies*, 1991, vol. 17, no. 4, pp. 313–326; P. Bilgin, K. Booth, and R. W. Jones, 'Security Studies: The Next Stage?', *Nacao e Defesa,* 1998, vol. 84, no. 2, pp. 131–157; R. W. Jones, *Security, Strategy, and Critical Theory*, Critical Security Studies, Boulder, CO: Lynne Rienner, 1999; K. Booth, 'Special Issue on Critical Security Studies', *International Relations*, 2004, vol. 18, no. 1; K. Booth (ed.). *Critical Security Studies and World Politics*, Critical Security Studies, Boulder, CO: Lynne Rienner, 2005; R. W. Jones, 'On emancipation: Necessity, capacity and concrete utopias', in K. Booth (ed.) *Critical Security Studies and World Politics*, Boulder, CO: Lynne Rienner, 2005; K. Booth, *Theory of World Security*, Cambridge: Cambridge University Press, 2008.
14 McSweeney, *Security, Identity and Interests*, p. 35.
15 O. Wæver, 'Insecurity, security, and asecurity in the West European non-war community', in E. Adler and M. N. Barnett (eds) *Security Communities*, Cambridge: Cambridge University Press, 1998, pp. 69–118.
16 Ibid.
17 O. Wæver, 'Securitization and desecuritization', in Ronnie D. Lipschutz (ed.) *On Security*, New York: Columbia University Press, 1995, pp. 58–62.
18 McSweeney, *Identity, Security and Interests*, p. 7.
19 Wæver, 'Insecurity, security, and asecurity in the West European non-war community', p. 86.
20 McSweeney, *Identity, Security and Interests,* p. 8.
21 Ibid.
22 S. Hoffmann, 'The European Community and 1992', *Foreign Affairs*, 1989, vol. 68, no. 4, p. 32.
23 McSweeney, *Identity, Security and Interests*, p. 7.
24 K. Deutsch, S. A. Burrell, R. A. Kann, M. Lee Jr., M. Lichterman, R. E. Lindgren, F. L. Loewenheim, and R. W. Van Wagenen (eds), *Political Community and the North Atlantic Area: International Organization in the Light of Historical Experience,* Princeton, NJ: Princeton University Press, 1957.
25 Ibid., p. 5.
26 Ibid., pp. vii, 3, 20–21.
27 Wæver, 'Insecurity, security, and asecurity in the West European non-war community'.
28 Ibid., p. 92.
29 I. Manners, 'Normative power Europe: A contradiction in terms?', *Journal of Common Market Studies*, 2002, vol. 40, no. 2 pp. 235–258; E. Adler and B. Crawford, 'Normative power: The European practice of region building and the case of the Euro-Mediterranean Partnership (EMP)', *Institute of European Studies Working Paper*,

Paper no. 040400, 2004; F. Bicchi, "Our size fits all': Normative power Europe and the Mediterranean', *Journal of European Public Policy,* 2006, vol. 13, no. 2, pp. 286–303; I. Manners, 'Normative power Europe reconsidered: Beyond the crossroads', *Journal of European Public Policy*, 2006, vol. 13, no. 2, pp. 182–199; P. Joenniemi, 'Towards a European Union of post-security?', *Cooperation and Conflict*, 2007, vol. 42, no. 11 pp. 127–148.

30 B. Buzan, 'Introduction: The changing security agenda in Europe', in O. Wæver, B. Buzan, M. Kelstrup and P. Lemaitre *et al.* (eds) *Identity, Migration and the New Security Agenda in Europe*, 1993, London: Pinter, pp. 1–2.

31 Wæver, 'Insecurity, security, and asecurity in the West European non-war community,' p. 91.

32 J. Huysmans, 'The European Union and the securitization of migration', *Journal of Common Market Studies*, 2000, vol. 38, no. 5, pp. 751–777; J. Huysmans, *The Politics of Insecurity: Fear, Migration, and Asylum in the EU*, The New International Relations, New York: Routledge, 2006; J. Huysmans, A. Dobson, and R. Prokhovnik (eds), *The Politics of Protection: Sites of Insecurity and Political Agency*, New York: Routledge, 2006.

33 Buzan, 'Introduction: The changing security agenda in Europe', p. 3.

34 Wæver, 'Insecurity, security and asecurity in the West European non-war Community', p. 91.

35 There was also the Cyprus 'Peace Operation' in 1974.

36 E. Yılmaz and P. Bilgin, 'Constructing Turkey's "Western" identity during the Cold War: Discourses of intellectuals of statecraft', *International Journal*, Winter 2005, vol. 6, pp. 39–59.

37 İ. Aytürk, 'Turkish linguists against the West: The origins of linguistic nationalism in Atatürk's Turkey', *Middle Eastern Studies* 2004, vol. 40, no. 6, pp. 1–25.

38 A. Davutoğlu, *Stratejik Derinlik*, İstanbul: Küre Yayınları, 2001.

39 P. Bilgin, 'Securing Turkey through Western-Oriented foreign policy', *New Perspectives on Turkey*, 2009, vol. 40, pp. 105–125.

40 Yılmaz and Bilgin, 'Constructing Turkey's 'Western' identity during the Cold War: Discourses of intellectuals of statecraft'.

41 For instance, in response to Valéry Giscard d'Estaing who declared that 'Turkey's capital [is] not in Europe, 95 per cent of its population [lives] outside Europe, and it [is] not a European country', various actors have pointed to Turkey's Cold War contributions to security in Europe and what it has to offer toward advancing European Security and Defence Policy (ESDP). Needless to say, both qualities are considered to be a function of Turkey's geographical location and its implications for politics. Their assumption being that, if not culture, religion, ideology or civilisation, geopolitics secures for Turkey a place in the 'West' and/or 'Europe'.

42 Bilgin, 'A return to "civilisational geopolitics" in the Mediterranean? Changing geopolitical images of the European Union and Turkey in the Post-Cold War Era', pp. 269–291.

43 P. Bilgin, '"Only strong states can survive in Turkey's geography": The "uses" of "geopolitical truths" in Turkey' *Political Geography*, 2007, vol. 26, pp. 740–756.

44 H. S. Türk, 'Turkish defense policy', Speech Delivered at the Washington Institute for Near East Policy, 3 March 1999. Online. Available http://www.washintgoninstitute. org/media/samiturk.htm (accessed 19 November 2001).

45 M. F. Tayfur, 'Turkish foreign policy towards Euro-Mediterranean Partnership and the Black Sea Economic Cooperation: A comparative analysis', *Dış Politika/Foreign Policy*, 1999, vol. 1, no. 4, 75.

46 See, for example, S. İlhan, *Jeopolitik Duyarlılık* [Geopolitical Vulnerability], Ankara: Türk Tarih Kurumu Basımevi, 1989; S. İlhan, *Avrupa Birliğine Neden Hayır* [Why 'No' to the European Union], İstanbul: Ötüken Neşriyat.

47 The Sèvres treaty (1917), which was never ratified, constitutes an attempt by the Allies to divide up the Ottoman Empire following World War I.

48 P. Bilgin, 'Turkey's "geopolitics dogma"': Searching for epistemological certainty at a time of ontological insecurity', in S. Guzzini (ed.) *Fixing Foreign Policy Identity: 1989 and the Uneven Revival of Geopolitical Thought in Europe*, (forthcoming).

49 Bilgin, 'A Return to "civilisational geopolitics" in the Mediterranean? Changing geopolitical images of the European Union and Turkey in the Post-Cold War era'.

50 Ç. Bir, 'Turkey's role in the new world order', *Strategic Forum*, 1998, 135. Online. Available http://www.ndu.edu/inss/strforum/forum135.html (accessed 19 November 2001).

51 J. Agnew, *Geopolitics: Revisioning World Politics*, London: Routledge, 1998; S. Dalby, 'Critical geopolitics: Discourse, difference and dissent', *Environment and Planning D: Society and Space*, 1991, vol. 9, pp. 261–283; G. Ó Tuathail and S. Dalby (eds), *Rethinking Geopolitics*, London: Routledge, 1998; G. Ó Tuathail, S. Dalby and P. Routledge (eds), *The Geopolitics Reader*, London: Routledge, 1998.

52 Dalby, 'Critical geopolitics', p. 274.

53 See T. Baytok, *Bir Asker Bir Diplomat: Güven Erkaya-Taner Baytok, Söyleşi* [One Officer One Diplomat], İstanbul: Doğan Kitapçılık, 2001, pp. 43–81, for an expose of some Turkish policy-makers' yearnings for the 'good old days' of the Cold War era.

54 O. Wæver, 'Conflicts of vision: Visions of conflict' in P. Lemaitre, E. Tromer and O. Wæver (eds) *European Polyphony: Perspectives Beyond East–West Confrontation*, New York: St Martin's Press, 1989, p. 301. Original emphasis.

55 D. Bigo, S. Carrera, E. Guild, and R. B. J. Walker, 'The Changing Landscape of European Liberty and Security: Mid-Term Report on the Results of the Challenge Project (Ceps)' *International Social Science Journal*, 2008, vol. 59, no. 192, pp. 283–308; D. Bigo, 'When two become one: Internal and external securitisations in Europe', in M. Keltsrup and M. C. Williams (eds), *International Relations Theory and the Politics of European Integration: Power, Security, and Community*, London, New York: Routledge, 2000; D. Bigo, 'The Möbius Ribbon of Internal and External Securit(ies)', in A. Mathias *et al.* (eds) *Identities, Borders, Orders: Rethinking International Relations Theory*, Minneapolis, MN: University of Minnesota Press, 2001; D. Bigo, 'Security and immigration: Toward a critique of the governmentality of unease', *Alternatives: Global, Local, Political*, 2002, vol. 27, no. 1, pp 63–92; D. Bigo and E. Guild, *Controlling Frontiers: Free Movement into and within Europe*, Aldershot: Ashgate, 2005.

56 'Turkey is not producing the [sic] security but rather consuming security and producing insecurity', then German minister Hans-Ulrich Klose is reported to have said at a conference organized by the Körber Foundation in İstanbul in 1997. See H. Bağcı, 'Changing security perspective of Turkey' in M. Aydın (ed.), *Turkey at the Threshold of the 21st Century: Global Encounters and/vs Regional Alternatives*, Ankara: International Relations Foundation, 1998, p. 81.

57 H. Kramer and F. Müller, 'Relations with Turkey and the Caspian Basin countries' in Blackwill and Stürmer, (eds), *Allies Divided: Transatlantic Policies for the Greater Middle East*, MIT Press, 1997, p. 185; R. Satloff, 'America, Europe, and the Middle East in the 1990s: Interests and policies', in Blackwill and Stürner (eds) *Allies Divided*, pp. 7–37

58 G. Aybet and M. Müftüler-Baç, 'Transformations in security and identity after the Cold War: Turkey's problematic relationship with Europe', *International Journal*, Autumn 2000, pp. 567–582.

59 For a discussion, see I. O. Lesser, *Bridge or Barrier? Turkey and the West after the Cold War*, Santa Monica, CA: Rand, 1992. The same crisis and the Gulf War that ensued highlighted the divisions within the EU regarding Turkey's role as a source of (in)security in 'Europe'. See F. S. Larrabee, 'U.S. and European foreign policy toward Turkey and the Caspian Basin', in Blackwill and Stürmer (eds) *Allies Divided*, pp. 160–161.

5 Elite opinion dimension

Behind the scenes of Turkey's protracted accession process: European elite debates[1]

Nathalie Tocci

Introduction

Turkey's long march to Europe and most pointedly the many obstacles encountered along the way are often attributed to contrary European public opinion[2] regarding Turkey's EU membership. However, European public opinion on EU–Turkey relations became a major agenda item only after the 2004 eastern enlargement, the 2005 opening of Turkey's accession negotiations and 2004–2009 travails over the EU's constitutional reform. Public opinion has been used and abused by several European elites to renege on their positions and commitments vis-à-vis Turkey. Furthermore, up until the turn of the century, Turkey, whose contractual ties with the EU date back to the 1963 association agreement, had rarely if ever been salient in European debates, only raising public and media attention in moments of foreign policy crisis such as the 1974 military intervention in Cyprus or the successive military coups in Turkey.

Notwithstanding, Turkey in general and EU–Turkey relations in particular have occupied a special place in the opinions and debates at elite levels within and across member states in so far as they have touched on a variety of domestic, European and global questions. These debates have shaped EU–Turkey relations over the decades and played a critical role in moulding the pace and shape of Turkey's accession process since it was launched in 1999. Elite debates have, on the one hand, filtered through to public opinion playing a role in explaining the widespread public opposition to Turkey's EU membership in recent years. On the other hand, elite debates have played a key role in explaining the *sui generis* and protracted nature of Turkey's long march to Europe. Indeed it is notable that although the political decision to grant Turkey candidacy was taken in 1999, the debates that followed focused on *whether* Turkey should join the European Union rather than on *how* Turkey's accession could take place. The claim advanced here is that the delay in Turkey's accession process is partly embedded in this disconnect between Turkey's accession process and European debates on Turkey–EU relations.

In view of the salience of European debates on Turkey in explaining Ankara's long march to Europe, the aim of this chapter is to explore the nature and substance of these debates, map who they are raised by as well as explain the underlying interests and beliefs motivating them. In what follows, this chapter first unpacks elite debates on Turkey, exploring how they have been pitched using domestic, European or global level of analysis. It then explains who the stakeholders are that articulate these debates within and across member states. Finally, it teases out the interests and ideas underpinning elite debates, pointing to their broader political significance. It addresses European elite debates on Turkey in the context of several member states, including those which reject Turkey's EU membership, member states which support Turkey's EU bid, as well as member states that are either lukewarm or divided on Turkey's EU prospects.

Elite debates on EU–Turkey relations: Non-communicating levels of analysis

Much of the complexity surrounding elite debates on EU–Turkey relations is explained by the fact that these debates are pitched at different levels of analysis, and have often failed to communicate with each other. Depending on the particular issue area subjectively deemed as most important by different stakeholders across the EU, debates have focused on a set of very different questions generating a very different range of opinions and positions on EU–Turkey relations. However, these opinions and positions have not been articulated in response to each other, but have rather developed and been exposed in isolation.

In debating EU–Turkey relations, different stakeholders within the EU have emphasised very different issues. In the economic sphere, the discussion has centred around a set of disparate issues ranging from Turkey's contribution to the EU's role in the global economy to Turkey's impact on the EU budget, labour markets and the Common Agricultural Policy (CAP). In the political and social spheres, the discussion has also touched upon a large variety of questions, including Turkey's impact on EU institutions, on European foreign policy as well as the effect of Turkey's membership on the articulation of the EU's identity. What explains how different actors go about analysing and opining about Turkey's accession? As elaborated below, a useful key to understanding which aspects and issues stakeholders choose to focus on is to assess the different levels at which these debates are pitched.[3]

The global level: The impact of Turkey's accession on the EU's role in the world

A first level of analysis is the global one, featuring debates about the EU's role in the world. Here elite debates have focused predominantly on the economic and foreign policy domains and have been rather positive about Turkey's future membership, highlighting the assets that Turkey's membership would bring to the EU's role in international relations and the global economy.

The EU, Turkey and the global economy

Particularly in the realms of business and foreign policy, stakeholders focus on Turkey's growth, its rising productivity, its young and growing labour force, its rising trade levels and growing foreign direct investment (FDI) inflows. They emphasise how these assets would contribute to the fulfilment of the EU Lisbon agenda, better equip the Union to face rising competition from emerging economic giants such as India or China, and sustain the EU in exiting successfully the global economic crisis. Stakeholders in this category also tend to emphasise how these economic benefits would risk serious dilution if the EU were to insert permanent derogations to the full liberalisation of the four freedoms for future member Turkey, as suggested by the European Council when launching Turkey's accession negotiations in October 2005.[4] Hence, the strong critiques about the prospects of permanent derogations in the liberalisation of agriculture markets or the free movement of persons and workers.[5]

The EU, Turkey and energy security

Another principal issue area for those stakeholders framing debates at the global level is related to energy security. Turkey's role as an energy and transport hub, facilitating the EU's much-sought-after energy diversification is underlined, especially by those member states that perceive acutely dependence on single and unpredictable sources of energy supplies – i.e. Russia – as well as by European stakeholders with commercial interests in oil and gas transit routes through Turkey.[6] Debates regarding Turkey and European energy security have risen on the agenda both in response to Russia's increasing use of energy leverage in Eastern Europe and the signing in July 2009 of the Nabucco gas pipeline agreement between Turkey, Romania, Bulgaria, Hungary and Austria.

The EU, Turkey and European foreign policy

Finally, elite stakeholders in this category highlight the assets that Turkey's inclusion could bring to bear on the fledging European foreign policy, in terms of location, logistics and ties to neighbouring regions such as Russia, the South Caucasus, Central Asia, the Balkans and the Middle East.[7] Many also highlight how Middle Eastern and Eurasian countries carefully watch the evolution of EU–Turkey relations, focusing especially on the expected growth in the EU's actorness in these regions in view of Turkey's accession.[8] Of particular interest for these elite debates has been the rising activism in Turkey's foreign policy under the Justice and Development Party (AKP) government's intent in increasing Turkey's presence in the Caucasus and the Middle East and improving relations with countries such as Armenia, Russia, Syria and Iran.[9]

The European level: The impact of Turkey's accession on EU institutions, societies and economy

A second level of analysis in elite debates on EU–Turkey relations regards the EU as such and focuses on the expected impact of Turkey's accession on the EU's internal institutional, political, social, cultural and economic make-up. Here the arguments emphasise the expected costs of Turkey's accession far more than the benefits.

Turkey and EU institutions

To start with, some elites have placed much attention on the impact of Turkey's accession on EU institutions.[10] The most common argument is that the EU would function less effectively with a greater number of member states, particularly large ones that allegedly do not share the Union's ill-defined '*esprit communautaire*'.[11] Here we essentially find a confluence of two mutually reinforcing arguments. The first is the classic EU debate on widening versus deepening, whereby an enlarged EU would imperil deeper integration particularly in the political sphere. The second argument is Turkey-specific and enmeshed in culturalist and essentialist views regarding Turkey, whereby a Turkey that is 'culturally distinct', politically sovereignist and economically less developed than the EU average would dilute the cultural, political and economic cohesion of the Union.

Those who follow this line of thinking claim that even in the area of foreign policy, where Turkey's membership is normally associated with key benefits for the Union's external projection, the greater internal diversity brought about by Turkey's accession would hinder the EU's external capabilities and actorness in the current institutional framework. Put metaphorically, precisely because Turkey represents an asset as a 'bridge' between Europe and the East, 'a bridge ... should never belong totally to one side. Turkey can fulfil its function as a bridge between Asia and Europe much better if it does not become a member of the EU'.[12] Moreover, if demography is to have a greater salience in determining member states' decision-making power within EU institutions, when Turkey becomes a full member she will have a decision-making power that is comparable to that of Germany, a situation which the Union's founding members in particular view with great unease. Hence, the argument goes, before even considering Turkey's membership, the Union has to put its house in order and equip itself with the necessary 'absorption capacity' to digest Turkey. Feeding these opinions is the widespread belief that the 2004 enlargement complicated the EU's institutional functioning, as well as the belief that the 2007 enlargement took place too hastily, with Romania and Bulgaria not being sufficiently prepared to enter the Union. The heightened perception that enlargement ought to take place with caution lest the EU project be imperilled has filtered straight through to elite debates on Turkey.

Others cast this reasoning into question.[13] Enlargement alone has not noticeably complicated the EU's institutional workings, they argue. Intra-EU divisions hindering effective policy-making remain the ones between 'old' member states. Several smaller member states have argued that it is easier to digest one big member than a number of small or micro states. They suggest that the entry of another large member state would make relatively little difference to the current balance between small and big members. Finally, still others highlight that the EU's institutional and constitutional reform is expected to take place well before Turkey's entry, and that Turkey's accession process can act as a further external push factor inducing a successful EU reform process.

Yet, the worries of many stakeholders go well beyond the concern that Turkey's accession would complicate the EU's institutional functioning. The fear – coupled with a strong sense of nostalgia for the past – is that Turkey's accession and ongoing enlargements will ring the death bell of the Union's federalist aspirations. More generally it would seal the end of the political project as conceived by the Community's founding fathers.[14] As European federalists would argue, it is only those who abhor the prospect of a federal Europe (e.g. British conservatives) or those who have lost all hope in it (e.g. German Christian Democrats or the Italian centre-left), who may be prepared to accept Turkey in the European fold. Indeed, if deepening were to become directly correlated to widening, some anti-federalists who are now favourable to Turkey's accession would turn against Turkey's EU aspirations. Their euroscepticism would easily trump their support for Turkey's accession.[15]

Turkey and the European electorate

Another argument against Turkey's EU accession emphasises public opinion. Here, the debate takes different tones. Some argue that the need to rectify the Union's disconnect from the demands, desires and expectations of EU publics is as great as ever.[16] The French and Dutch 'no' to the Constitutional Treaty and the increasingly low turn-outs at European Parliament elections are attributed to the rejection by European citizens of an increasingly elitist EU project. By the same token, others argue that 'enlargement fatigue', first and foremost with respect to Turkey, is partly explained by the inability of EU elites to engage the publics in the debate over the eastern enlargement.[17] The Union, it is argued, went through its biggest enlargement ever in 2004 and 2007, with the entry of twelve member states which almost two decades ago constituted Europe's much-feared 'other'. A plethora of Western Balkan states and Turkey are now channelled in the same accession process. Beside them are a number of aspiring applicants, insistently knocking at the Union's door. Yet, all this has happened and continues to happen without the remotest engagement of the public, a lack of engagement which has rendered 'Brussels' ever more alien and distant in the minds of EU citizens. It is with these arguments in mind that some criticise the Commission's technical progress in enlargement and its alleged stifling of the European-wide debate on Turkey's accession.[18]

Others, including Enlargement Commissioner Olli Rehn, rebuke many of these points.[19] Rehn, in a speech at the University of Helsinki on 27 November

2006, forcefully suggested that the political debate on Turkey runs the risk of undermining the credibility of EU policies towards Turkey. If the Union's right hand lectures Turkey on the Copenhagen criteria arguing that these are the *sine qua non* for EU entry, while the left hand engages in highly politicised and often populist debates over the desirability of Turkey's entry, the Union's credibility in Turkey risks being seriously undermined. Others argue that the need to engage with European public is certainly real and pressing and is, incidentally, a need that has always accompanied the highly elitist EU project. Yet those very actors who keep stressing the importance of taking European citizens into account are doing little to insert greater clarity and cool-headedness in European public debates on Turkey. Less still do they foster European solidarity towards Turkey. Far more often, raising the issue of contrary public opinion, and calling for national referenda on the Turkey question, appears to be more of a shield to hide the absence of strong leadership than a genuine concern for the Union's democratic deficit.

Turkey and the EU's identity

Turning to another EU-level debate, a common strand of argument links Turkey's accession to debates about the EU's multiculturalism and the question of a 'European identity'. In several elite debates Turkey's EU integration is mirrored with the integration of Muslim migrant communities in Europe, with positive and negative repercussions.[20] Here, views differ depending on the different understandings of a European identity. By those highlighting the essentialist features of a European identity, including culture, religion and history, Turkey's membership is strongly rejected. Turkey, it is argued, cannot integrate into the EU, just as 'non-European' Muslim migrants have failed to integrate into their respective host European countries. Hence, accepting Turkey into the European fold would entail abandoning aspirations to forge a cohesive EU identity, defined through history, culture and religion.[21] Others refute the claims that a European identity is and can be premised on monocultural interpretations. They emphasise the importance of fostering unity in diversity, encouraging the development of an EU identity based precisely on multiculturalism. Following a different line instead, others doubt Turkey's membership not on the basis of its religion or culture *per se*. Rather, they express concerns on the one hand about Turkish secularism which is viewed as contrary to a European – read French – understanding of *laïcité*, and on the other hand about the threat of resurging political Islam in Turkey.[22]

A related question which receives increasing attention across the EU is the link between identity and borders. To those viewing a European identity through culturalist lenses, geographical borders represent an integral element separating and defining 'us' and the 'other'. Hence, Turkey should be kept out of the EU on the basis of its different culture, religion and history. Its otherness would be physically expressed through the delineation and consolidation of the EU's borders well within the boundaries of the European continent. Unsurprisingly, member states in the hinterland of Europe are far more receptive to this interpretation of borders than members lying on the periphery of the Union.

Others, while also placing much emphasis on the question of borders, have downplayed its cultural dimension.[23] The definition of the EU's borders, the argument goes, is a critical political step in the formation of a European identity. But the delineation of these borders is conceptualised as an arbitrary and purely political fact, rather than as a preordained cultural inevitability. In other words, for reasons of political interest, the European polity would choose for reasons of political expediency not to extend its borders to Iraq, Iran and Syria by refuting Turkey's accession. The EU's borders would be determined on the basis of their functional political utility in pursuing the Union's interests, defining a European identity and allowing the European polity to live in a comfort zone, protected by friendly buffer states such as Turkey. The underlying political outlook permeating these views is strongly eurocentric. Europe's world would be predominantly confined to itself and its neighbouring other, in contrast to the more global outlook espoused by arguments highlighting the EU's role in the world.

Turkey and the EU budget

A last set of arguments pitched at the EU level relates to the economic realm. As opposed to the rather pro-Turkey elite arguments embedded in analyses focusing on the EU's role in the global economy, more inward-looking economic arguments tend to be far more sceptical of Turkey's accession. A prime issue relates to the budgetary costs of Turkey's accession, given Turkey's size and level of economic development which stands below the EU average.[24] Yet, rather than the absolute cost to the EU budget, which in terms of individual member state contributions is unlikely to change radically, it is the relative distribution of Community funds which would alter as a result of Turkey's accession. Hence, structural funds would be redirected away from current recipients in eastern Europe and the Common Agricultural Policy (CAP) would risk being seriously affected by the entry of a large new member state with a significant agricultural sector. Arguments focusing on budgetary issues are especially speculative and prone to populist fear-mongering. Not only is it fictional to speculate about the EU budget or the CAP in 2020, but the rate of change in Turkey's economy is such that predicting Turkey's impact on the EU's budgetary, cohesion or agricultural policies with any reasonable degree of precision is almost impossible.[25]

The national level: The impact of Turkey's accession on the member states and Turkey

Turkey and immigration[26]

A final level of analysis favoured by many stakeholders within the EU is the national one: the effect of Turkey's accession on national economies, societies and security. Here, the first and most important source of member state concern is that of Turkish immigration, particularly within member states which already host large Turkish communities such as Germany, Austria and the Netherlands. In these countries, populist leaders rouse economic fears warning that Turkey's membership will bring with it an invasion of 'Turkish plumbers'. In countries such as the UK, Italy or Poland, which have not witnessed high levels of Turkish immigration, these concerns are still dormant, but could ignite in future tilting the now relatively favourable attitudes towards Turkey against it. In member states such as Germany and Austria instead, migration worries are also linked to wider fears about economic globalisation and the erosion of the welfare state, despite the fact that the immigration of young Turkish migrants could help ageing European states confront their monumental pension system problems.[27] Still others in member states like France, Austria and Holland cast their arguments about Turkish immigration in the more emotional language of societal integration or lack thereof.[28] Unlike arguments based on global considerations, these arguments focusing on Turkey's impact on member state economies and societies view Turkey's size and demography as a threat rather than an asset. It is these concerns that induce member states to pre-empt the future by inserting the possibility of permanent derogations to the full liberalisation of the four freedoms in future member Turkey, opening the worrying prospect of Turkey's second-class membership.

Turkey and national security

Another element of member states' interest in EU–Turkey relations concerns the realm of security. For some countries such as Greece or Cyprus, the understanding of national security principally hinges on relations with Turkey itself. Indeed for Greece, national security is the primary reason why Turkey's accession is accepted, yet only on the basis of Turkey's fulfilment of what Greece would like to see framed as clear-cut conditionalities relating to Greek security interests.[29] These conditions would include issues directly related to Greek interests such as the Aegean, Cyprus or the rights of the Orthodox community in Turkey, as well as issues indirectly connected to Greek interests such as the rebalancing of Turkey's civil–military relations which would allow, inter alia, Greece to cut its defence budget. It is precisely because Turkey's accession is conceptualised through the lens of national security that other 'unsecuritised' issues pertaining to Turkey–EU relations, irrespective of whether they are viewed as assets or liabilities, are considered non-issues in Greece. A similar argument applies to Cyprus, where the impact of Turkey's accession is discussed exclusively within the framework of the Cyprus conflict. Far more so than Greece however, Greek Cyprus is more inclined to use all means at its disposal lest Turkey refuses to toe the Greek Cypriot line on the conflict.

In the case of other member states such as the UK, the security impact of Turkey's accession is framed in relation to other threats and interests. Turkey's accession process and the impact of its membership are viewed positively because of the prospects for deepening Anglo-Turkish police and intelligence cooperation over terrorism.[30] The 2003 Al-Qaeda bombings in Istanbul created a close bilateral tie between the Turkey and the UK, inducing London to emphasise the security benefits of Turkey's accession to member state Britain.

EU–Turkey relations and Turkey's reform process

A last national level argument is the impact of Turkey's accession on Turkey itself. The primary observation to make here is that the impact of the accession process on Turkey hinges upon the nature and extent of the domestic transformation engendered by the accession process, thus creating a critical link between the effectiveness of the EU's transformative role and the expected impact of accession. The impact of the accession process on Turkey is already being felt, not only in the domestic political realm, but also in the economic and foreign policy domains. Since the beginning of Turkey's accession process, the levels of trade between Turkey and the EU have steadily risen, European FDI in Turkey has gathered steam, and Turkey's production cycles are increasingly following those of the EU economies.[31] Also in the realm of foreign policy, Turkish foreign policy allegedly approximates increasingly that of the EU, as revealed by positions adopted by Turkey and the EU in multilateral forums such as the UN.[32] In other words, the accession process is already influencing the Turkish domestic political system, economy and foreign policy in a manner that could make the question of membership and its impact far less salient over the accession years.

This is not to say that Turkey's accession process and the expected impact of membership is cost-free. It is striking that little attention is paid not only in the EU but also in Turkey to the potential losers of membership in Turkey. The impact of the accession process on ordinary citizens is seriously under-researched, yet the waning support for membership in Turkey (as in other candidates before it) suggests that key sectors of society could seriously lose out from the accession process.[33] Turkish citizens are already being deeply affected by rising living costs and economic restructuring. These changes, while being generally associated to the consequences of modernisation and economic globalisation, are more specifically linked to the EU accession process in the minds of the public. Unless carefully tackled, these costs could seriously undermine the public support necessary for a monumental transformationist project such as EU membership.

Table 5.1 summarises the plethora of European debates on Turkey, categorising them according to the level at which they are articulated. The mapping of European debates on Turkey's accession process explained above and summarised in Table 5.1 highlights a first reason for its protractedness. Not only are EU–Turkey relations intertwined with a set of highly sensitive and longstanding European debates, which at times are only tangentially linked to Turkey but have nonetheless been associated with Turkey's accession process; but also, these debates have been pitched at different levels, explaining their often non-communicating nature. A second factor underpinning Turkey's long march to Europe to which we now turn relates to the fact that these debates have been held by a relatively wide array of elite stakeholders across the member states and Turkey.

Table 5.1 European debates on EU–Turkey relations

Level of Analysis	Global	European	National
Thematic debates on EU–Turkey relations	Global economy	EU institutions	Immigration
	Energy security	EU democracy and public opinion	National security and defence
	European foreign policy	European identity and borders	Turkish democracy, reform and adjustment
		EU budget	

Elite stakeholders on EU–Turkey relations: Who espouses the different debates?

Part of the reason why debates on EU–Turkey relations have been so varied and at times non-communicating lies in the fact that a very wide set of stakeholders within the EU have articulated these debates. These elite debates, particularly when presented by governmental or political actors, have certainly been constrained and moulded by public opinion. However, much of the direction of causality lies in the reverse: public opinion is primarily formed through the messages delivered by elite stakeholders, which in turn often hide behind public opinion when adopting defensive positions in a classic Putnamite 'two-level game'.[34]

State institutions

The first type of stakeholder on EU–Turkey relations includes official institutions: governments, foreign ministries and civil services, parliaments and other relevant state actors. These stakeholders tend to have greater influence on EU–Turkey relations in those member states in which Turkey is a low-level political issue, such as in Poland or the UK, as well as in countries where there is a relatively strong bi-partisan support for Turkey's accession to the EU, such as the UK or Italy, and thus where Turkey has not become an issue of domestic political competition and debate. State actors tend to focus their debates on EU–Turkey relations on questions related to foreign policy and Turkey's reform process. In turn their views regarding Turkey's prospective membership have tended to be rather positive. This is because actors within state institutions dealing with Turkey are normally located in foreign ministries or in foreign affairs committees in parliaments.[35] Furthermore, civil services are sensitive to *pacta sunt servanda* arguments,[36] whereby Turkey, having been granted candidacy in 1999, ought to proceed with the accession process on the exclusive basis of its compliance with EU conditions and its adoption of the *acquis communautaire*, as also argued by the Turkish foreign ministry and government.

Political parties

Next we find political parties. This is the domain where we see the largest degree of variance across member states in terms of favoured debates and ensuing positions on Turkey's accession process. It is these differences, rooted in the domestic politics and trajectories of each member state, which above all else explain the absence of a single European debate on Turkey. The area of similarity and overlap across member states lies in the extremes. Far-right parties tend to oppose resolutely Turkey's membership on the grounds of identity, interpreted in strongly essentialist terms focused on religion and culture. These parties are also backed by some segments within strongly Catholic parties across the EU. Hence, the similar rhetoric permeating the *Lega Nord* in Italy, FPÖ in Austria, the *Dansk Folkeparti* in Denmark, the *Mouvement pour la France* and LAOS in Greece, as well as some elements within Law & Justice in Poland, the CDU/CSU in Germany or the Union of Christian Democrats in Italy.[37]

Parties on the far-left instead often tend to mildly oppose Turkey's accession while being open to change. They reject Turkey's membership for reasons linked to Turkey's reform process, which they consider to be still incomplete and deficient. They oppose Turkey's accession in view of Turkey's ongoing human rights record, its treatment of the Kurds, its reluctance to recognise the Armenian genocide and its deregulated labour markets. However, they would be ready to accept Turkey's accession if the country were to fully reform and are enthusiastic of the assets Turkey would bring to a multicultural Europe. Following this line of thinking we find *Rifondazione Comunista* in Italy, *Socialistisk Folkeparti* in Denmark as well as the Greens in Austria.[38]

When it comes to the mass centre-left and centre-right parties in the EU, differences prevail and no single debate or line of argument dominates. In some member states we find strong bipartisan support in favour of Turkey's accession for reasons ranging from foreign policy (Italy and the UK) to national security (Greece). In other member states there is weak bipartisan support for Turkey's accession (Denmark, Poland) or alternatively stark divisions cutting within and between party lines (Germany), in so far as mainstream political parties are persuaded about the foreign policy gains to be reaped by Turkey's membership while being concerned about the identity implications for the EU (Denmark and Poland). Finally in a third group of member states there is a strong bipartisan rejection of Turkey's EU bid for reasons related to EU institutions, immigration, identity, and borders (Austria and France).

Business

Business, across all member states, represents the single most ardent, committed and undivided supporter of Turkey's EU cause for reasons inextricably linked to debates about the enlarged EU's competitiveness in the global economy. While claims that Turkey is 'already in Europe' in view of its participation in the EU customs union since 1996 may give rise to doubts regarding the degree to which

European businesses are truly committed to Turkey's full membership, most business stakeholders across the member states confirm the importance attributed to Turkey's reform process, which they view as being intrinsically tied to the anchor of membership.[39] In other words, while EU business stakeholders consider Turkey to be already 'in Europe', as confirmed by their trade and investment decisions, their expectation as well as their desire is that Turkey will become a full member state. Interestingly, this is largely true also of the most sceptical member states: France and Austria.[40] This said, European businesses have been relatively silent stakeholders in the EU–Turkey debate, having sway on government positions, but not exposing themselves in public debate. With few and far between exceptions such as the report published by *Dansk Industri* in Denmark, the activities of TÜSİAD in Germany, or the *Saison de la Turquie* financed by French business, the strong and committed support of business stakeholders has not translated into a vocal EU-wide economic lobby in support of Turkey's cause.[41]

Trade unions and professional associations

Next we find trade unions, professional associations and economic interest groups. Here, the story to be told is fairly consistent across member states, and most notably in Germany, Italy and France.[42] While far from being vocal, trade unions tend to take an interest in Turkey and are open to the prospect of Turkey's accession – or at the very least they are not against Turkey's EU bid – for reasons related to religion, culture and identity in view of their general embrace of the notion of a multicultural European identity.

However, trade unions in particular are concerned with the state of labour rights in Turkey and the deregulation of the Turkish labour market, which, they fear, could either spill into the EU or may generate unfair competitive pressures on member state workers. This is particularly true of some sectors, such as the agricultural sector in member states such as Italy or the FNSEA in France. As far as debates surrounding Turkey's reform process are concerned, trade unions thus tend to be rather sceptical of the progress made by Turkey to date regarding the protection of workers' rights.

The media

Of critical importance is also the media. On the whole the media tends to paint a rather negative image of Turkey, driven above all by its commercial logic whereby stereotypes, sensationalism and alarmism 'sell'. This is certainly true of the tabloid press in cases like Poland and the UK, television in Germany, but also, to a lower degree, of the principal national dailies across member states, with the possible exceptions of Germany and the UK.[43] Cross-cutting tendencies in member states' media include 'culturalising' political issues and reporting Turkey's accession to the EU in the context of Islam and migration, as well as focusing on tragic incidents or crises, and linking these back to the depiction of Turkey as the unknown 'other' and its inability to conform to 'European standards of civilisation'.[44]

Churches

Another important set of stakeholders is the Church. The position of the churches is fairly consistent across member states. As far as the Catholic Church is concerned, the message of the Vatican has been cautious, yet some Catholic personalities have expressed a resolutely negative stance on the Turkey question. Reasons include broad-brush arguments related to Europe's 'Christian identity', as well as more subtle arguments related to Turkey's reform process and in particular the rights of Christians in Turkey.[45] Protestant churches in Germany and France in particular have discussed Turkey both in the context of religious freedoms in Turkey as well as in terms of secularism and its meaning in Europe.[46] This fairly homogenous message of churches across member states must however be mapped against the different degrees of influence that the churches yield within them. At one end of the spectrum we find Italy and Poland, where the views of the Vatican hold considerable sway on public opinion. At the other end, we find the UK, Denmark and, interestingly, Greece, where the Church either has been conditionally favourable to Turkey's accession (Greece) or has little sway over public opinion (UK and Denmark). In the middle we find Austria, France and Germany, where both Catholic and Protestant churches have spoken about Turkey but have influence on specific sectors of society rather than on public opinion writ large.

Diasporas

A final group of stakeholders in EU–Turkey relations include diaspora communities. Here again the arguments raised are fairly consistent across member states, with Turkish diaspora communities being viewed as relatively 'silent stakeholders'. This is either because of their small numbers (Poland, Italy), because they are weakly organised (Austria, France, Denmark), because they are relatively well-integrated and thus 'disappear' in the public space (Italy), or because the political system reduces the prospects for community groups to make an impact through electoral politics (UK). Only in Germany, in view of the sheer size of the Turkish community, is the EU–Turkey cause promoted by well-known personalities of Turkish origin and associations (often organised as 'Muslim' rather than specifically Turkish organisations).[47] This notwithstanding, in member states such as France, Denmark, Germany and Austria, the real and perceived non-integration of these 'silent stakeholders' becomes a prime source of debate against Turkey's EU bid by other vocal stakeholders. This relates to and contrasts with another diaspora community: the French of Armenian origin. While not being one monolithic community, the level of integration and organisation of the French Armenians has allowed them to occupy much of the space left vacant by a poor, irresponsible and unresponsive leadership regarding the EU–Turkey question.[48] Unsurprisingly, attitudes towards Turkey's EU membership have been rather negative and centred on Turkey's deficient reforms, in particular with regard to its non-recognition of the Armenian genocide and its relations with Armenia.

Table 5.2 Elite stakeholders and debates in EU–Turkey relations

Stakeholders	Debates	Positions
State institutions	European foreign policy Turkey's reforms	Conditionally in favour
Political parties	Identity and borders Turkey's reform and democracy Foreign policy National security EU institutions Immigration	Varied
Business	The EU in the global economy	Strongly in favour
Unions, Professional associations and civil society	Turkey's reform and labour rights The EU's multicultural identity Foreign policy, energy and the global economy	Conditionally favourable to strongly in favour
Churches	Turkey reforms and the rights of the Christian minorities EU identity and Christianity	Resolutely against to conditionally in favour
Media	Identity and culture Immigration	Sceptical or against
Diaspora communities	Turkey's reforms, Armenia and the Armenian genocide Immigration EU identity	Resolutely against to conditionally in favour

Table 5.2 summarises the different elite stakeholders in EU–Turkey relations within member states as well as Turkey, attributing to each set of stakeholders the debates that tend to be prioritised.

Conditioning factors shaping elite debates: Interests, perceptions and prejudices

Having mapped EU–Turkey debates and identified elite stakeholders engaged in them, let us turn to a third and final question: why do particular stakeholders prioritise particular debates and hold a particular position on EU–Turkey relations? What are the underlying motivations underpinning these debates and positions? Tackling this final question adds a layer of complexity to the topic at hand. Turkey's accession process has been complex and protracted not only because of the multiplicity of debates it has interlocked with and the multiplicity of elite stakeholders involved. The protractedness and complexity of Turkey's accession process is also due to the multiplicity of interests, perceptions and prejudices informing these debates. Naturally interests, perceptions and prejudices are closely interlinked: the underlying interests of different stakeholders shape the formation of perceptions and prejudices on Turkey and the EU; those interests in turn are moulded on the basis of prevailing perceptions and misperceptions about the EU and Turkey.

Domestic politics and interests

A first conditioning factor influencing the debate in different European countries is the manner in which EU–Turkey relations intersect with the interests of the elite stakeholders within their domestic political systems. One key factor influencing these interests is the extent and manner in which Turkey's accession process is linked to national identity politics in different member states. Wherever EU–Turkey discussions become part and parcel of the debates on national identity, EU–Turkey relations tend to become an issue in domestic politics. In France for example, the Turkey debate is inextricably tied to the domestic political 'battle' between secularists and Catholics within political parties, civil society, academia and the media, whereby the former appreciate Turkey's secularism while being wary of the Turkish state's control of religion, while the latter highlight Turkey's religion as an argument either in favour of Turkey's accession in a multi-religion Europe or against Turkey's membership on essentialist grounds relating to Turkey's different religion.[49] In Germany, Austria and Denmark, the debates on national identity are instead related to the different views on the role of existing Turkish and Muslim migrant communities in the definition of national identities.[50] In other words, particularly in Germany – the member state with by far the largest Turkish diaspora in Europe – the debate about Turkey's accession to the EU reflects the different views about the German identity itself, ranging from former Chancellor Helmut Kohl's explicit emphasis on Christianity as opposed to former Foreign Minister Joschka Fischer or the Greens' emphasis on multiculturalism, the latter being linked in no small measure to Germany's change in its citizenship law in 1999.[51] By contrast, and in view of the small Turkish communities in Finland, Italy, Poland, Slovenia, Spain, Sweden or the UK, debates about national identity in these countries have little or nothing to do with Turkey, explaining in part the lack of public debate on Turkey beyond expert elite levels. However, if EU–Turkey relations were to become an issue in the contested definitions of national identities in these countries, the level of attention in public debate on this question could rise, not necessarily to the benefit of Turkey's accession process.

Another issue shaping stakeholder interests in EU–Turkey relations is the level and type of contact with Turkey. Again, depending on the degree and nature of contact and acquaintance with Turkey, views on EU–Turkey relations may radically change. In countries such as the UK and Poland, Turkey is debated predominantly within private elite circles, in which expert discussion encourages a relatively detached and fine-tuned assessment of the pros and cons of Turkey's accession. In other contexts, the contacts and interests of specific groups shape the nature of the debate on Turkey. The large Armenian diaspora in France or the defence establishment in the UK feed and generate ideas shaping national views on EU–Turkey relations, leading in the first case to an acute awareness of the question of the Armenian genocide and in the latter case on the national security gains to be reaped from Turkey's EU membership. Geographical proximity also plays a role in determining the degree and type of contact between different EU actors and Turkey, shaping interests regarding EU–Turkey relations. For obvious geographical reasons, Turkey plays a far more prominent role in the public debate in Greece or Bulgaria than it does in Finland. Despite incomparable differences in terms of absolute size and weight, to Finns the importance of Estonia's accession was far greater than that of Turkey, explaining the differences in the levels of public debate and attention in Finland about the former case compared with the latter. Economic and social contact is also important. The rising trade levels between the UK or Germany on the one hand and Turkey on the other, the growing British and German business and property investments in Turkey, and the rising levels of British and German tourism in Turkish coastal resorts, all contribute in diffusing ideas about the expected positive impact of Turkey's membership in Britain and Germany.[52] This contrasts with other member states such as Austria, whose business and trade links with Turkey are still rather low. Finally historical ties also play a critical and often negative role, rendering Austria or Greece's instinctive attitudes towards Turkey far more sceptical than those of other member states.

Perceptions of 'Europe'

A second conditioning factor shaping elite debates on EU–Turkey relations is the different perceptions of Europe within the EU and Turkey. Different ideas of what the EU is or should be critically shape the manner in which different stakeholders view Turkey's accession. Simply put, differences in attitudes depend on whether the EU is perceived as a matter of domestic or foreign policy.

Where the EU is viewed through the lens of domestic policy, the focus of attention rests on the 'inside': on factors affecting the EU's internal set-up in terms of institutions, society, economics, identity and culture. It is the widespread perception of the EU as a matter of domestic policy that raises the stakes of questions such as Turkey's impact on EU institutions, budget, social cohesion and agriculture. This is especially the case in member states such as France and Germany, whose mandate deals primarily with internal EU policies. The perception of the EU as an internal political project by many in France and Germany also heightens the importance attributed to such issues as Turkey's impact on migration flows within the enlarged EU. Rising and changing migration patterns have implications on the formation of the EU's internal identity, an identity emphasised much by those who focus on the Union as a political project. For others, such as British conservatives, it is precisely the dilution of the European political project entailed by ongoing enlargements that consolidates support for Turkey's accession.

By contrast, those who view the EU primarily through the lens of foreign and security policy tend to focus on different issues, with correspondingly different positions on EU–Turkey relations. Many in the UK, Finland, Poland, Slovenia and Turkey itself, perceive the EU as a matter of foreign policy. As such, they are far more inclined to highlight the impact that future member state Turkey would have on the EU as an international actor in neighbouring regions such as the Middle East, the Caucasus and Central Asia. As opposed to those who view the Union as a matter of domestic policy and express concern about extending the Union's identity and borders to Iraq, Iran or Syria, viewing this very fact through the lens of foreign policy encourages different and often more positive views about Turkey's EU membership. Seen from a foreign policy angle, the Poles, Germans and Slovenes praise Turkey as an asset in promoting Europe's energy security; the British and Danes emphasise Turkey's collaboration in the fight against terrorism; the British argue that EU member Turkey would strengthen EU–NATO cooperation as well as EU–US relations; and security specialists highlight Turkey's contribution to EU defence capabilities, referring to Turkey's participation in European defence efforts in Lebanon, Afghanistan, Bosnia, Macedonia and the Congo. To these stakeholders, the internal dimension of the EU is of secondary importance. Hence, for example, even if a Polish security specialist appreciates that Turkey's membership may entail a redistribution of structural funds away from Poland, he/she may well favour Turkey's accession in view of the positive implications it would have for the EU as a foreign policy actor.

Misperceptions and prejudices about Turkey

A third conditioning factor shaping views on EU–Turkey relations are perceptions, misperceptions and prejudices about Turkey itself. Particularly after the attacks on 11 September 2001, Turkey is frequently viewed both by supporters and opponents of its EU membership as a Muslim or 'Islamic' country.[53] The current geopolitical context encourages many in Europe and Turkey to highlight religion as a main defining feature of what Turkey is, what it can contribute to Europe and what instead it detracts from it. Yet, this essentialist understanding of Turkey makes these arguments, whether in favour or against Turkey's membership, equally problematic. Either way, viewing Turkey primarily through the lens of 'Islam' means assuming that Turkey is the 'other'; an assumption which ultimately hinders Turkey's European integration.[54]

Most frequently, viewing Turkey as 'Islamic' works directly to the detriment of EU–Turkey relations. Particularly in the post-Cold War context when civilisational prisms often shape Europe's self-understanding, Turkey falls into the 'wrong' category, grouped together with millions of other people, with their respective religions, traditions, languages and cultures, into the black box of the 'other'. Turkey's European integration is resisted by those who associate it with the failure of integrating Muslim migrant communities in Europe.[55] This expected failure of integration fans fears about the negative impact of Turkey's accession to the EU, as well as the inability of EU conditionality to transform the inherently 'different' Turkey into accepting European values, beliefs and codes of action. In some instances, these arguments verge on outright racism and xenophobia. This is often the case when the understanding of Turkey as the 'other' is transposed into the realm of security, encouraged by fears about 'Islamic terrorism'.[56] In other instances, these arguments are simply ill-founded. There is no concrete reason why Turkey's integration into the EU should mirror in any way the integration of Pakistanis in the UK, Algerians in France or Moroccans in Spain. Believing this to be the case not only arbitrarily ascribes primary importance to one definition of identity – religion – but also presumes causal links which simply do not exist.

Less frequently, Turkey's 'otherness' is used as an argument in favour of its accession to the EU. To those viewing the EU as a matter of domestic policy, the integration of Muslim Turkey could aid the integration of Muslim migrants into the EU, regardless of whether these communities have any connection to Turkey beyond the loose link of religion. To those viewing the EU as a domain of foreign policy instead, the integration of a 'different' member state such as Turkey could help the EU confront its security threats and seize the opportunities in the turbulent East. Turkey, the argument goes, could act as a 'litmus test' demonstrating that Islam and democracy can be compatible, and can thus represent a 'model' or an 'inspiration' to other 'Islamic' countries. Premised on the assumption that there is an inherent tension between Islam and democracy, Turkey is mentioned as the quintessential test case demonstrating how this tension can be resolved; Turkey becomes the exception that confirms the rule. To others instead, Turkey can act as a 'bridge' to the 'Islamic world'. Many have suggested that Muslim Turkey could help the Union 'enter' the East, allowing it to hedge and confront the security threats emanating from this region, ranging from terrorism to illegal migration. Yet these 'positive' arguments about Turkey's potential role in the EU are based on precisely the same mental categories, the same forms of othering, as negative arguments shunning Turkey in view of its identity. In other words, the mental categories used are the same, irrespective of whether the arguments are set in the framework of the 'clash of civilisations' or benign variants of an 'alliance' or 'dialogue' of civilisations.[57] In both cases, two main identity boxes are artificially classified and defined, leaving Turkey in the uncomfortable position of having to act as a litmus test reconciling the two or as a tenuous bridge between these hypothesised juxtaposed worlds. These arguments are problematic not only because they are superficial and prejudiced, but also because they hinder a deeper understanding between the EU and Turkey, necessary for the accession process to succeed.

Conclusions

This chapter has explored a critical factor underpinning Turkey's *sui generis* relations with the EU and their turbulent evolution over the decades: European debates on EU–Turkey relations. It has done so by tackling three interlinked questions: What are the debates surrounding Turkey's accession process? Who are the stakeholders engaged in these debates? Why are these debates selected and conducted in particular ways? The answers to these three questions highlight a key reason explaining why Turkey's accession process has been so complex and protracted: Turkey's accession process has been complicated by the fact that it has interlocked with a multiplicity of debates, conducted by a multiplicity of stakeholders for multiple critical motivations grounded in interests, perceptions as well as prejudices. These debates have varied widely, as a reflection of different interests and ideas, which are either directly or indirectly related to the EU–Turkey question. These debates have also oscillated over time, whereby particular issues are sparked and others diffused by different stakeholders at different points in time, again as the result of the changing configurations of domestic, regional and international interests and ideas.

The major contention advanced in this chapter is that one of the reasons explaining the *sui generis* nature of Turkey's accession process is that the elite debates surrounding the question have acted as proxies for broader views on Turkey, Europe and international affairs rather than on the specific relationship between Turkey and the EU. Within member states, the debate on Turkey has largely reflected different ideas about the desirable evolution of the Union and its place in the world as well as of the member state in question. Unlike any other candidate, Turkey's membership prospects have thus become deeply enmeshed with broader debates regarding the very essence and future of Europe, explaining to a large extent the complexity and protractedness of Turkey's journey to the EU.

Notes

1 This chapter draws on the research results of the two-year research project 'Talking Turkey' carried out by the Rome-based Istituto Affari Internazionali (IAI) and the Ankara-based Turkish Economic Policy Research Foundation (TEPAV) which resulted in two edited volumes: N. Tocci (ed.), (2007) *Conditionality, Impact and Prejudice in EU–Turkey Relations*, Quaderno IAI. Online. Available http://www.iai.it/sections/pubblicazioni/iai_quaderni/Indici/quaderno_E_09.htm; and N. Tocci (ed.), (2008) *Talking Turkey in Europe: Towards a Differentiated Communication Strategy*. Available http://www.iai.it/sections/pubblicazioni/iai_quaderni/Indici/quaderno_E_13.htm.

2 For an analysis of European public opinion on Turkey, refer to the chapter by E. Ş. Canan-Sokullu and Ç. Kentmen in this volume.

3 I am indebted to Richard Whitman for raising this point during a 'Talking Turkey' workshop held in Rome on 23 March 2007.

4 European Council (2005) *Turkey's Negotiating Framework*, 3 October 2005, Luxembourg. Online. Available http://ec.europa.eu/enlargement/pdf/turkey/st20002_05_TR_framedoc_en.pdf.

5 M. Emerson, 'Vade Mecum for the Next Enlargements of the European Union', *Policy Brief*, No. 61, December, Brussels: CEPS, 2004, pp. 2–3.

6 B. Grgic, 'Conditionality, impact and prejudice in EU–Turkey relations: A view from Slovenia and "New Europe"', in N. Tocci (ed.), 2007, op. cit.

7 M. Emerson and N. Tocci, 'Turkey as Bridgehead and Spearhead: Integrating EU and Turkish Foreign Policy', *EU–Turkey Working Paper*, No.1, Brussels: CEPS, 2004.

8 See for example Open Society Foundation Turkey, *Reflections of EU–Turkey Relations in the Muslim World*, İstanbul, July 2009.

9 K. Kirişci, N. Tocci, and J. Walker, 'A neighborhood rediscovered: Turkey's transatlantic value in the Middle East', *Brussels Forum Paper*, March 2010.

10 A. Le Gloannec, 'Conditionality, impact and prejudice in EU–Turkey relations: A view from France', in N. Tocci (ed.), 2007, op. cit.

11 S. Goulard, 'Contre l'entrée de la Turquie dans l'Union européenne – L'Union européenne de nos mérites', *Pouvoirs*, No. 115 – La Turquie, November 2005, pp. 139–151.

12 A. Merkel, 'Speech by A. Merkel, German Parliament, plenary debate on EU–Turkey relations', 16 December 2004.

13 A. Ananicz, 'Conditionality, impact and prejudice in EU–Turkey relations: A view from Poland', in N. Tocci (ed.), 2007, op. cit.

14 Le Gloannec, 2007, op. cit.

15 R. Whitman, 2007, 'The United Kingdom and Turkish accession: The enlargement instinct prevails', in N. Tocci (ed.), 2007, op. cit.

16 Le Gloannec, 2007, op. cit.

17 D. Devrim, and E. Schulz (2009) *Enlargement fatigue in the European Union: From enlargement to many unions*, Real Istituto Elcano Working Paper, Madrid: Elcano, Online. Available http://www.realinstitutoelcano.org/wps/portal/rielcano_eng/Content?WCM_GLOBAL_CONTEXT=/elcano/elcano_in/zonas_in/europe/dt13-2009.

18 Le Gloannec, 2007, op. cit.

19 L. Narbone, 'Conditionality, impact and prejudice in EU–Turkey relations: A view from Brussels', in N. Tocci (ed.), 2007, op. cit.

20 D. Jung, 'Conditionality, impact and prejudice in EU–Turkey relations: A "Northern"view', in N. Tocci (ed.), 2007, op. cit.

21 H. Yılmaz, 'Turkish identity on the road to the EU', in S. Verney and K. Ifantis (eds), *Turkey's Road to EU Membership*, London: Routledge, 2009, pp. 81–91.

22 Le Gloannec, 2007, op. cit.

23 Le Gloannec, 2007, op. cit.

24 Ananicz, 2007, op. cit.

25 K. Derviş, D. Gros, F. Öztrak, and Y. Işık (2004) *Turkey and the EU Budget: Prospects and Issues*, EU–Turkey Working Paper Series, Brussels: CEPS. Online. Available http://shop.ceps.eu/BookDetail.php?item_id=1148.

26 For a discussion of the immigration issue in the context of security, see the chapter by P. Bilgin in this volume.

27 C. Günay, 'Conditionality, impact and prejudice in EU–Turkey relations: A view from Austria', in N. Tocci (ed.), 2007, op. cit.

28 Jung, 2007, op. cit.

29 K. Ifantis, 'Conditionality, impact and prejudice in EU–Turkey relations: A view from Greece', in N. Tocci (ed.), 2007, op. cit.

30 R. Whitman, 'The United Kingdom and Turkish accession: The enlargement instinct prevails', in N. Tocci (ed.), 2007, op. cit.

31 L. Narbone and N. Tocci, 'Running around in circles? The cyclical relationship between Turkey and the European Union', *Journal of South European Politics and Society*, 2007, vol. 9, no. 3, pp. 233–246.

32 P. Luif, S. S. Senyücel, and C. Z. Ak (2009) *How common is the Common Foreign and Security Policy of the European Union? Where Does Turkey Fit In?* TESEV Publications, March, Online. Available http://www.tesev.org.tr/UD_OBJS/Foreign AndSecurityPolicy.pdf.

33 Transatlantic Trends (2009) *Topline Data*, p. 24. Online. Available http://www.gmfus.org/trends/2009/docs/2009_English_Top.pdf.

34 R. Putnam, 'Diplomacy and domestic politics: The logic of two-level games', *International Organization*, 1988, vol. 42, no. 3, pp. 427–460.

35 See A. Balcer, 'Polish stakeholders in the EU–Turkey debate', in N. Tocci (ed.), 2008, op. cit.; R. Whitman, 'Member state stakeholders, views and influence: The case of the UK', in N. Tocci (ed.), 2008, op. cit.

36 For another analysis in this context, see the chapter by T. Diez in this volume.

37 See E. Alessandri, and E. Canan, '"Mamma Li Turchi!": Just An Old Italian Saying' in N. Tocci (ed.), 2008, op. cit; D. Jung, 'Danish stakeholders in the EU–Turkey debate', in N. Tocci (ed.), 2008, op. cit; A. Le Gloannec, 'Marcus Aurelius' foot: Looking for Turkey's project in the EU. An interpretation of the French debate on Turkey', in N. Tocci (ed.), 2008, op. cit; E. Fotiou, and K. Ifantis, 'Greek stakeholders in the EU–Turkey Debate' in N. Tocci (ed.), 2008, op. cit; A. Balcer, 'Polish stakeholders in the EU–Turkey debate', in N. Tocci (ed.), 2008, op. cit; B. Lippert, 'Wait-and-see attitudes of German stakeholders towards EU–Turkey relations' in N. Tocci (ed.), 2008, op. cit.

38 See Alessandri, and Canan, 2008; Günay, 2008; Jung, 2008, op. cit.

39 See Alessandri and Canan, 2008, op. cit.

40 Le Gloannec, 2008, op. cit.; Günay, 2008, op. cit.

41 Jung, 2008, op. cit.; Lippert, 2008, op. cit.; Le Gloannec, 2008, op. cit.

42 Le Gloannec, 2008, op. cit.; Alessandri and Canan, 2008, op. cit.; Lippert, 2008, op. cit.

43 Balcer, 2008, op. cit; Whitman, 2008, op. cit.; Lippert, 2008, op. cit. In the case of the UK however a growing link has been drawn by the media between the Turkish–Kurdish Diaspora and organised crime.

44 E. Svendsen, '"The Turks Arrive!" European Media and public Perceptions of Turkey', *ZEI EU–Turkey Monitor*, vol. 2, no. 3, November 2006, pp. 3–5. Online. Available http://www.zei.de/download/zei_tur/ZEI_EU-Turkey-Monitor_vol2no3.pdf.

45 Alessandri and Canan, 2008, op. cit.; Balcer, 2008, op. cit.

46 Lippert, 2008, op. cit.; Le Gloannec, 2008, op. cit.

47 Lippert, 2008, op. cit.

48 Le Gloannec, 2008, op. cit.

49 Le Gloannec, 2007, op. cit.

50 European Stability Initiative (2006), *The German Turkey Debate Under the Grand Coalition*, Berlin–Istanbul, Online. Available http://www.esiweb.org/pdf/esi_document_id_94.pdf; European Stability Initiative (2008) *A referendum on the unknown Turk? Anatomy of an Austrian debate*, Berlin–Istanbul, Online. Available http://www.esiweb.org/index.php?lang=en&id=156&document_ID=101.

51 C. Stelzenmueller, 'Turkey's EU bid: A view from Germany', in N. Tocci (ed.), 2007, op. cit.

52 Whitman, 2007, op.cit.; Stelzenmueller, 2007, op. cit.

53 B. Challand, 'From hammer and sickle to star and crescent: the question of religion for European Identity and a political Europe', *Religion, State & Society*, 2009, vol. 37, no. 1–2, 2009, pp. 65–78; D. Kuzmanovic, 'Civilization and EU–Turkey Relations', in D. Jung and C. Raudvere (eds), *Religion, Politics and Turkey's EU Accession*, New York: Palgrave Macmillan, 2008, pp. 41–63.

54 J. Casanova, 'The long, difficult, and tortuous journey of Turkey into Europe and the dilemmas of European civilization', *Constellations*, 2006, vol. 13, no. 2, pp. 234–247.

55 S. Goulard (2004) 'Challenge Europe Issue 12: Europe how wide? How deep? Turkey and the European Union: seeking an illusion', European Policy Centre 13 September, Online. Available http://www.epc.eu/en/ce.asp?TYP=CE&LV=177&see=y&t=42&PG=CE/EN/detail&l=3&AI=377

56 Jung, 2007, op. cit.

57 B. Rumelili, 'Negotiating Europe: EU–Turkey relations from an identity perspective', *Insight Turkey*, 2008, vol. 10, no. 1, pp. 97–110.

6   Public opinion dimension

Turkey in the EU? An empirical
analysis of European public opinion
on Turkey's 'protracted'
accession process

Ebru Ş. Canan-Sokullu and
Çiğdem Kentmen

Introduction

This chapter provides an in-depth cross-time analysis of European citizens' attitudes towards Turkey's accession to the European Union (EU). Our goal is to identify the direction of European opinion patterns concerning Turkey, and to explain key determinants of variation in popular support for Turkey's possible membership of the EU. The opinions and preferences of the mass public play a key role in Turkey's EU accession as EU member states require consent from the populace to accept candidate countries as members.[1] Turco-sceptic citizens might halt Turkey's accession to the EU by voting against it in referenda or by electing Turco-sceptic policy-makers at national and European levels who would work against Turkey. Thus, there is no doubt that understanding the nature and determinants of European public opinion is essential to future Turkey–EU relations.

For more than 20 years, despite political controversies on enlargement in the 1960s in some member states,[2] a majority in the European Community (EC) welcomed the entry of new countries in a mood of 'collective appraisal'. The first round of enlargement took place in the early 1970s when Denmark, the Republic of Ireland, Norway and the UK successfully negotiated accession treaties. Denmark, Ireland and UK joined the EC in 1973, though Norway remained outside. After the military dictatorships in Greece had been ousted and democratic government restored in 1974, Greece joined the EC in 1981, and Portugal and Spain joined in 1986 after they successfully accomplished the democratic transition from authoritarian regimes to democratic government. In 1995, Austria, Sweden and Finland became members of the EU.[3] Europeans (EU12) were extremely supportive of this wave of enlargement.[4] While the accession of Central and Eastern European Countries (CEECs) after the breakdown of communist regimes was viewed favourably, there has been a lack of a clear-cut, overwhelming support regarding Turkey's accession.[5] A significant majority in the EU has had clear and persistent reservations about Turkey's accession.

In the late 1980s, Eurobarometer (EB) polls, which have regularly monitored European public opinion since 1973, incorporated for the first time relevant indicators to understand popular attitudes towards EC enlargement with Turkey. In 1988, Europeans were asked explicitly about their opinion on whether Turkey should be admitted to the EC (EB No: 30), and only 3 per cent of respondents expressed support. Among them, the Dutch were the most supportive of Turkey's accession with only 5 per cent favouring Turkey, whereas for 42 per cent of Greeks, Turkey's membership of the EU would be an important problem. Even after Turkey's acceptance as an official candidate for EU membership in 1999, public support for Turkey was low in Europe (EU15). Results from the EB No: 53 (conducted in 2000) revealed that, among the 13 applicant countries Turkey had the lowest public support with 30 per cent in 2000.[6] The European Council adopted the EU–Turkey Accession Partnership document on 8 March 2001, providing a road map for Turkey's EU accession process. On 19 March, the Turkish Government adopted the National Programme for the Adoption of the *Acquis*, reflecting the Accession Partnership. In this progressive political mood, there was an increase of support to 34 per cent. However, this increase failed to continue in the following years and stayed far below 50 per cent (EB No: 56).

In 2005, after the 2004 enlargement, when the European Council decided to open membership talks with Turkey, a majority (52 per cent) of Europeans (EU25) opposed Turkey's membership, with only 35 per cent supporting (EB No: 63). In this climate the question of Turkey became more complicated. Turkey's membership gave rise to certain reservations in and across Europe. Europeans were clear on the idea that Turkey's accession should be subject to two main conditions: 'systematic respect for human rights' (84 per cent) and 'significant economic development' (76 per cent). Sixty-three per cent of Europeans feared that 'Turkish accession would encourage further unavoidable immigration to wealthier European countries', although 50 per cent considered 'Turkey a European country because of geographical reasons'. A similar proportion of Europeans was worried about 'cultural differences between Turkey and Europe', while only a minority of respondents considered that Turkey's membership would help 'mutual comprehension of European and Muslim values'. By 2008, Europeans (EU27) opposed integration with Turkey due to a common reservation: 'Turkey needs to comply with all membership conditions' (EB No: 69.2).

Research on European public opinion enhances our understanding of trends in European mass attitudes, and generates significant political insights in, among other things, enlargement policies. If European decision-makers had had a better picture of the dynamics of citizen attitudes, the results of the Norwegian, Greenlander or Irish referenda might have been different.[7] Since the early 1980s, there has been a flood of research on European attitudes toward European integration. Most of these studies have been motivated by questions including – but not limited to – the following: Do citizens perceive European integration as a good or a bad thing? When do citizens think that their country has benefited from integration? Is xenophobia a motive behind opposition to integration with other countries? Do personal economic expectations, human capital, age and gender affect attitudes toward the EU? However, it must be noted that most of the literature on public opinion deals with either what member state citizens think about the progress of European integration or under which conditions candidate country citizens support accession to the EU. Cross-time and cross-country analyses, which mostly rely on survey data, seek to find answers to those questions and provide a map of individual preferences for academic and political analysts.

A particularly important gap in the literature is the lack of empirical research that focused on why and to what extent member state citizens support a candidate country's bid to join the EU. This is an important question since after the European Council approves of, and the European Parliament gives assent to, an accession treaty, it is sent to member states for ratification. These states either ratify the accession treaty in their parliaments or submit it to referendum. Either way, a candidate country's accession is subject to the consent of a member state's citizens. In sum, there is a need to frame theoretical explanations and generate empirical evidence on the dynamics of public attitudes toward candidate countries.

This chapter contributes to the burgeoning literature on European public opinion by testing different competing theories developed to explain attitudes of member states' citizens toward Turkey's accession to the EU in the 2000s. Although the European *vox populi* has been monitored closely in recent years, the type of cross-country and cross-time study reported here is a missing element in the literature. We investigate the question of whether it is viable to talk of a European consensus on Turkey's much debated protracted accession process. We also compare the explanatory powers of mainstream theories of public opinion on EU enlargement. Given that public opinion is not a *monomorphous* organism, it shows change in structure and exists in a variety of forms. Hence as *it is erroneous to reduce the popular thinking in Europe to a single dimension*, this chapter provides an empirical examination of different theories of public opinion on EU enlargement.

We first analyse whether the European public adopts a utilitarian perspective derived from the perceived costs and benefits of enlargement. Does instrumental justification of costs and benefits encourage or discourage people from supporting Turkey's membership? Do Europeans value Turkey's EU membership with utilitarian calculations of egocentric or sociotropic costs and benefits in a wide range of considerations? Second, we turn to identity-related explanations and ask whether Turkey's accession is perceived in connection with a shared 'European' identity that is defined with cultural, religious or universal values. To what extent do shared values and principles characterise Europeans' popular position on Turkey? Do they prioritise Christian values and principles, and thus evaluate Muslim Turkey's credentials in this line? This second point also stresses the importance of shared European norms such as democratic values, rule of law and the protection of and respect for human and minority rights in an applicant country. We also delve into whether and how European public opinion has changed over time and across countries with different experiences of EU membership. All in all, we aim at implying possible policy implications of analysing the 'essential domino' – the public opinion – of the European enlargement project for the study of Turkey–EU relations. In our analysis, we rely on Eurobarometer survey data, using descriptive and multinomial logistic regression analysis to estimate the dynamics that explain the cross-time evolution of European public opinion on Turkey's EU membership.

Theoretical overview of public opinion on enlargement of the European Union

In this section, we briefly review two main sets of theories on public opinion – utilitarian and identity-based theories – and review some of the empirical literature on attitude formation in Europe. We discuss how well these theories apply to the Turkish case and posit our hypotheses.

Utilitarian theories

Scholars have long debated whether utilitarian calculations are important ingredients of public opinion about the EU. Earlier literature on international political economy claimed that citizens were usually uninformed about national economic conditions and thus they were not adequately equipped to make strategic decisions about economic and financial matters.[8] However, empirical evidence shows that public opinion is driven by economic issues that directly affect citizens' daily lives, such as the replacement of national currencies with the Euro or the introduction of the Schengen visa regime.[9]

Recent research has generated two theories that predict how such utilitarian calculations shape public opinion, namely sociotropic (macro-economic) utilitarianism and egocentric (micro-economic) utilitarianism. Both share the assumption that individuals are rational actors who make cost/benefit calculations when making decisions. Individuals are capable of understanding what options are available for them, can put these options in an order from the most beneficial to the least, and prefer the option with the most advantages. Regarding EU membership, there are two main options available for individuals: to support or not to support their country's EU membership. Utilitarian assumptions imply that, if the economic benefits of integration with the EU exceed the costs, individuals are inclined to support EU membership. National economic factors and/or personal economic discontent should modify how people view the implications of EU membership.

More specifically, sociotropic theory suggests that citizens' attitudes toward the EU are based on how European Economic and Monetary Union (EMU) affects national economic conditions. If, for example, EMU raises inflation and/or unemployment rates, citizens will blame the EU. European citizens might view negative economic policy outcomes as a product of member states' actions or inaction at the EU level and therefore hold national governments as well as European integration responsible for worsening economic conditions.[10] On the other hand, member states have lost power within EU's multi-level governance structure. National governments are no longer the only decision-making actor; today, they share jurisdiction with local, regional and European level actors within the EU.[11]

Moreover, national economic spaces have been widely modified to comply with EU rules. This approach also points to the need that the integration project would not engender costs on member state economies. Based on these arguments, the sociotropic approach claims that individuals evaluate the performance of the EU policies on an economic basis. Given that objective evaluations of the national and European economy have a positive and statistically significant influence on support for European integration, we argue that support for enlargement depends on (Hypothesis 1) perceived macro-economic costs of enlargement on European and member state economies, (Hypothesis 2) compatibility between the levels of economic development of the candidate country and the EU, and (Hypothesis 3) the continuation of perceived financial benefits for member states.

Unlike sociotropic theory, egocentric theory claims that individuals support European integration if their personal economic and financial situation gets better as a result of integration. Personal benefits of the integration vary from one individual to another with differences in human capital (skills and knowledge). Citizens who have the skills required to take advantage of freedom of movement will more easily adapt themselves to the new conditions of the EU's internal market. For example, those who have higher occupational skills and education levels, such as engineers and college instructors, can look for jobs with better pay and working conditions in another state. Models of the pocketbook economy expect such citizens to have more positive views of the EU compared with low-skilled individuals, who are not in demand as much.[12] These models also predict that expensive lower-skilled workers should be especially against the internal market and the EU.[13] One reason is that economic integration allows firms to move production to member states with cheap unskilled labour, leaving local costly labour jobless. Another reason is that, in skill-scarce member states, unskilled workers can demand relatively higher wages prior to integration with other countries. However, after integration with new members, increased trade with unskilled member states will lower their wages, so they will develop unfavourable attitudes toward integration.

What expectations flow from the egocentric utilitarian model regarding European citizens' attitudes toward Turkey's EU membership? The answer to this question largely rests in the perceived fear of influxes of immigrants from candidate countries.[14] In the context of EU enlargement, immigration poses a significant perceived threat to individual's pocket economy. McLaren describes how individuals feel about competing with foreigners for jobs available in the home country as 'realistic threats'.[15] According to her, 'members of the dominant group may come to feel that certain resources belong to them, and when those resources are threatened by a minority group, members of the dominant group are likely to react with hostility'.[16]

Based on the assumptions of egocentric utilitarianism and the perceived fear of immigrants, we argue that member states' unskilled workers should be against Turkey's membership of the EU since (they might believe) it would result in an influx of Turkish unskilled workers into Europe. As research shows, Europe's population is declining due to its ageing population and low birth rates. This trend causes several economic and social problems in European countries, including decreases in production efficiency, global competitiveness and sustainable economic development.[17] Scarcity of unskilled young workers compels European member states to import foreign workers. However, even if importing cheap labour from Turkey decreases production costs, increased efficiency and lowered consumer prices, European unskilled labour might still oppose the free movement of Turkish workers since cheap Turkish labour would 'steal' their jobs as Western companies would prefer cheap Turkish labour over the costly Western unskilled labour force. In contrast, European skilled labour should support Turkey's EU membership because Turkey would import skill-intensive goods and services from skill-abundant Western European states. This would increase the demand for, and the wages of, skilled EU citizens. Therefore we expect that (Hypothesis 4) the perceived fear of immigrants because of employment concerns and (Hypothesis 5) the level of occupational skills, determines the level of support for Turkey's membership in EU member states.

Identity-based theories

Studies of social identity posit that utilitarian theories are reductionist since they assume that people are motivated only by economic incentives ignoring how identities, values and social status affect individual attitudes and behaviour. Social identity theories fill this gap by claiming that people act in accordance with their social identity, meaning individuals' acknowledgement of their membership of a social group. The main argument of social identity theory is that, even when the motivation behind the group formation is trivial, people tend to develop social identities, make distinctions between their group and outsiders, have favourable feelings towards their in-group, and maintain beliefs about in-group supremacy.[18] For example, Levine et al. found that fans of an English soccer team are more likely to help an injured person wearing their team's shirt than someone wearing a rival team's shirt.[19] Although a soccer team's thousands of fans do not personally know each other, rooting for the same team creates a bond among them, leading to feelings of connectedness. Studies suggest that 'we-feeling' and a sense of in-group supremacy also boost individual self-esteem; people think that if they are worthy enough to become a member of a positively distinctive group, they have positive personal characteristics.[20] Individuals therefore act in ways to preserve the inter-group distinctiveness that provides them with such psychological rewards, and so they are sceptical and hostile towards outsiders who threaten their group identity.[21]

Studies on identity claim that if supporting the same soccer team has the potential to lead to inter-group discrimination, then long-established identities, such as European identity, should also be associated with inter-group discrimination and increases in self-esteem.[22] Thus, like any other group identity, European identity should lead to increased protection of the in-group and favourable attitudes toward group members that share some common cultural, geographical and historical traits. It might be questioned whether EU citizens actually share a 'we-feeling', as member states' cultural and linguistic differences might prevent them forming a collective identity,[23] and, as Smith argues, the EU lacks historical roots in the psyche of European citizens.[24] As regards European cultural identity we argue that (Hypothesis 6) the level of vicinity to Turkey and Turkish cultural, geographical or historical traits determines the level of attitudes towards EU enlargement with this country.

On the other hand, as some scholars claim, Europeans do share common values based on constitutional patriotism, liberal democracy, and respect for universal and human rights. Such values might create a bond among EU citizens and differentiate them from other regions, so that Europeans might view those who do not share the common traits of European culture as 'others', viewing them as a threat to their European identity.[25] Scholars suggest that Europeans do not view Turkey as European since it does not have a consolidated democracy or it did not experience the Renaissance or reformist movements at the same time as Western Europe.[26] On the contrary, Casanova pronounces that 'Muslim democracy is as possible and viable today in Turkey as Christian democracy was half a century ago in Western Europe'.[27] As Alessandri and Canan argue '[t]he contested nature of Islam and democracy in Europe among public inextricably relates to the EU membership of Turkey – a predominantly Muslim but secular state founded on democratic values and principles'.[28] We join this debate over how right-based European identities affect individuals' attitudes concerning Turkey's accession to the EU by arguing that (Hypothesis 7) if a candidate country meets the criteria about rights and democracy then public opinion in the EU becomes more pro-enlargement.

Identity-related research also tackles the religious identities that might be conducive to shape individual political attitudes. Scholars claim that the norms and values attached to religious identities provide uninformed individuals with heuristics for understanding the political domain and explaining which actions and attitudes are socially preferable.[29] For example, studies show that Christian voters tend to support the political party that shares the world view of their church.[30] Religion also provides individuals with feelings of certainty, affirmation and stability in a rapidly changing world, since religions are based, to a large extent, on concrete doctrines. This suggests that people should be keen to preserve their religious identity as it elevates positive feelings about the self and disseminates information about the political process.[31] According to Casanova, the issue of Europe's cultural and religious identity, and the prospect of Turkey's joining the EU cause increasing unease among Europeans, Christian and 'post-Christian' alike.[32] Along this line, we expect (Hypothesis 8) religious identities to affect public opinion in Europe on predominantly Muslim Turkey's EU membership.

The final strand of identity-centric public opinion research focuses on attitudes concerning political incorporation and social visibility of the out-group – the 'immigrants' – with reference to protection of shared in-group identity and xenophobia. Some scholars focus on the perceived threat of other cultures for in-group identity and its protection.[33] Carey expects individuals who favour in-group protection to be less supportive of immigration into Europe.[34] He claims that '[s]ome individuals are more concerned with the degradation of the nation state than with the personal costs and benefits to their own lives'.[35] They prefer the 'the protection of the in-group and the group identity from the out-group'.[36]

In the context of EU enlargement, immigrants pose a significant perceived 'symbolic' threat to the collective (national/European) identity. McLaren conceptualises threats posed to in-group identity with specific reference to 'symbolic' threats.[37] She argues that 'symbolic threat' is associated with a fear that others will change the domestic culture. Kinder and Sears argue that the notion of symbolic threats, whereby people perceive that the 'other' (or 'minority') group have different morals, values, beliefs and attitudes than their own majority group, will enhance prejudice.[38] To sum up, as McLaren also argues, 'threats are likely to be at play in explaining extreme anti-immigrant hostility in Europe', and so are likely to be a factor in the popular debate on Turkey's EU membership bid.[39] As a corollary to this debate around symbolic threats, we examine whether (Hypothesis 9) the direction of European public attitudes depends on the fear that Turkish immigrants pose a threat to the in-group European identity.

Methodology

In this chapter, we utilise the data that come from EB surveys that explore European public attitudes towards Turkey's membership. We include surveys that specifically dealt with aspects of Turkish enlargement, as discussed previously. Firstly, we carry out a cross-time and cross-country contextual descriptive examination with survey data dating back to December 1988 (EB No: 30). Secondly, we utilise a quantitative analysis that covers the opinion patterns between 2000 and 2008. The selected surveys in this period allow us to analyse European attitudes toward Turkey at the EU15, EU25 and EU27 levels.[40] These surveys comprise the questions that enable us to measure our dependent and independent variables discussed in theoretical framework. Our analysis reveals cross-time patterns and thematic aspects of Turkish enlargement so long as survey data are available.

The dependent variable in our analysis is 'public opinion on Turkey's EU membership'. To operationalise it, we use the EB question: '*For each of the following countries, would you be in favour of or against [Turkey] becoming part of the European Union?*' (see Appendix). The binary response to the dependent variables was whether individuals were in favour of (Y = 1) or against (Y = 2) Turkey's EU membership.[41]

In this chapter we aim at delving into the question of how public opinion differed with reference to utilitarian calculations (egocentric and sociotropic), and identity-based concerns and evaluations. We also look at whether opinions changed over time. Since the EB surveys do not systematically incorporate the same questions every year and have even addressed some of them only once, our models for different years have different independent variables. Each model includes the same control variables: age, gender, ideological self-placement, occupation and country of origin.[42] We chose these controls because literature on public opinion claims that they affect political attitudes.[43] Measurement of independent and control variables are explained in the Appendix.

Six regression models are constructed with the variables using data from the selected EB surveys. Since our dependent variable is categorical, each model is tested through multinomial logistic regression to detect the multinomial distribution and to calculate different effects of predictors.[44] The association between public opinion on Turkey's EU membership and the potential impacts of utilitarian and identity-related perceptions are examined through multinomial logistic regression analysis.[45] Thus, a positive coefficient of independent and control variables would indicate an increasing likelihood of favourable (pro-Turkish) opinion on EU enlargement with Turkey.

Empirical analysis

Descriptive overview of trends in European public opinion on enlargement and Turkey's 'protracted' accession process

European public opinion has been monitored since 1974 with the inception of the systematic EB surveys. The earliest EB surveys devoted attention to the thematic coverage of Europeans' (EC6) priorities about issues such as the Common Market (EB No: 3, 1975), the then upcoming European Parliament elections in 1979, or the institutional formula of the EC6. In 1975, after the first enlargement of the EC6 to the EC9, European public opinion became variegated about these issues. For instance, the new EC citizens – the British, Danish and Irish – expressed a lower willingness to support the Common Market, benefits of EC membership and plans for a future European unification than the citizens in the original six members (EB No: 3). Given the higher salience attached to issues like coordination of social policies, regional development differences or the common fight against inflation, Turkey's relations with the Common Market was neither on the political nor on the public agenda.

In 1981, at a time when the EC enlarged with Greece (the 'EC10'), diffuse support for western European unification was worrisome, especially in the UK and Denmark.[46] The general mood suggested that supporters of the EC membership were in shorter supply between 1973 and 1981. This decline in support for the Common Market membership persisted over years. After the Spanish and Portuguese enlargement in 1986, the so-called 'Mediterranean Europeans' were remarkably more supportive of the EC membership than the 'old' Europeans. A year after the third enlargement of the EC, when Turkey applied for full membership of the EC in 1987, whether it would be 'a good or a bad thing' if a new state joined the EC was still *not* the issue at stake for Europeans (EC12).

Twenty-five years after European unification and with experiences of different phases of enlargement, Europe and integration was not in the forefront of ordinary people's concerns (EB No: 17). Citizens in the EC10 were more concerned with international developments as well as national politics. On the issue of Western European unification, there was a rather vague emotional consensus at around 54 per cent level of support (EB No: 18). Driven by utilitarian motivations, majorities were rather frustrated with the costs and benefits of Community membership for their own country. In other words, this feeling of frustration could be explained with the simple logic of the 'zero-sum game' that people associated the EC with and with perceptions about material benefits.

Prior to the second Mediterranean enlargement with Spain and Portugal, enlargement again became an issue at stake on survey agenda. On average, 6 out of 10 Europeans in the EC10 welcomed this enlargement (EB No: 23).[47] Variations of support for enlargement were largely dependent on individual's support for his/her own country's membership of the EC, perceived benefits from the EC and expectations from enlargement. All in all, the second Mediterranean enlargement generated Euro-optimism, which was evident in positive assessment of benefits embedded in the EC membership. Spanish and Portuguese accessions and the discussions on the ratification of the Single European Act created a popular interest in Community matters. Given this climate, attitudes towards European unification were very positive (80 per cent) (EB No: 26).

Europeans (EC12) were asked for their opinions in 1988 about which countries should be admitted to the EC (EB No: 30) and explicitly whether Turkey should be admitted. Turkey was among countries like Austria, Finland, Norway, Sweden and Switzerland.[48] While public opinion at large combined an expression of confidence about neighbouring people with consent about uniting all democratic countries of Western Europe, support for Turkey's admittance was expressed only at 3 per cent level (EB No: 30). The expansion of the EC towards Turkey was considered to be 'a very important problem' by 27 per cent of Europeans.

In the immediate aftermath of the end of the Cold War, Europeans were faced with the prospect of a new wave of immigration. This made European citizens (EU15) concerned about the plight of Central and Eastern European immigrants. Fear of immigration and its economic burdens dissuaded Europeans' positive opinions on the CEECs. As far as a European architecture in the year 2000 was questioned, for 55 per cent of Europeans there was an expectation that only Poland, Hungary and Czechoslovakia would become members of the EC by 2000 (EB No: 35).[49] As a remedy, the majority of European people (72 per cent) perceived the necessity of speeding up economic, political and monetary integration (EB No: 34) for a wider and democratic Western unification. Conditionally, for 66 per cent of Europeans once democracy and an open economy were established in Central and Eastern Europe, eastward expansion could be thought to be over.[50]

On the contrary, a larger majority (63 per cent) favoured the EC membership of EFTA members – Austria, Switzerland, Norway, Sweden and Finland – which would be more burden-free for the European economy and would bring more advantages to the EC (EB No: 37). Absolute majorities of European (EC12) citizens expressed their desire that the EC in the year 2000 should consist of 21 countries: the EC12, six EFTA countries, Poland, Hungary and Malta (EB No: 38). In this hypothetical composition Turkish membership was opposed (42 per cent) more than it was favoured (41 per cent) by Europeans.

Eight countries had applied to join the EC by 1992 – Turkey (1988), Austria (1989), Cyprus (1990), Malta (1990), Sweden (1991), Finland (1992), Norway (1992) and Switzerland (1992).[51] At a time when Austria, Finland and Sweden successfully finished their negotiations with the Commission and Council in 1993, overwhelming majorities (over 80 per cent) of European public opinion welcomed them as new members of the EU (EB No: 42). All in all, the overall effects of the 1995 enlargement on the EU were generally positive (64 per cent) (EB No: 43). Yet, enthusiasm for the CEECs enlargement was more circumspect and Europeans (EU15) were noticeably prudent about Turkey.

In 1998, the EU started accession negotiations with the Czech Republic, Cyprus, Estonia, Hungary, Poland and Slovenia, and set up Accession Partnerships with Bulgaria, Latvia, Lithuania, Romania and Slovakia, which would help speed up these countries' preparations for membership. In 1999, at the Helsinki Summit, the European Council gave Turkey the status of candidate country for EU membership. On this eventful enlargement agenda, Europeans were quite positive on the idea of enlarging the EU to include new European countries mostly because an enlarged EU would be more important in the world (72 per cent), enlargement would contribute to cultural enrichment (64 per cent) and would guarantee more peace and security (64 per cent). However, people were pessimist about the economic aspects of enlargement as it would cost their own country more money (47 per cent), less financial aid and more unemployment (35 per cent) (EB No: 50).

There was an extensive consensus that the EU should enlarge with countries that respected human rights and the principles of democracy (94 per cent) (EB No: 50). Support for Turkey among the 13 applicant countries that were in the accession process scored the lowest (30 per cent) (EB No: 53). Contrary to the highest public support for enlargement with Norway and Switzerland (70 per cent), Turkey's membership of the EU started receiving the lowest support (29 per cent) after 1999 (EB No: 51). The Spanish (42 per cent), Irish (45 per cent), Portuguese (38 per cent) and British (36 per cent) were more in favour of Turkey, contrary to the Greeks (77 per cent) and Austrians (66 per cent) continuous opposition to Turkish membership. In 2000, Greek and Austrian opposition dropped around five points (EB No: 53). Against the majority opposition in EU15 to Turkey's membership, the Spanish, Irish, Portuguese and British continued to express that they would be in favour of Turkey's becoming a part of the EU.[52]

European public opinion has been quite selective about candidate countries. For instance, in 2000, almost 44 per cent of Europeans (EU No: 15) believed that the enlargement should take place with some of the countries wishing to join, and 21 per cent gave outright support for enlargement (EB No: 55). Yet only 16 per cent of respondents believed that the EU should not be enlarged to any additional countries.[53] Previous concerns about economic costs prevailed over issues like the EU's global role (EB No: 55). By the end of 2001, Europeans were eight points more (51 per cent) in favour of the enlargement of the EU to include new countries and 30 per cent were against this.[54] In about a year's time, unlimited support for enlargement increased by three points. Even though a strong majority (68 per cent) held the view that after enlargement their personal lives would be about the same, for 10 per cent enlargement would ameliorate their personal lives. The main reasons for deterioration were all economic-based such as 'immigrants', 'occupation of job opportunities', 'unemployment', 'high costs of funding new members' and 'less community funds allocated to current members of the EU'.

At the outset of the twenty-first century, a positive political mood was about to emerge in terms of Turkey–EU relations, which was also followed by a positive opinion climate. The European Council adopted the EU–Turkey Accession Partnership on 8 March 2001 and it provided a road map for Turkey's EU accession process. In its immediate aftermath, on 19 March, the Turkish Government adopted the National Programme document for the Adoption of the *Acquis*, which reflected the Accession Partnership. Later, a regulation the Council adopted on 17 December 2001 increased EU financial support through a pre-accession instrument. In this positive political mood there was a four-point increase in public support (34 per cent) and yet a one-point increase in opposition (46 per cent) for Turkish accession (EB No: 56).[55]

It is also noteworthy to mention that the level of awareness of Europeans about enlargement was also increasing. For instance, in 2002, Turkey was the second most often quoted country among 13 candidate countries, after Poland. Poland was named by 27 per cent and Turkey by 20 per cent of Europeans. Given that 44 per cent of Europeans could not quote even one candidate country, such awareness about Turkey was remarkable (Flash EB No: 132 / 1, 2002). By the end of 2002, Turkey became the most remembered and most often quoted candidate country (31 per cent) ahead of Poland. Not surprisingly, the ongoing debates about Turkey's membership and the 2002 elections in Turkey might explain this 11-point increase in the level of Europeans' knowledge (Flash EB No: 132/2, 2002).

During the Copenhagen Summit, on 12–13 December 2002, it was decided that negotiations with Cyprus, the Czech Republic, Estonia, Hungary, Latvia, Lithuania, Malta, Poland, Slovakia and Slovenia would be completed; that Bulgaria and Romania were to join in 2007; and that accession negotiations with Turkey would be opened if, by December 2004, the European Council decided that Turkey would meet the Copenhagen political criteria. The lack of a predetermined membership date for Turkey, however, rekindled the debate on Turkey. This reflected itself in the mood of increased Turco-scepticism at mass public level. Between 2000 and 2002, the level of support for EU enlargement increased by eight points from 44 to 52 per cent, yet as far as Turkey's accession was concerned, public support continued to decrease while opposition remained relatively widespread (49 per cent) (EB No: 57).

Before the EU's historical enlargement to the East, support for enlargement, in general, remained slightly stagnant and Turkey was the least supported applicant country. On the other hand, the degree of awareness about Turkey's candidacy exceeded the 95 per cent level. Almost every European citizen (EU15) had already heard about this candidate country. This was the highest level of awareness of among all candidate countries (EB No: 59). Yet, a contradiction emerged regarding the likelihood of Turkey's joining the EU in 2004. The probability of Turkey joining the EU in 2004 among all candidate countries (accession countries included) was 42 per cent (Flash EB No: 140).

The year 2004 was a milestone, with the CEECs enlargement of the EU and the Treaty establishing a Constitution for the Union. As far as the enlargement forecasts for 2010 were concerned, a certain scepticism prevailed regarding the possibility of Europe becoming the world's leading economy by 2010 (EB No: 63).[56] In 2005, one out of two citizens was in favour of EU enlargement at a future date – the 10 new member states' citizens being even more supportive of a future enlargement. As in previous years, many people (42 per cent) expressed the opinion that enlargement would be on a selective basis, by integrating only some countries that wanted to join the EU. The majority (52 per cent) was also opposed to Turkey. Although in 2004 the European Council decided to open membership talks with Turkey, Turkey's accession was the least preferred accession by European (EU25) public opinion (32 per cent support) (EB No: 63).

During the post-2004 enlargement climate, the question of Turkey became even more complicated. Turkey's membership gave rise to certain reservations in and across Europe. Europeans were already clear on the idea that Turkey's accession should be subject to two main conditions: 'systematic respect for human rights' (84 per cent) and 'significant economic development' (76 per cent). Moreover, Europeans (63 per cent) feared that 'Turkish accession would encourage further unavoidable immigration to wealthier European countries' (EB No: 63). Half of them considered Turkey to be a European country because of 'geographical reasons'. A considerable number of Europeans were worried about 'cultural differences between Turkey and Europe'. There was a minority of Europeans who considered a *positive* aspect of Turkey's membership that it would help 'mutual comprehension of European and Muslim values'. Lastly and more optimistically, 45 per cent of Europeans thought that Turkey's accession would have an 'added value for Europe's security and defence' (EB No: 63). All in all, in 2005, support for enlargement decreased by one point in the EU25. A significant majority (55 per cent) of the EU25 public opinion remained against Turkey's membership (EB No: 64).

On the eve of the last wave of enlargement with Bulgaria and Romania, in 2006, European (EU25) public opinion remained divided about the enlargement.[57] The majority of Europeans persistently indicated that respect for human rights (85 per cent) and systematic economic development (77 per cent) were the two most important considerations for Turkey's accession. Fears about Turkish immigration were very widespread (66 per cent). For 61 per cent of Europeans, the problem was a significant cultural divergence between Turkey and the EU (EB No: 66). As in previous years, half of Europeans considered Turkey to be a European country, because it was geographically in Europe or historically belonged to Europe. On the other hand, from a security perspective, one third of Europeans were supportive of Turkey's EU accession given that it would strengthen European security in the region. Only one third of Europeans favoured Turkey's membership because they thought that it would be a remedy for ageing Europe (EB No: 66).

In conclusion, a descriptive examination of trends in public opinion on Turkey revealed that Europeans have constantly become more Turco-sceptic in past decades. In 2008, enlargement with Turkey's accession once again scored the lowest support.[58] Europeans were for integrating and enlarging with Turkey with a reservation: complying with all the conditions. If Turkey complied with all the conditions proposed by the EU, European public opinion would give a green light for Turkey's membership (46 per cent) (EB No: 69.2).

Multinomial logistic regression analysis

The association between public opinion on Turkey's EU membership and the potential impacts of utilitarian and identity-based perceptions are examined through multinomial logistic regression analysis using Eurobarometer data from 2000–2008. A positive coefficient of independent and control variables indicates an increase in the likelihood of favourable (pro-Turkish) or unfavourable (anti-Turkish) opinions on EU enlargement with Turkey. We test eight models where the predictors had different units.[59] Standard errors provide the parameter estimates (log-odds) that we requested 95 per cent confidence intervals (CI) for the odds-ratios.[60]

Public opinion on Turkey's EU membership in EU15: Cost-aversion vs. cultural richness

To start with the public opinion climate in EU15, our findings of the first model (Model EB53) showed that Europeans' support for their own country's EU membership and perceived benefits for their home country from the EU also had a significant and positive impact on EU enlargement with Turkey. High support for welcoming new member countries as an EU priority also translated into public support for Turkey's membership. Concerns about the level of economic development of a candidate country deterred Europeans' support for Turkey's accession to the EU (see Table 6.1). European citizens who thought that a candidate country should not join the EU if its level of economic development was not close to that of member states opposed Turkey's accession to the EU. This finding was in line with our sociotropic utilitarian expectation (Hypothesis 1) that macro-economic concerns drove public perceptions on enlargement. Those who opposed immigration from Muslim countries to work in the EU were also negative towards Turkey's membership. On the contrary, those who supported the idea that immigrants should be unconditionally accepted into the EU were significantly supportive of Muslim Turkey's EU membership. We contend that in this finding the central concern was more in line with religious identity assumptions. Hence we can partially confirm our expectation of the fear that Muslim and Turkish immigrants posed a threat to the in-group European identity (Hypothesis 9).

In our second model (Model EB54.1) we tested the impacts of costs and benefits of EU enlargement in general and individuals' perceived fears about the EU on their support for enlargement with Turkey. There was a direct and positive impact

Table 6.1 Multinomial logistic regression of European (EU15, EU25 and EU27) public opinion on Turkey's EU membership

	EU15		EU25		EU27	
	Model EB53 (2000)	Model EB54.1 (2000)	Model EB58.1 (2002)	Model EB63.4 (2005)	Model EB66.1 (2006)	Model EB69.2 (2008)
	B (SE)	B (SE)	B (SE)	B (SE)	B (SE)	B (SE)
Intercept	−2.105 *** (.371)	−2.944*** (.451)	−1.736*** (.297)	−1.504*** (.410)	−3.356*** (.393)	−1.011*** (.200)
Support for EU integration						
EU membership of own country 'good'	.376*** (.105)	.186 (.129)	.080 (.141)	−.153 (.161)	.519*** (.151)	.227** (.090)
Benefit from EU membership	.208* (.096)	.047 (.113)	−.206 (.115)	−.042 (.138)	−.231 (.130)	.267*** (.082)
Support for enlargement policy						
Enlargement: EU priority	.983*** (.059)	.594*** (.078)	.294*** (.081)	a	.307 (.235)	a
Enlargement: EU proposal	a	1.056*** (.090)	.844*** (.110)	.791*** (.109)	1.336*** (.098)	1.988*** (.056)
Enlargement: with all countries	a	a	1.614*** (.086)	1.545*** (.104)	a	a
Enlargement: with 'no' countries	a	a	−.843*** (.136)	−.693*** (.140)	a	a
Utilitarian Variables						
Sociotropic Utilitarianism						
Enlargement criterion: Economic development	−.526*** (.074)	−.403*** (.088)	a	a	a	a
Enlargement criterion: Costless for member states	.087 (.080)	−.103 (.095)	a	a	a	a
Enlargement outcomes: No costs for member states	a	.362*** (.075)	.298*** (.077)	a	a	a

(continued on the next page)

Table 6.1 continued

	EU15			EU25		EU27
	Model EB53 (2000)	Model EB54.1 (2000)	Model EB58.1 (2002)	Model EB63.4 (2005)	Model EB66.1 (2006)	Model EB69.2 (2008)
	B (SE)	B (SE)	B (SE)	B (SE)	B (SE)	B (SE)
Enlargement outcomes: Less financial aid to member states	a	-.162* (.078)	-.191 (.078)	a	a	a
Turkey's responsibility: Improving its economy	a	a	a	.162 (.163)	.179 (.159)	a
Fears about the enlargement: Cost of too much money for member states	a	-.311*** (.079)	a	-.071 (.091)	a	a
Egocentric Utilitarianism Enlargement outcomes: More unemployment:	a	-.094 (.080)	-.189* (.078)	a	a	a
Fears about the enlargement: Transfer of jobs to countries with lower costs	a	.042 (.078)	a	-.130 (.099)	a	a
Benefits of Turkey's accession: Regional security	a	a	a	1.265*** (.094)	1.697*** (.087)	a
Benefits of Turkey's accession: Rejuvenation of population	a	a	a	.477*** (.089)	.685*** (.085)	a
Costs of Turkey's accession: Risk of immigration	a	a	a	-.313** (.101)	-.528*** (.100)	a
Immigrants from Muslim countries 'not accepted'	-.651*** (.090)	a	a	a	a	a
Immigrants from Muslim countries 'unconditionally accepted'	.521*** (.072)	a	a	a	a	a

(continued on the next page)

Table 6.1 continued

| | | EU15 | | | EU25 | EU27 | |
| | | Model EB53 (2000) | Model EB54.1 (2000) | Model EB58.1 (2002) | Model EB63.4 (2005) | Model EB66.1 (2006) | Model EB69.2 (2008) |
		B (SE)	B (SE)	B (SE)	B (SE)	B (SE)	B (SE)
Identity-based Variables							
Cultural values	Enlargement outcomes: Cultural richness	a	.492*** (.091)	.352**** (.100)	a	a	a
	Fears about the enlargement: Loss of national / cultural identity	a	.006 (.078)	a	−.141 (.096)	a	a
	Benefits of Turkey's accession: Mutual understanding of values	a	a	a	1.061*** (.093)	a	a
	Cost of Turkey's accession: Significant cultural differences	a	a	a	−1.527*** (.089)	−1.640*** (.089)	a
Common traits	Turkey part of European geography	a	a	a	.861*** (.106)	.818*** (.102)	a
	Turkey part of European history	a	a	a	.425*** (.097)	.426*** (.092)	a
Rights	Enlargement criterion: Rights and Democracy	.337 (.306)	1.078** (.369)	a	a	a	a
	Turkey's responsibility: Respect for human rights	a	a	a	.062 (.202)	.570** (.198)	a
	Democracy represents EU	a	a	a	a	−.016 (.082)	−.072 (.045)
Religion	Religion important for society	a	a	a	a	.013 (.088)	a

(continued on the next page)

Table 6.1 continued

		EU15			EU25		EU27
		Model EB53 (2000)	Model EB54.1 (2000)	Model EB58.1 (2002)	Model EB63.4 (2005)	Model EB66.1 (2006)	Model EB69.2 (2008)
		B (SE)	B (SE)	B (SE)	B (SE)	B (SE)	B (SE)
Religion represents the EU		a	a	a	a	.135 (.241)	.152 (.127)
Religious: Strong		a	a	a	-.037 (.130)	.120 (.127)	a
Religious: Weak		a	a	a	.059 (.106)	.046 (.106)	a
Control Variables							
Ideology	Left	.257*** (.075)	-.058 (.082)	.024 (.082)	-.020 (.103)	-.034 (.103)	.246*** (.053)
	Right	.276*** (.071)	-.064 (.086)	-.187* (.090)	-.239** (.100)	-.232** (.096)	-.176*** (.053)
Gender	Male	-.096 (.060)	-.095 (.075)	-.037 (.074)	-.153 (.088)	.065 (.085)	-.029 (.045)
Age	15–24 years	.007 (.128)	.136 (.165)	.254 (.160)	.570*** (.215)	.497** (.206)	.301** (.113)
	25–39 years	-.203* (.096)	.050 (.119)	.156 (.121)	-.058 (.144)	.256 (.137)	.144* (.074)
	40–54 years	-.068 (.095)	.114 (.116)	.008 (.116)	.069 (.139)	.055 (.129)	.161** (.071)

(continued on the next page)

Table 6.1 continued

		EU15			EU25		EU27
		Model EB53 (2000)	Model EB54.1 (2000)	Model EB58.1 (2002)	Model EB63.4 (2005)	Model EB66.1 (2006)	Model EB69.2 (2008)
		B (SE)	B (SE)	B (SE)	B (SE)	B (SE)	B (SE)
Occupation	Self-employed	.199 (.150)	.287 (.188)	.056 (.187)	.118 (.249)	-.092 (.244)	.186 (.135)
	Managers	.098 (.141)	.066 (.179)	-.113 (.173)	.136 (.227)	.021 (.228)	.217 (.125)
	Other white collars	.097 (.136)	.209 (.172)	.007 (.169)	.193 (.233)	-.079 (.230)	.145 (.123)
	Manual workers	.303* (.126)	.100 (.158)	.181 (.155)	.212 (.214)	.031 (.215)	.151 (.116)
	House persons	.114 (.155)	.002 (.200)	-.002 (.197)	.127 (.260)	-.109 (.255)	.078 (.143)
	Unemployed	.355* (.167)	.009 (.226)	-.338 (.221)	.161 (.259)	.089 (.263)	.161 (.144)
	Retired	.245 (.153)	.294 (.194)	.087 (.190)	.196 (.246)	.050 (.240)	.090 (.131)

Dependent variable is 'For each of the following countries, would you be in favor of or against or against [Turkey] becoming part of the European Union?" (1) favour vs. (2) against'. Reference category of dependent variable is 'against'.

Notes

1 Model EB53: R^2 = .149 (Cox and Snell), .201 (Nagelkerke), .119 (McFadden). Model χ^2 (35) = 1003.543***, *** $p < .001$, ** $p < .01$, * $p < .05$

2 Model EB54.1: R^2 = .203 (Cox and Snell), .274 (Nagelkerke), .168 (McFadden). Model χ^2 (41) = 1026.009***, *** $p < .001$, ** $p < .01$, * $p < .05$

3 Model EB58.1: R^2 = .281 (Cox and Snell), .376 (Nagelkerke), .241 (McFadden). Model χ^2 (37) = 1598.123***, *** $p < .001$, ** $p < .01$, * $p < .05$

4 Model EB63.4: R^2 = .480 (Cox and Snell), .651 (Nagelkerke), .490 (McFadden). Model χ^2 (56) = 3696.625***, *** $p < .001$, ** $p < .01$, * $p < .05$

5 Model EB66.1: R^2 = .404 (Cox and Snell), .565 (Nagelkerke), .412 (McFadden). Model χ^2 (52) = 2815.340***, *** $p < .001$, ** $p < .01$, * $p < .05$

6 Model EB69.2: R^2 = .232 (Cox and Snell), .315 (Nagelkerke), .197 (McFadden). Model χ^2 (44) = 3159.636***, *** $p < .001$, ** $p < .01$, * $p < .05$

a These variables are not included in the data and analysis.

of support for enlargement as an EU priority and support for EU enlargement with new member states on Turkey's membership. When people had personal fears about costs of enlargement for current member states, such as less financial aid or extra economic burdens, Turco-scepticism increased significantly. If enlargement did not bring about any costs for member states, Turkey's membership was also favoured. These confirmed our expectations (Hypothesis 2 and Hypothesis 3) about sociotropic utilitarian calculations. On the contrary, evaluation of the importance of democratic values and human rights as enlargement criteria and prospects for cultural richness in an enlarged Europe created a source of support for Turkey. This finding contradicted our expectation (Hypothesis 6) that cultural and linguistic differences might decrease Europeans' support for Turkey's membership.

In 2002 (Model EB58.1), Europeans were asked about their preferences about immediate future enlargement of the EU: whether the EU should be enlarged to include all countries wishing to join or should not be enlarged to any additional countries. Our results showed a direct relation between preferences about an enlargement with all countries wishing to join the EU and support for Turkish membership. In contrast, opposition to enlargement with any of those countries wishing to become EU members also resulted in a significant opposition to Turkey. Model EB58.1 confirmed once again that Europeans were in favour of Turkish accession in so far as the expansion would not yield any costs for member states (Hypothesis 1). In line with sociotropic and egocentric utilitarian assumptions Europeans were cost-averse if enlargement brought more unemployment and less financial aid from the EU budget to its member states (Hypothesis 4 and Hypothesis 3, respectively). On the contrary, the fact that enlargement would contribute to Europe's cultural richness motivated Europeans (EU15) to become enthusiastic about Turkey's accession.

Public opinion on Turkey's EU membership in EU25: Re-considering the impacts of values and utilities of enlargement

According to the results of the equations estimated using EB No: 63.4 (2005) and EB No: 66.1 (2006) data for 25 EU member states (see Table 6.1), those who thought that Turkey was geographically a part of Europe and that it shared a common history with European countries were more likely to support Turkey's EU membership (Hypothesis 6). In contrast, those who thought that Turkey had significant cultural differences were more likely to oppose Turkey's membership. These findings supported our arguments that European identity is based on a common heritage so that those who do not share those common traits will be considered as the out-group. We found that holding the belief that democracy represents the EU had an insignificant effect on support for Turkey's accession. On the other hand, our results demonstrated that those who think that to join the EU Turkey should systematically improve its human rights records and that Turkey's accession would have an added value on mutual understanding of values tended more to support Turkey's EU membership. In this regard, we could partially confirm our expectation (Hypothesis 7) that if a candidate country met the criteria about rights and democracy then public opinion in the EU became more pro-enlargement.

We next observed that utilitarian calculations regarding not only egocentric economic concerns but also security benefits affected attitudes towards Turkey. Europeans who tended to believe that Turkey's accession would contribute to regional security and would offer a remedy to the ageing European population expressed favourable opinions about Turkey's membership (Hypothesis 4). Regarding the impact of religion, we found, perhaps surprisingly, that attitudes toward Turkey were uninfluenced by individuals' opinions on whether religion is important for society, whether it represents the EU, and individuals' personal attachment to religion. Thus, we rejected our hypothesis about religion (Hypothesis 8) in Europe on predominantly Muslim Turkey's EU membership.

Public opinion on Turkey's EU membership in EU27: Drifting away from religion and rights

Lastly, our results for the EB No: 69.2 (Model EB69.2) data showed that, in EU27, support for European integration, the perceived national benefits of EU membership, and a general favourable opinion of EU enlargement policy had significant positive impacts on Europeans' opinions towards Turkey's membership. Given the variegated configuration of European public opinion in the aftermath of the 2007 enlargement, we found no effect on support or opposition to Turkey's EU membership of respondents' believing that democracy (Hypothesis 7) and/or religion (Hypothesis 8) represent the EU. This finding is conducive to studying public opinion on Turkey's EU membership with reference to explanations other than religious or right-based identities.

Conclusion

This chapter aimed to investigate the nature, determinants and trends of European public opinion on the debate over Turkey's EU accession. To do this, we concentrated our attention on two mainstream approaches prevalent in the literature. First, we suggested that utilitarian calculations might play a role in the formation of European citizens' attitudes toward Turkey. Individuals care about how European unification affects their national and personal economic conditions. Thus, if they are content with the economic benefits they receive from European integration, and if they believe that Turkish accession would not cost them much, they will have favourable attitudes toward Turkey joining the integration.

Our findings indicate partial support for our expectations as discussed within the theoretical debate. To start with, as far as sociotropic utilitarian calculations are concerned, we contend that an increase in macro benefits of enlargement, in general, and with Turkey in particular, triggers an increase in public support for Turkey's EU membership. In contrast, calculations based on unemployment fears due to large numbers of immigrants decreases the Turco-sceptic preferences of enlargement. However, our analysis reveals that personal occupational concerns have a non-significant impact on attitudes toward Turkey.

Second, we claimed that identity-based considerations might affect public opinion on Turkey's EU membership. Social identities, such as European cultural and religious identities, provide individuals with feelings of group supremacy, high self-esteem and some shared values, such as respect for democracy, freedoms and rights. Members of the same group might also share a common history and geography. Those outsiders who do not share such characteristics will be prevented from blending in, in order to preserve in-group distinctiveness. Based on this assumption, we argued that, since Europeans believe that Turkey does not yet have a consolidated democracy or full guarantees for human and minority rights, and since its population is predominantly Muslim, EU citizens will not wish it to join the EU.

Our analysis discerns that religion does not have a significant effect on support for Turkey. In a different fashion, European demos are not driven with right-based concerns such as democracy or human rights. Rather, the European *vox populi* is more concerned about whether Turkey shares the same cultural and geographical traits and values with Europe, and whether this enlargement provides an added value to Europe's cultural richness and mutual understanding of values.

In conclusion, we intended to produce an all-inclusive cross-time study of the trends in Turco-scepticism versus Turco-enthusiasm in Europe, as shaped by popular debates on Turkey's EU membership. This study offered a multidimensional approach to understanding the European *vox populi* that is contingent on a complex set of factors rather than a single one. The general implication of this chapter is as straightforward as it is important: utilitarian considerations, in concert with a pre-existing sense of Europeanness based on identity and values, have persistent effects on public opinion.

On the other hand, our study, and also public opinion research in Europe in general, faces a significant challenge. That is, data limitations prevent us from making a thorough analysis of the determinants of European support for Turkey's EU membership covering the whole 50 years of Turkey–EU relations. Methodologically, because Eurobarometer surveys – albeit the richest cross-country and cross-sectional trend data – do not ask the same questions each year, we could not specify a pooled time-series model. Nevertheless, despite this drawback, our descriptive analysis covered trends in public opinion over the last thirty years and our quantitative analysis was able to shed light on how Turkey has been perceived in the EU during the last decade. We are satisfied that this length of period allows us to offer strong insights into how European public opinion during each enlargement phase varied in line with the debate over Turkey's 'protracted' EU accession process. Prescriptively, this study offers policy implications for decision-makers, given that the opinions and preferences of the mass public play a critical role in Turkey–EU relations. The variation in these attitudes not only symbolises a deterioration that has evolved over a long period of time but also shows that the state of mind of the European *vox populi* on Turkey's protracted accession to the EU is a heavily utility-driven design.

Appendix

Operationalization of variables

	Variable	Survey Question	Response categories
Dependent variable			
	Public opinion on Turkey's EU membership	For each of the following countries, would you be in favour of or against it becoming part of the European Union? Turkey (EB No: 53, EB No: 54.1, EB No: 58.1, EB No: 63.4)	1 in favour 2 against[a]
		For each of the following countries and territories, would you be in favor or against it becoming part of the European Union in the future? Turkey (EB No: 69.2)	1 in favour 2 against[a]
Independent variables			
Support for EU integration	EU membership of own country 'good'	Generally speaking, do you think that (our country's) membership of the European Union is .... (EB No: 53, EB No: 54.1, EB No: 58.1, EB No: 63.4, EB No: 66.1, EB No: 69.2)	1 good thing 2 bad thing 3 neither good nor bad
	Benefit from EU membership	Taking everything into consideration, would you say that (our country) has on balance benefitted or not from being a member of the European Union? (EB No: 53, EB No: 54.1, EB No: 58.1, EB No: 63.4, EB No: 66.1, EB No: 69.2)	1 benefited 2 not benefited
Support for enlargement policy	Enlargement: EU priority	I am going to read out a list of actions that the European Union could undertake. For each one, please tell me, if in your opinion, it should be a priority, or not? Welcoming new member countries (EB No: 53, EB No: 54.1, EB No: 58.1, EB No: 66.1)	1 priority 2 not priority
	Enlargement: EU proposal	What is your opinion on each of the following statements? Please tell me for each proposal, whether you are for it or against it: The European Union should be enlarged and include new countries (EB No: 54.1, EB No: 58.1, EB No: 63.4, EB No: 66.1, EB No: 69.2)	1 for 2 against

(continued on the next page)

Appendix continued

Variable	Survey Question	Response categories
Enlargement: with all countries (1) / Enlargement: with no countries (2)	Which of these 3 options do you prefer for the immediate future of the European Union? The European Union should … (EB No: 58.1, EB No: 63.4)	1 be enlarged to include all countries wishing to join 2 not be enlarged to any additional countries 3 be enlarged to include only some of the countries wishing to join
Utilitarian Variables		
Sociotropic utilitarianism Enlargement criterion: Economic development	For each of the following criteria, please tell me if it seems important to you, or not in deciding whether a particular country should join the European Union, or not? Its level of economic development should be close to that of other member states (EB No: 53, EB No: 54.1)	1 important 2 not important
Enlargement criterion: Costless for member states	For each of the following criteria, please tell me if it seems important to you, or not in deciding whether a particular country should join the European Union, or not? Its joining should not be costly for existing member countries (EB No: 53, EB No: 54.1)	1 important 2 not important
Enlargement outcomes: No costs for member states	Thinking about the enlargement of the European Union to include new countries, do you tend to agree or tend to disagree with each of the following statements? The enlargement will not cost more to existing member countries like (our country) (EB No: 54.1, EB No: 58.1)	1 tend to agree 2 tend to disagree
Enlargement outcomes: Less financial aid to member states	Thinking about the enlargement of the European Union to include new countries, do you tend to agree or tend to disagree with each of the following statements? Once new countries have joined the European Union, (our country) will receive less financial aid from it (EB No: 54.1, EB No: 58.1)	1 tend to agree 2 tend to disagree
Turkey's responsibility: Improving its economy	For each of the following please tell me whether you totally agree, tend to agree, tend to disagree or totally disagree: To join the European Union in about ten years, Turkey will have to significantly improve the state of its economy (EB No: 63.4, EB No: 66.1)	1 totally agree 2 tend to agree 3 tend to disagree 4 totally disagree[b]

(continued on the next page)

Appendix continued

Variable	Survey Question	Response categories
Fears about the enlargement: Cost of too much money for member states	Some people may have fears about the building of Europe, the European Union. Here is a list of things which some people say they are afraid of. For each one, please tell me if you - personally - are currently afraid of it, or not? Other countries joining the European Union will cost member countries too much money (EB No: 54.1)	1 currently afraid of 2 currently not afraid of
Egocentric utilitarianism		
Enlargement outcomes: More unemployment:	Thinking about the enlargement of the European Union to include new countries, do you tend to agree or tend to disagree with each of the following statements? The more countries there are, the more employment there will be in (our country) (EB No: 54.1, EB No: 58.1)	1 tend to agree 2 tend to disagree
Fears about the enlargement: Transfer of jobs to countries with lower costs	Some people may have fears about the building of Europe, the European Union. Here is a list of things which some people say they are afraid of. For each one, please tell me if you - personally - are currently afraid of it, or not? The transfer of jobs to countries which have lower production costs (EB No: 54.1, EB No: 63.4,)	1 currently afraid of 2 currently not afraid of
Benefits of Turkey's accession: Regional security	For each of the following please tell me whether you totally agree, tend to agree, tend to disagree or totally disagree: Turkey's accession to the European Union would strengthen the security in this region (EB No: 63.4, EB No: 66.1)	1 totally agree 2 tend to agree 3 tend to disagree[b] 4 totally disagree[b]
Benefits of Turkey's accession: Rejuvenation of population	For each of the following please tell me whether you totally agree, tend to agree, tend to disagree or totally disagree: Turkey's accession would favor the rejuvenation of an ageing European population (EB No: 63.4, EB No: 66.1)	1 totally agree 2 tend to agree 3 tend to disagree[b] 4 totally disagree[b]
Costs of Turkey's accession: Risk of immigration	For each of the following please tell me whether you totally agree, tend to agree, tend to disagree or totally disagree: Turkey's joining could risk favoring immigration to more developed countries in the European Union (EB No: 63.4, EB No: 66.1)	1 totally agree 2 tend to agree 3 tend to disagree[b] 4 totally disagree[b]

(continued on the next page)

Appendix continued

Variable	Survey Question	Response categories
Immigrants from Muslim countries 'not accepted' / 'unconditionally accepted'	If people from Muslim countries wish to work here in the European Union, do you think that they should... (EB No: 53)	1 not be accepted 2 accepted without restriction 3 accepted with restriction
Identity-based Variables		
Cultural values — Enlargement outcomes: Cultural richness	Thinking about the enlargement of the European Union to include new countries, do you tend to agree or tend to disagree with each of the following statements? With more member countries, Europe will be culturally richer (EB No: 54.1, EB No: 58.1)	1 tend to agree 2 tend to disagree
Fears about the enlargement: Loss of national / cultural identity	Some people may have fears about the building of Europe, the European Union. Here is a list of things which some people say they are afraid of. For each one, please tell me if you - personally - are currently afraid of it, or not? The loss of our national identity and culture (EB No: 54.1, EB No: 63.4)	1 currently afraid of 2 currently not afraid of
Benefits of Turkey's accession: Mutual understanding of values	For each of the following please tell me whether you totally agree, tend to agree, tend to disagree or totally disagree: Turkey's accession to the European Union would favor the mutual comprehension of European and Muslim values (EB No: 63.4)	1 totally agree 2 tend to agree 3 tend to disagree 4 totally disagree[b]
Cost of Turkey's accession: Significant cultural differences	For each of the following please tell me whether you totally agree, tend to agree, tend to disagree or totally disagree: The cultural differences between Turkey and the European Union Member States are too significant to allow for this accession (EB No: 63.4, EB No: 66.1)	1 totally agree 2 tend to agree 3 tend to disagree 4 totally disagree[b]
Common traits — Turkey part of European geography	For each of the following please tell me whether you totally agree, tend to agree, tend to disagree or totally disagree: Turkey partly belongs to Europe by its geography. (EB No: 63.4, EB No: 66.1)	1 totally agree 2 tend to agree 3 tend to disagree 4 totally disagree[b]

(continued on the next page)

Appendix continued

Variable	Survey Question	Response categories
Turkey part of European history	For each of the following please tell me whether you totally agree, tend to agree, tend to disagree or totally disagree: Turkey partly belongs to Europe by its history (EB No: 63.4, EB No: 66.1)	1 totally agree 2 tend to agree 3 tend to disagree 4 totally disagree[b]
Rights		
Enlargement criterion: Rights and Democracy	For each of the following criteria, please tell me if it seems important to you, or not in deciding whether a particular country should join the European Union, or not? The country has to respect Human Rights and the principles of democracy (EB No: 53, EB No: 54.1)	1 important 2 not important
Turkey's responsibility: Respect for human rights	For each of the following please tell me whether you totally agree, tend to agree, tend to disagree or totally disagree: To join the European Union in about ten years, Turkey will have to respect systematically Human Rights (EB No: 63.4, EB No: 66.1)	1 totally agree 2 tend to agree 3 tend to disagree 4 totally disagree[b]
Democracy represents EU	Which three of the following values, best represent the European Union? Democracy (EB No: 66.1, EB No: 69.2)	1 mentioned 2 not mentioned
Religion		
Religion important for society	For each of the following propositions, tell me if you…? The place of religion in our society is too important (EB No: 66.1)	1 totally agree 2 tend to agree 3 tend to disagree 4 totally disagree[b]
Religion represents the EU	Which three of the following values, best represent the European Union? Religion (EB No: 66.1, EB No: 69.2)	1 mentioned 2 not mentioned
Religiosity	Apart from weddings or funerals, about how often do you attend religious services? (EB No: 66.1)	1 more than once a week 2 once a week 3 about once a month 4 about each 2 or 3 months 5 only on special holy days 6 about once a year 7 less often[c]

(continued on the next page)

Appendix continued

Variable	Survey Question	Response categories
Fear: Own country pay more to the EU	Some people may have fears about the building of Europe, the European Union. Here is a list of things which some people say they are afraid of. For each one, please tell me if you - personally - are currently afraid of it, or not? Our country paying more and more to the European Union (EB No: 63.4,)	1 currently afraid of 2 currently not afraid of

Control Variables

Variable	Survey Question	Response categories
Age	Age	1 15-24 2 25-39 3 40-54 4 55+
Gender	Gender	1 male 2 female
Ideology	Ideological self-placement on a 10-scale spectrum	1 left (1-4) 2 right (5-6) 3 centre (7-10)
Occupation	Occupation (self-reported)	1 self-employed 2 manager 3 other white collar 4 manual worker 5 houseperson 6 unemployed 7 retired 8 student
Country of origin	Country of origin (dummy)	For each survey country.

Notes
a 'Don't know' category is treated as missing value.
b This scale is recoded into a categorical one with values of (1) 'agree' and (2) 'disagree'
c This scale is recoded into a categorical one with values of (1) 1 to 2 into 'strong religiosity', (2) 6 to 7 into 'weak religiosity', and (3) 3 to 5 into 'moderate religiosity.

Notes

1 At time of elections and referenda mass public opinion plays a decisive role in decision-making. This is reflected in, for instance, the French Constitution that requires a referendum prior to a country's EU accession if it represents more than 5 per cent of the overall EU population.

2 An example of political controversy reveals itself in the cases of President de Gaulle's veto of British application in 1963 and 1967.

3 The EU was launched with the Treaty on European Union (1992). This point onwards European public opinion will be abbreviated as 'EU' public opinion.

4 EU12 includes the 12 member states of the EU and their citizens until 1995 enlargement.

5 See Eurobarometers No: 34, 35 and 39 for details.

6 Applicant countries were Bulgaria, Cyprus, the Czech Republic, Estonia, Hungary, Latvia, Lithuania, Malta, Poland, Romania, Slovakia, Slovenia and Turkey.

7 Although European Economic Community (EEC) decision makers concluded and signed accession treaties with Norway twice, Norwegian voters rejected the membership of the EU in referendum once in 1972 and later in 1994. Greenland joined the EEC together with Denmark in 1973 but after Greenland received home rule from Denmark, Greenlanders voted to withdraw from the EC in a 1985 referendum. Voters in Ireland rejected the Nice Treaty in 2001 but then they approved it in another referendum in 2002. Recently, the Irish voted against the Lisbon Treaty in 2008 and thus halted the plans of governing elites to remove some of the existing political and economic constraints on integration. However, later, the majority of Irish changed their minds and voted 'yes' to the Lisbon Treaty in a second referendum.

8 P. Conover and S. Feldman, 'Emotional reactions to the Economy: I'm mad as hell and I'm not going to take it anymore', *American Journal of Political Science,* 1986, vol. 30, no.1, pp. 50–78.

9 For example, voter turnout rate in a referendum in Denmark in 2000 on joining the Euro was almost 88 per cent, which implies that the majority of Danish citizens were concerned with the costs and benefits of economic integration and wanted to take part in the historical decision of joining the single currency. See, M. Gabel and S. Hix, 'Understanding public support for British membership of the Single Currency', *Political Studies*, 2005, vol. 53, no. 1, pp. 65–81; M. Gabel and G. Whitten, 'Economic conditions, economic perceptions, and public support for European integration', *Political Behavior,* 1997, vol. 19, no. 1, pp. 81–96.

10 M. Mattila, 'Contested decisions: Empirical analysis of voting in the European Union Council of Ministers', *European Journal of Political Research,* 2004, vol. 43, no. 1, pp. 29–50.

11 L. Hooghe and G. Marks, 'Unraveling the central state, but how? Types of multi-level governance', *American Political Science Review*, 2003, vol. 97, no. 2, pp. 233–243; G. Marks, L. Hooghe, and K. Blank, 'European integration from the 1980s: State-centric v. multi-level governance', *Journal of Common Market Studies,* 1996, vol. 34, no. 3, pp. 341–378.

12 M. J. Gabel, 'Economic integration and mass politics: Market liberalization and public attitudes in the European Union', *American Journal of Political Science* 1998, vol. 42, no. 3, pp. 936–953; M. J. Gabel, 'Public support for European integration: An empirical test of five theories', *Journal of Politics*, 1998, vol. 60, no. 2, pp. 333–354.

13 L. Hooghe and G. Marks, 'Does identity or economic rationality drive public opinion on European integration?', *PS: Political Science & Politics,* 2004, vol. 37, no. 3, pp. 415–420; L. Hooghe and G. Marks, 'Calculation, community and cues: Public opinion on European integration', *European Union Politics*, 2005, vol. 6, no. 4, pp. 419–443.

14 S. De Master and M. K. Le Roy, 'Xenophobia and the European Union', *Comparative Politics* 2000, vol. 32, no. 4, pp. 419–436; J. S. Fetzer, *Public Attitudes towards Immigration in the United States, France and Germany,* Cambridge: Cambridge University Press, 2000; J. S. Fetzer and C. J. Soper, *Muslims and the State in Britain, France and Germany,* Cambridge: Cambridge University Press, 2005; M. Hoskin, *New Immigrants and Democratic Society: Minority Integration in Western Democracies,* New York: Praeger, 1991.

15 L. M. McLaren, 'Public support for the European Union: Cost/benefit analysis or perceived cultural threat?', *Journal of Politics,* 2002, vol. 64, no. 12, p. 557.

16 L. M. McLaren, 'Anti-immigrant prejudice in Europe: Contact, threat perception, and preferences for the exclusion of migrants,' *Social Forces,* 2003, vol. 81, no. 3, p. 915.

17 See W. Lutz, B. C. O'Neill and S. Scherbov, 'Europe's population at a turning point', *Science* 2003, vol. 299, no. 5615, pp. 1991, 1991–1993.

18 J. Turner *et al.,* 'Social comparison and group interest in intergroup favouritism', *European Journal of Social Psychology,* 1979, vol. 9, pp. 187–204; J. C. Turner, 'Social comparison and social identity: Some prospects for intergroup behavior', *European Journal of Social Psychology,* 1975, vol. 5 no. 1, pp. 5–34.

19 M. Levine, A. Prosser, D. Evans and S. Reicher, 'Identity and emergency intervention: How social group membership and inclusiveness of group boundaries shape helping behavior', *Personality and Social Psychology Bulletin,* 2005, vol. 31, no. 4, pp. 443–453.

20 M. A. Hogg and D. Abrams, *Social Identifications: A Social Psychology of Intergroup Relations and Group Processes*, London: Routledge, 1988; A. D. Cast, and P. Burke, 'A theory of self-esteem', *Social Forces*, 2002, vol. 80, no. 3, pp. 1041–1068; A. D. Cast, J. E. Stets and P. J. Burke, 'Does the self conform to the views of others?', *Social Psychology Quarterly*, 1999, vol. 62, pp. 68–82; J. E. Stets and P. J. Burke, 'Identity theory and social identity Theory', *Social Psychology Quarterly* 2000, vol. 63, no. 3, pp. 224–237.

21 C. L. Pickett and M. B. Brewer, 'Assimilation and differentiation needs as motivational determinants of perceived in-group and out-group homogeneity', *Journal of Experimental Social Psychology,* 2001, vol. 37, pp. 341–348.

22 L. Hooghe and G. Marks, 'Calculation, community and cues'; L. M. McLaren, *Identity, Interests and Attitudes to European Integration*, Basingstoke: Palgrave Macmillan, 2006.

23 T. Risse, 'The Euro between National and European Identity', *Journal of European Public Policy*, 2003, vol. 10, no. 4, pp. 487–505; A. D. Smith, 'National identity and the idea of European unity', *International Affairs,* 1992, vol. 68, no. 1, pp. 55–76.

24 Smith, 'National Identity and the Idea of European Unity', p. 62.

25 J. A. Caporaso, 'The possibilities of a European identity', *Brown Journal of World Affairs,* 2005, vol. 12, no. 1, pp. 65–75; J. Habermas, *The Divided West*, trans. Ciaran Cronin, Cambridge: Polity Press, 2006.

26 H. Flam, 'Turkey and the EU: Politics and economics of accession', *CESifo Economic Studies*, 2004, vol. 50, no. 1, pp. 171–210; S. Laçiner, 'Possible impacts of Turkey's full membership of EU's Common Foreign Policy' in S. Laçiner, M. Özcan and İ. Bal (eds), *European Union with Turkey: The Possible Impact of Turkey's Membership of the European Union*, Ankara: Usak Yayınları, 2005, pp. 15–86.

27 J. Casanova, 'Religion, European secular identities and European integration' in T. A. Brynes and P. J. Katzenstein (eds), *Religion in an Expanding Europe,* Cambridge: Cambridge University Press, 2006, p. 73.

28 E. Alessandri and E. Ş. Canan '"Mamma li Turchi!" Just an old Italian saying' in N. Tocci (ed.), *Talking Turkey in Europe: Towards a Differentiated Communication Strategy*, Quaderno IAI no. 13, Rome: Istituto Affari Internazionali, 2008, p. 28; E. Ş. Canan-Sokullu 'Perceptions of Islam, Turkey and the European Union – Islamophobia and Turcosceptism in Europe? A four nation study in Europe' in C. Flood, S. Hutchings,

G. Miazhevich and H. Nickels (eds), *Islam in the Plural: Identities, (Self-)Perceptions and Politics* Amsterdam: Brill (forthcoming).

29 T. G. Jelen, 'The political consequences of religious group attitudes', *The Journal of Politics* 1993, vol. 55, no. 1, pp. 178–190; M. Rokeach, 'The role of values in public opinion research', *The Public Opinion Quarterly* 1968, vol. 32, no. 4, pp. 547–559.

30 N. J. Kelly and J. M. Kelly, 'Religion and Latino partisanship in the United States,' *Political Research Quarterly*, 2005, vol. 58, no. 1, pp. 87–95.

31 The issue of Europe's religious identity that bred Turco-scepticism also has resonance in the field of international relations. As Huntington asserts, 'The identification of Europe with Western Christendom provides a clear criterion for the admission of new members to the western organizations'. S. P. Huntington, 'The Clash of Civilizations?' *Foreign Affairs*, 1993, vol. 72, no. 3, p. 158.

32 Casanova, 'Religion, European Secular Identities and European Integration', p. 71.

33 S. Carey, 'Undivided loyalties: Is national identity an obstacle to European integration?', *European Union Politics* 2002, vol. 3, no. 4, pp. 387–413; L. M. McLaren, 'Public Support for the European Union', pp. 551–556; McLaren 'Anti-immigrant prejudice in Europe: Contact, threat perception, and preferences for the exclusion of migrants', p. 917.

34 Carey, 'Undivided Loyalties'.

35 Carey, 'Undivided Loyalties', p. 393.

36 Carey, 'Undivided Loyalties', p. 394.

37 McLaren, 'Public support for the European Union'.

38 D. R. Kinder and D. O. Sears, 'Prejudice and politics: Symbolic racism versus racial threats to the good life', *Journal of Personality and Social Psychology* 1981, vol. 40, no. 3, pp. 414–431; R. D. Ashmore, 'Prejudice: Causes and cures' in B. E. Collins (ed.), *Social Psychology: Social Influence, Attitude Change, Group Processes, and Prejudice,* Addison-Wesley, 1970; J. Citrin, B. Reingold and D. P. Green 'American identity and the politics of ethnic change' *Journal of Politics* 1990, vol. 52, pp. 1124–1154.

39 McLaren 'Anti-Immigrant Prejudice in Europe', p. 917.

40 Empirical analysis of public opinion data is carried out with the following EB surveys: EB No: 53 (April–May 2000); EB No: 54.1 (November–December 2000); EB No: 58.1 (October–November 2002); EB No: 63.4 (May–June 2005); EB No: 66.1 (September–October 2006); and EB No: 69.2 (March–May 2008). EB No: 53 to EB No: 58.1 (April–May 2000) includes 15 EU member states; EB No: 63.4 to EB No: 66.1 (September–October 2006) includes 25 EU member states and EB No: 69.2 (March–May 2008) includes 27 member states. For reasons of practicality, the abbreviations EU15, EU25 and EU27 are used if necessary.

41 The 'don't know' (3) category was assigned as 'missing category' and the 'against' category was assigned as 'reference category' because the main issue at stake was positive assessment of Turkish membership rather than the respondent's rejection or indifference.

42 Dummies for the country of origin are not reported in the Appendix to make the interpretation of the table easier. However, these data and results are available on request to the authors.

43 M. J. Gabel, 'Economic Integration and Mass Politics', 1998.

44 Multinomial logistic regression is also suitable with binary dependent variables. See M. J. Norušis, *SPSS 14.0 Advanced Statistical Procedures Companion,* Upper Saddle River, NJ: Prentice Hall, 2005, p. 43; A. Field *Discovering Statistics Using SPSS*, London: Sage, 2005.

45 Logistic regression is the most appropriate technique for categorical response data. For a binary/categorical dependent variable Y and an explanatory variable X, the regression model is $\pi(x)\dfrac{\exp(\alpha+\beta x)}{1+\exp(\alpha+\beta x)}$. See N. Leech, K. C. Barrett and G. A.

Morgan, *SPSS for Intermediate Statistics: Use and Interpretation*. Mahwah, NJ: Lawrence Erlbaum Associates, 2005, p. 109.

46 The Danes and the British were strongly in favour of withdrawal from the EC.

47 More specifically, in 1983, 48 per cent of EC citizens were in favour of Spanish accession, this figure raised to 61 per cent in 1985. Likewise, the Portuguese accession was supported by 46 per cent of Europeans in 1983, which increased to 61 per cent in 1985 (EB No: 23). Remarkably, indifference was also very high in many member states. There were also large country-specific variations in these estimations.

48 The question addressing the issue of expanding the European Community was put in EB No. 30 (1988).

49 For the first time in the history of EB polling, an individual section on 'enlargement' was included in the reports, which clearly showed the importance attached to the issue at the European level.

50 Even though the EC budget would increase to assist these countries, expansion was favoured by 63 per cent of Europeans (EB No: 33 and 34).

51 On 6 December 1992, Switzerland rejected by referendum joining the European Economic Area.

52 Economic implications of enlargement deterred Europeans. 50 per cent of EU citizens believed that enlargement would cost their own country more money. Danes (67 per cent), Dutch (66 per cent), Germans (64 per cent) and Austrians (62 per cent) were particularly inclined to feel this way. Many people also suspected a smaller financial aid share once new countries had joined, especially Irish and Portuguese (both 67 per cent), Danes (66 per cent), Greeks (64 per cent), Swedes and Finns (both 62 per cent). On the other hand, Europeans also perceived (61 per cent) cultural enrichment and more peace and security (55 per cent) (EB No: 54).

53 A new question that measured support for enlargement was included on the first fieldwork wave of EB No: 55. Respondents were asked: *'Which of these three options do you prefer for the immediate future of Europe? a) The European Union should be enlarged to include all the countries wishing to join; b) The European Union should be enlarged to include only some of the countries wishing to join; c) The European Union should not be enlarged to any additional countries?'*

54 EB No: 56 reworded the enlargement question as: *'What is your opinion on each of the following statements? Please tell me for each proposal, whether you are for it or against it. 'The enlargement of the European Union to include new countries'*. Previously, the wording was: *'The European Union should be enlarged and include new countries'*.

55 The French were becoming more anti-Turkish accession, whereas the Swedes or Dutch were incessantly more pro-Turkish in their evaluation of Turkey's membership (EB No: 56).

56 Two years after the Iraqi war, Europeans (EU25) were willing to have a common position in the event of an international crisis. Yet, majorities were not happy about an increase in the budget for political objectives of the EU (EB No: 63).

57 The gap between the supporters (46 per cent) and opponents (42 per cent) of enlargement was four points (EB No: 66).

58 This trend of lack of support for Turkey was more visible in the original six members of the EU (with the only exception of the Netherlands) (EB No: 69).

59 For instance, 1 unit of ideological self-positioning is not equal to 1 unit of cost perceived.

60 Confidence intervals and expected (B) values are not reported the Appendix to make the interpretation of the table easier. However, these data and results are available on request to the authors.

7 Identity dimension

Postwesternisation: A framework for understanding Turkey–EU relations

Chris Rumford and Hasan Turunç

Introduction

The lack of European credentials which maintain Turkey as a perpetual outsider is a familiar motif in the literature on EU enlargement. Yet the picture of Turkey painted in these accounts is frequently inaccurate and does little to dispel the cliché that Turkey is a bridge between East and West, an unfortunate location which implies that Turkey can never truly become 'one of us'. However, the inaccuracy of accounts built upon these foundations cannot simply be explained by the way Turkey is positioned (or positions itself) vis-à-vis the EU. Although there are many failings in existing accounts of Turkey's faltering attempts to join the 'EU club' over the past 50 years, deriving from essentialist views of Turkish identity and/or simplistic civilisational histories, a bigger problem is to be found in overly optimistic characterisations of the EU and its relationship with its near abroad and the rest of the world, coupled with clichéd approaches to the dynamics of Turkish politics.

The breakdown of the previously foundational (and global) East–West cleavage is of considerable importance to the European Union's relations with Turkey, whose national identity in the Republican period is almost always represented in the literature as being founded on a desire to be wholly Western, an identity reinforced by Turkey's Cold War role in the architecture of Western defences against the Communist East. According to this narrative, in the wake of the Cold War Turkey had to reorient itself around new principles as its staunch Western vocation was no longer the same geo-strategic asset.[1] Moreover, Turkey's tentative Europeanisation was complicated by the fact that countries that had previously identified themselves as Eastern (for example, Hungary, Poland and Bulgaria) jumped the EU queue and obtained full membership, while Turkey, an aspirant member since 1963, was still struggling to be formally recognised as an accession country.

The old notion of Turkey as a bridge between East and West has thankfully lost much purchase (except in travel brochures it can be noted) because these realms are revealed as no longer separated by a deep division. Indeed, in the case of enlargement the countries of Eastern Europe were so intent on emulating the West that they happily shed their geopolitical identity in order to become more quickly integrated within the EU's governance structures. At the same time, the West itself began to fragment without the cohesion generated by a common external enemy. The end result is that it is no longer possible to identify a common Western position on a range of international issues: Iraq, global warming, debt relief for Africa, agricultural subsidies. As an index of these postwestern shifts, the Turkish government's refusal (despite massive financial inducements) to allow the US to launch military operations into Iraq (in 2003) from Turkish bases is especially significant.

The postwesternisation of Turkey has been aided by domestic political changes within Turkey where the quasi-Islamicist Justice and Development Party (JDP) forms the current government and achieved much during its first term in office to bring Turkey closer to the EU. Importantly, the rise of liberal-conservative Islamic politics in Turkey has given voice to a contending view of modernity and progress. It is possible to argue that whereas the traditional Kemalist (secular) political elites equated modernisation with Westernisation, the Islamicist-tinted government equates modernisation not only with Europe and human rights but with a 360° neighbourhood policy and a global consciousness. The JDP sees Turkey as both Western and Eastern, European and Middle Eastern, and, for that matter, local and global.

European integration is usually narrated as a matter internal to EU states with the development of the EU, its enlargement, and future trajectory conveyed in developmental and quasi-teleological terms. EU integration is seen as the destiny for the continent and each country, including non-EU members, is compelled to seek a place in the unfolding order. Turkey's attempts to slot into the EU project are generally seen to have been unsuccessful, for one of two interrelated reasons. The first is that the EU has been guilty of 'shifting the goalposts' in respect of Turkey's accession criteria (requiring Turkey to jump through more hoops than other aspirant members). The second is that Turkey has found it impossible to 'hit a moving target' either because of a blatant (at times) refusal to conform to EU accession criteria (protection of minorities, human rights) or because of Turkey's rather inadequate assessments of the opportunity for EU accession, such as still seeking Customs Union in the 1990s while former Warsaw Pact countries were negotiating accession agreements: in other words, 'Ankara Agreement Syndrome'.[2] Similarly, approaches to understanding Turkey's attempts to orientate itself towards the EU and fulfil the Copenhagen criteria are frequently undermined by a tendency to polarise domestic political actors into two main contending groups: the modernising, secular Kemalist elites traditionally pro-Western and pro-EU, but favouring a top-down rather authoritarian style of democracy; and the pro-Islamicist grass-roots alternative which offers a conservative approach to social issues and a critical appraisal of the Kemalist project.

This chapter takes issue with these conventional understandings of the dynamics of Turkey's domestic politics. Relying upon tired models of domestic political cleavages is not sufficient to understand the key dynamics of Turkey's EU orientation. The argument advanced in this chapter is that we require a broader perspective in order to understand contemporary transformations, one which situates a changing Turkey in the historical context of a changing Europe and a changing world. To this end we propose the idea of postwesternisation or, more specifically, the idea that postwestern Turkey is engaging with a postwestern Europe. This is a Europe in which East and West are no longer solid reference points or identity markers, and in which a previously marginalised East has become central to political developments.[3] Importantly, the 'postwesternisation thesis' enables us to understand political changes within Turkey, and Turkey's relationship with a changing Europe within the same interpretive framework.

This chapter is organised as follows. The first section introduces the theoretical foundations and analytical potential of the idea of postwesternisation, and in so doing outlines the framework which is employed throughout the chapter. The following sections focus in some detail on the postwesternisation of Turkish politics, dealing mainly with the erroneous but widely held belief that Turkey represents a clash between Republican modernists and conservative Islamicists. The chapter rejects conventional approaches to understanding Turkey that depend upon the existence of a range of polarisations (for example, traditional/modern, Kurd/Turk), the most important in the present context being that between secular and Islamic tendencies.[4] The argument developed here is that the emerging 'Islamic secularism' reveals the extent of Turkey's postwesternisation. In this sense, postwesternisation is much more than a designation for a post-Cold War geopolitical constellation. Viewing Turkey through the lens of postwesternisation allows us to comprehend the changing political landscape at the national and sub-national level, and how this connects with, and cannot be dissociated from, global processes. At the same time, the analysis of Turkey's domestic politics advanced here extends the repertoire of the 'postwesternisation thesis', previously applied to global processes of change.[5] Turkey's relations with the EU are conventionally located within a historical narrative of stalled integration; in this chapter the same relations are interpreted according to a broader history of postwesternisation.

Postwesternisation

The idea of postwesternisation has become important in recent years,[6] and cannot simply be equated with the ending of the Cold War and the bipolar world order, and the decreasing salience of the idea of 'the West' as a reference point for political identification and global leadership. Postwesternisation suggests a process, or series of processes, which is leading to the de-unification of the West, and, at the same time, a displacement of the idea of 'the West' from a central position in the way we think about self, others and the world. Postwesternisation is a designation which suggests that the West has ceased to exist as a meaningful entity, and that it has been superseded, or at least that it is undergoing serious transformation. Whereas it was once possible to view the West as a coherent geopolitical presence, it is no longer possible to do this. There is no longer a unity to the West, with Europe and the United States diverging in important respects, and elements of what was previously the non-West are now indistinguishable from it. But postwesternisation is not intended as a new description of geopolitical realities. It is a process which informs social scientific thinking in such a way as to de-universalise the West and increase awareness of other non-Western developments and perspectives.

Examining postwesternisation in more detail it is possible (following Delanty) to identify several developments which have contributed to its emergence. First, the recognition that Europe is a meeting place for different modernities – Western, post-communist, Islamic[7] – rather than the site of a singular Western modernity. In one of his earliest papers on the theme, Delanty sees the emergence of post-westernisation as being linked to the confluence of Europe's 'three civilisation-al constellations': the Occidental Christian constellation; the Byzantine–Slavic Eurasian constellation; the Ottoman Islamic constellation.[8] These civilisational constellations allow for the possibility of multiple modernities; 'European moder-nity has been shaped in the image of not one modernity but all three'.[9] Delanty thus warns against assuming the singularity of European history or origins. Eu-rope's multi-civilisational heritage has produced different traditions of modernity, experienced as Western capitalism/liberalism, Communism, and statist Westerni-sation exemplified by Turkey, which also offered a challenge to the dominant Western model.

Second, the emergence of a new East shaping the continent[10] means that Europe can no longer equate itself with the West when much of what used to be the Eastern bloc is now part of the European Union, for example. The incorporation of Central and Eastern Europe into the EU continues to orientate the EU around a new set of concerns, for example the European Neighbourhood Policy.[11] One consequence of all this is that Europe has come to possess an identity distinct from that of the West. Europe is moving eastwards as the axis shifts from the Baltic and Adriatic towards the Black Sea.[12] At the same time is possibly developing a strong cosmopolitan character,[13] which also suggests that there exists contestation over the meaning and identity of Europe. In his discussion of the opening up of Europe to the world and the emerging cosmopolitan relationship between Europe and Asia, Delanty advances the claim that, 'Europe may be becoming less Western at precisely the time Eurasia is becoming less Eastern and that something like a "post-Western" Europe is emerging'.[14] The association between Europe and the West is being transformed and one of the most important reference points for European identity has been undermined.

Third, postwesternisation signals the increasing lack of unity within those countries formerly considered to have a common 'Western' world view; examples include divisions over the invasion of Iraq in 2003, or action on climate change which divided Europe from Australia and the United States, for example. For Delanty it is impossible to sustain the idea of the West as a coherent ideological, cultural, or geopolitical entity partly because 'Western civilisation' has been globalised and partly because its underlying unity is rapidly fragmenting: 'Europe, America and the West have become disentangled'.[15] This dimension of postwesternisation is reproduced in the EU's project of enlargement, which not only involves becoming bigger but also means that the EU is becoming more diverse. At the same time as the EU is becoming more internally differentiated it is also becoming arguably less exclusively European in its sphere of operation, with an increasing interest in developing mechanisms of global governance, exporting its Social Model, seen as major badge of identity vis-à-vis the United States,[16] and developing what some see as a more cosmopolitan set of concerns.[17]

The development of postwestern Europe can be traced historically through a series of events which point to either a lack of Western unity (fascism and dictatorship, Marshall Aid, the Suez crisis), the mélange of modernities which have shaped Europe (for example, post-colonialism), or a new East influencing the continent (exemplified by the oil crisis or the legacy of the Iranian revolution). This alternative history of post-war Europe calls into question the usual chronology of significant dates by which Europe knows itself: 1957 (Treaty of Rome), 1968 (the 'year that made us who we are'),[18] 1989 (Eastern European revolutions), 1992 (Single Market) etc. Rather than the generally accepted 'turning points' of, say, 1957, 1968 and 1989 and their significance on the road to 'ever closer Union' postwestern Europe has its own key dates, 1956, 1973 and 1979, for example. It is worth dwelling for a moment on the dates that punctuate the (alternative) history of postwesternisation because they reveal a compelling narrative of change which continues to shape Europe and which provides a context within which to better understand Turkey–EU relations. For example, the Suez crisis, or 'last imperial offensive from Europe' as Therborn terms it,[19] was a decisive moment for the idea of a West rooted in colonialism. The non-alignment pact signed in 1956 by Egypt, Yugoslavia and India which 'explicitly dissociated Egypt from any dependence on the West'[20] was greeted initially by the US, Britain and France, the West's three most interested parties, with a common front of opposition. The shared position disguised suspicions that the three parties had of each other and their longer-term plans in the region, Britain and France attempting to hold on to colonial gains and the US attempting to establish itself in the region (possibly at the expense of Britain). Britain's interest was most immediately focused on the Suez Canal, vital if Britain was to continue to benefit from cheap oil supplies from the Middle East. Without the USA's knowledge Britain and France made secret plans for a joint military invasion of Egypt using an Israeli military excursion into Sinai as a justification for their occupation of the Canal Zone. The Americans were angry at the attempted deception by Britain and France, and resentful at the way their support had been taken for granted.[21] The Americans were also angry that Anglo-French adventurism had drawn the world's attention away from the Soviet Union's invasion of Hungary, which had happened at the same time. In this sense they 'had placed their own – as it seemed to Washington, anachronistic – interests above those of the Western alliance as a whole'.[22] In the face of American opposition, Britain and France withdrew from Suez.

The French experience of Suez is seen by historians as a catalyst for their increasing support for the EEC[23] and possibly also marks the point that the then-EEC chose to dissociate itself from the imperial past of many member states (and soon to become member states). While the history of colonialism continues to exercise its influence on both Europe and the rest of the world, this history tends to be excluded from the EU's self-image, emerging only in discussions of the flows of peoples into the EU from former colonies.[24] The EU likes to see itself as the 'epitome of goodness' and a force for positive political change in the world but in promoting the ideology of 'European goodness', 'the political process of identity construction tries to hide the corpse of colonialism while it continues, of course, to partake of the material inheritance of the same colonialism'.[25]

Another key date in the postwestern timeline is 1973, the year of the oil crisis and the recognition that the West depended upon an East which was more than capable of flexing its economic muscles. The impact of OPEC raising the price of crude oil dramatically, from 3.6 USD per barrel in 1973 to 10.4 USD in 1974,[26] led directly to an economic downturn in European Community countries leading to what became known as 'stagflation', the memory of which would later catalyse the drive for the Single Market. In the 1970s oil had become central to the European economy due to 'tens of millions of new cars on the roads of Western Europe',[27] and the consumer boom of the late 1950s and 60s more generally had exposed a dependency on cheap (imported) oil. Therefore, Europe felt the impact of this price hike much more keenly than the USA which benefitted from large domestic oil reserves. According to Ladrech, 'the manner in which Europe and the US responded to this event added another division in intra-West foreign-policy cohesion',[28] thereby supporting the idea that this period saw a growing lack of unity within the West.

The Iranian Revolution and the Soviet invasion of Afghanistan both occurred in 1979 making it a key date in the history of the present, and one linked to the 'rise of Islam' and arguably to contemporary forms of Jihadism. In any case, both Iran and Afghanistan have witnessed the construction of Islamic regimes which have resulted in major confrontations with the West and a shifting of political influence towards the East, both key prerequisites of postwesternisation. In the case of Iran (and also Iraq) it has been argued that the rise of political Islam represented a form of nationalism and, more importantly from the perspective of the discussion of Turkish politics that forms the bulk of this chapter, 'facilitated a convergence between secular nationalism and political Islam based on their antagonism to Western domination'.[29]

What has been presented so far is postwesternisation in broad brush strokes: the lack of Western unity from the Suez crisis to the invasion of Iraq; a new East shaping the West viewed in terms of a series of challenges (post-colonialism, antagonistic states, rising economic power). A more finely-grained analysis is also possible, hinted at above in the example of the rise of political Islam allowing for the possibility of convergence between secular and religious forces. What we now need to establish is how processes of postwesternisation (viewed not simply as the rise of political Islam, or the JDP looking towards the Middle East) have shaped Turkey and what the likely implications of this are for the future of Turkey–EU relations.

Turkey's relationship with the EU has long been a puzzle for social and political scientists, except where essentialised civilisational differences are evoked[30] or geopolitical clichés reinforcing East–West dichotomies are relied upon.[31] The difficultly of understanding Turkey from a conventional EU studies perspective stems from the retention of an East–West dichotomy which structures thinking about European development. But Turkey's key position in the West's defensive architecture was not consolidated by the collapse of the communist East, it was made less secure. In fact, it is no longer possible to apply an East–West model to the Turkish context. Rather, in this chapter it is argued that understanding the shifting political orientations of Turkey's ruling JDP and the Kemalist elites they have to a large extent displaced can be only understood in the context of postwesternisation, which should be understood as a two-way process: postwestern Turkey meets postwestern Europe. The process of postwesternisation is of course not limited to the interactions between the EU and Turkey. It is a much wider process taking in the whole of the continent (and beyond) and incorporating major changes to Europe/Asia relations.[32]

Much scholarship on Turkey's fraught relationship with the EU still works with Cold War notions of Turkey's position in the world, and corresponding model of the dynamics of Turkey's domestic politics. It is the position here that Turkey is playing a leading role in the postwesternisation of Europe and has alternative ports of entry into global politics which do not depend upon the EU as a gateway. Rather than seeing the EU as an agent of the westernisation of Turkey, it would be more accurate to see Turkey as one agent of Europe's postwesternisation. The idea that Turkey might be considered postwestern may be thought to be contentious by some, the JDP's attempts to 'relocate' Turkey in both Europe and the Middle East notwithstanding. However, what may be thought more contentious still is the idea that Europe has long been postwestern, or, more accurately, the processes of postwesternisation which are shaping Europe have a history which reveal it not simply as a contemporary trend which can be dated from the fall of the Berlin Wall or the break-up of the Soviet Union, but can be traced over the past 50 years or so, or longer if we include the rise of fascism. In this sense postwesternisation should be seen as an important historical process rather than a twist of 'postmodern' social science.

A concrete example of what is meant by postwesternisation in the Turkish context may be useful. The European Stability Initiative (ESI), a Berlin-based think-tank, carried out a year-long field study in Kayseri during which time it interviewed hundreds of conservative business people. ESI discovered that 'individualistic, pro-business currents have become prominent within Turkish Islam' and a 'quiet Islamic Reformation' was unfolding with Muslim entrepreneurs.[33] Konya, a sister city to Kayseri, has also witnessed a similar embrace of economic mobility, liberal culture, gender freedom and secularism.[34] These developments have been termed 'Islamic Calvinism', drawing a parallel between the values contributing to the rise of the Anatolian Tigers and the Protestant values of thrift, piety, and hard work which Max Weber famously identified as underpinning capitalist emergence in Western Europe. As one commentator has noted, Kayseri demonstrates that 'Islam and Western values can coexist without problems in Turkey, and Kayseri is the best answer to those who oppose Turkey's EU membership because of cultural, religious and social differences'.[35] The idea of Islamic Calvinism is much contested it should be noted, not least in Turkey, where critics have argued that it is a European attempt to westernise or 'Christianise' Islam.[36] Other commentators have pointed to the clear continuity between what are seen as traditional Christian values and the contemporary conservative Anatolian values which Islamic Calvinism embodies.[37] From the perspective of this chapter, the phenomenon of 'Islamic Calvinism' can be read as a sign that Turkey is simultaneously 'Eastern' and 'Western', inside and outside: in short, postwestern.

What follows in an extended analysis of Turkey's postwesternisation. This analysis lends support to the argument that the 'postwesternisation thesis' is not simply another way of looking at Turkey's changing political complexion and/or explaining the rise and success of the JDP. Rather, the argument here is that viewing Turkey within a postwestern frame is the only way to adequately understand political developments, Turkey's troubled relations with the EU, and Turkey's changing place in the world.

Europe and Turkey: Reciprocal misconceptions

Scholars have portrayed Turkey as a country hampered by the legacy of an early-Republican period characterised by top-down modernity without broad popular approval. The main protagonist in this story is Mustafa Kemal Atatürk who, enamoured of the scientific and intellectual achievements of European rivals, sought to catapult a 'primitive' society away from the superstitions of universalist Islam towards positivism and humanism by means of a radical secularisation and state-building programme. Naturally, the narrative goes, the antagonist, the Turkish public, rebelled against the sustained assault on their traditions and religious beliefs, thereby laying the foundations for interminable conflict between an elite, progressive-thinking, Western-oriented, secular establishment and tradition-bound, Islamic-leaning Turks. From this conflict arose another protagonist, the Islamicist political movement, challenging the mores of the Kemalist state. This movement, after undergoing various formulations and permutations, is now embodied in the Islamic-rooted JDP.

Scholars of Turkish politics have already pronounced judgement upon the nature of the JDP. To quote Narlı, a typical exponent of this view:

> [t]he Islamist movement is an outlet to express political dissatisfaction with the existing order on the part of the geographical periphery and specific social groups and classes with grievances or different interests. At least five types of relationships are represented here: centre–periphery conflict; class cleavages; regional cleavages; Islamist–secularist conflict; and sectarian antagonism [i.e., Sunnis vs. Alevis].[38]

Lest it be thought that Narlı represents a minority position, one need only peruse the works of a range of Turkish Studies scholars.[39] Arguably, the die was cast by Şerif Mardin whose seminal 1970s insights placed Turkish politics and society within the Marxian prism of centre–periphery relations.[40] He considers that the rise of Islamic movements is a reaction to Turkish 'modernisation' and the alienation of the Muslim population.[41]

Generally, Turkey has been described as trapped between 'East and West',[42] a 'torn country',[43] possessing a perpetual 'identity crisis',[44] a decidedly Western-oriented power despite internal opposition from 'neutralists' and 'Islamic fundamentalists'.[45] Most academics and commentators have invariably perceived contemporary Turkey as an Islamic-oriented, state-secular country, ambivalent about its Ottoman past, and aspiring for membership of the European Union. Turkey seems to be cast as a prisoner of geography, neither European nor Eastern, culturally akin to the Middle East yet ideologically attached to European values and bifurcated along the secular-Islam axis. This binary image of the modern Turkey is best encapsulated by the popular refrain: 'Turkey's heart is in the east; its head is in the west.'

This chapter will contend that Mardin's centre–periphery analysis and its related theories of a secularism-Islam rupture never correctly reflected the actual realities of Turkey's political and socio-economic development, and that this misconception lies at the root of the mutual misunderstandings between Turkey and Europe, or more accurately the contemporary European Union. It is argued that an analysis informed by the framework of theory associated with postwesternisation can explain much more accurately the internal dynamics of a country at the doorstep of Europe, the Middle East, Caucasus and the Black Sea region.

A common appraisal of Turkey's essence posits a bedevilled nation of Kemalists and Islamicists who together are unable or unwilling to arrive at an agreed-upon meaning of what constitutes a 'Turk'. Toprak explains the issue thus:

> [t]he first consequence of republican secularism ... was to produce important groups who were committed to minimising the role of Islam in public life. The second consequence was to produce groups who stood in contrast to the former, who had been marginalised by the Republic and pushed out of the centres of political power, social status and intellectual prestige, because of their opposition to the republican reforms and/or their provincial/religious backgrounds. This division of the Turkish population into 'secularist' versus 'Islamist' camps led to serious political polarisation after 1980 as the urban poor joined the ranks of the Islamists.[46]

Unsurprisingly, the conceptual framework of identity conflict between Kemalists and Islamicists has translated easily into a dogmatic perception of Turkey as a conservative Islamic society incompatible with the European values of democracy, human rights and civil liberties – the 'Copenhagen criteria' in EU parlance. It is, therefore, not surprising that French President Nicolas Sarkozy, a staunch opponent of Turkey's EU membership, has stated that 'Turkey has no place in Europe', asserting instead that its real home is 'Asia Minor'.[47] Mirroring Sarkozy's employment of religious–cultural language, Turkish Prime Minister Recep Tayyip Erdoğan has suggested that '[w]ithout Turkey the EU is a Christian Club'.[48]

Notwithstanding the seductive appeal of the identity-based explanation of Turkey's development, the crucial question to ask is whether it can withstand scrutiny. But before doing so, the ideological foundations of Republican Turkey must first be identified so as to appreciate the source of the cognitive dissonance between Europe and Turkey.

Perceptions of the ideological foundations of the Turkish Republic

The conventional picture of modern Turkey as a state-led, top-down project dominated by nationalism and secular ideals governed by a narrow group of Kemalist elites is well established in popular discourse. However, this account rests on one critical assumption; that secularism was a key driver of Turkey's ideological progress. But is this in fact the case? And what kind of secularism is being referred to?

Contrary to what most scholars imply, Turkey is not a secular country in the sense of fully complying with the three criteria derived from the classical, Western definition of the word: (1) a state administration equidistant from all religions, that is strict state–religion separation; (2) religion not representing a source of law and public policy; and (3) a divorce between private morality and religion.[49] Turkey satisfies criteria (2) but neither (1) nor (3). While Article 4 of the Turkish constitution stipulates that Turkey is a Republic based on secularism, social equality and equality before the law, the state prescribes mandatory (mostly Sunni Islamic) religion classes and finances adult *Qu'ranic* courses.[50] Moreover, there is a state body called the *Diyanet İşleri Başkanlığı* (Directorate of Religious Affairs) under the control of the Prime Minister's Office empowered 'to execute works concerning the beliefs, worship, and ethics of Islam, enlighten the public about their religion, and administer sacred places of worship'.[51] This body exclusively organises the *Hanifite* school of Sunni Islam, supervises all the mosques, educates and appoints the Sunni Islamic clergy (imams), who are classified as civil servants. A state foundation, the *Diyanet Vakfı* (Turkish Foundation for Religious Affairs), answerable to the Prime Minister, finances mosque-building, and the Ministry of Education is involved in promoting Sunni Islamic *İmam Hatip* schools.[52] Clearly, the existence of such state institutions and state practices violate criteria (1), that is state neutrality in religious practice, and (3), the separation of religion from private morality; in Turkey no political party is permitted to advocate the abolition of the Diyanet.[53]

Toprak is in no doubt that the institutional integration of the Sunni Islam with the Turkish state flies in the face of unequivocal secularism:

> [w]hether Islam is compatible with democracy is a legitimate question to ask about Islamic states where the legal system is based on shari'a [Islamic law and jurisprudence]. Islam envisions a political order which is founded on its fundamental principles about community life and moral behaviour. Such a conception blurs the distinction between politics, law and theology

as well as between the public versus private spheres. A system where there is community control over the individual lives, backed by the legislative authority of the Islamic state, seems especially ill-equipped for the emergence of liberal democracy. Moreover, neither the status of women nor the status of non-Muslims under Islamic law allows, under an Islamic state, the exercise of full democratic rights and equal participation by all citizens.[54]

Turkey is, at best, a quasi-secular state. As such, the Republican reforms of Kemal Atatürk and the subsequent polarisation between Kemalists and Islamicists is grossly mischaracterised as a secular–Islamicist fissure. None of the major political parties – the JDP, the (Kemalist) Republican People's Party (RPP), and the Nationalist Movement Party (NMP) – campaign on a platform of downgrading or abolishing the Diyanet İşleri Başkanlığı. In fact, including the arch-Kemalist military establishment there is near complete consensus on this particular point. So, can Kemalists, nationalists, and the military be correctly referred to as secularists?

Statistical evidence also challenges the 'secularist thesis', not by disputing the secular character of the Turkish state, but by indicating that the Turkish public cannot be separated into 'secularists' and 'Islamicists'. Throughout the political roller-coaster ride of the past 40 or so years – elected governments falling to military interventions – Turkey has largely succeeded in nurturing secular democratic principles that seem to have penetrated the national consciousness by virtue of positive methods of propagation (mass education, military, and media) as opposed to repression and fear. According to surveys carried out by Turkish academics Ali Çarkoğlu and Binnaz Toprak in 1999 and 2006, the percentage of Turks who favour a state based on *Shari'a* Islamic law collapsed from 21 per cent to 9 per cent.[55] This implies that the approval rates for broad-spectrum secularism stand at 91 per cent. Such a conclusion is consistent with findings by Gallup Polling in 2006. Remarkably, the number of women wearing headscarves declined by 9 per cent, with much higher figures recorded for more conservative forms of headwear than looser styles, despite the perception of two-thirds of the respondents to the contrary. At the same time, however, their findings revealed that 46 per cent of the population now identifies itself as 'Muslim' rather than 'Turkish', 10 per cent more than in 1999.

Hazama (2007) studied the voting patterns of Turks to find out whether and to what extent the traditional ideological cleavage in Turkish society played a part in the electoral choice of the average voter.[56] He attempted to analyse two types of volatilities – cleavage-type volatilities based on social cleavages and retrospective-type volatilities based on voter punishment of the incumbent – using separate regression models. The results demonstrate several things. First, deep social cleavages previously increased electoral volatility but since the 1990s voting behaviour has stabilised. Second, electoral volatility as a whole nonetheless remains high because of a growing trend toward retrospective voting. Low economic growth and high unemployment are the major reasons for this. The apparent instability in the party system stems not from a lack of representation in parliament of major social groups but rather from poor government performance. Persistently high electoral volatility thus does not necessarily indicate an absence of party system institutionalisation. This current phenomenon in Turkey appears to be analogous with the world trend toward declining trust in government and growing trust in democratic and party systems.

Akarca and Tansel studied the results of 25 Turkish elections for parliament and local administrations between 1950 and 2004.[57] Turkish voters were found to take the government's economic performance into account but are inclined only to consider the performance over the past year. Furthermore, voters hold the major incumbent party responsible for both growth and inflation, but minor incumbent parties only for inflation. Also, they appear to vote strategically, especially in local and parliamentary by-elections, resulting in a diffusion of power. Finally, all parties exhibit a steady depreciation in their political capital while in office. These conclusions are essentially in conformity with the literature on other countries. This study demonstrates that economic factors are increasingly determinative of Turkish voting patterns, which is consistent with the decline of ideological differentiation in society.

Tepe explored the outcomes of elections in Turkey and undertook a survey of left-wing (i.e. mainly Kemalist) voters, centrist voters and right-wing voters (i.e. conservative and religious).[58] On most major issues, whether on military intervention in politics, political liberalisation, secularism, and state support to the Alevi faith, there is remarkable consensus. Where there is disparity on a minority of issues like allowing headscarves to be worn in the Turkish parliament, a respectable third of secularists would agree that the ban should be removed. Tepe goes further, arguing that since the 1990s the influence of ideological voting manifested by identity issues – headscarf, liberal positions on the role of Islam – have assumed much less prominence in predicting the voting behaviour of the majority of Turks:

> [t]he voters' position on the role of the military shows that a discussion of Islam versus secularism does not necessarily create a polarized public. Conventionally, the military regards itself as the custodian of secularism and inserts itself into the debates on issues related to the public role of Islam. In fact, the public evaluates differently the military's role in politics, which is often included in debates on secularism. More than half of the respondents in each bloc support restrictions on the military's role in politics, perhaps because the military has often been associated with austerity measures and an authoritarian application of state-centred policies. Interestingly enough, a significant number of both left- and right-wingers (31 per cent and 21 per cent, respectively) do not completely rule out the idea of opposing the military's involvement in politics, often to protect secularism and social order.[59]

Furthermore, Tepe argues that right-wing parties would lose votes if they chose to cater exclusively or principally to the wants, demands and expectations of their core voters: 'The history of pro-Islamic politics in Turkey indicates that the pro-Islamic right-wing parties' political success rests on their ability to deepen their popular support without falling into the trap of appeasing their hard-core, right-wing, religiously conservative supporters at the expense of other social groups.'[60] Tepe's reasoning explains why the first-term JDP was able to enjoy election success by forming a 'big tent' of the Anatolian business and peasant communities, urban poor, Kurds and, refreshingly, liberal voters – 17.7 per cent of the JDP's constituency are self-described 'Atatürk's followers' and 18.1 per cent describe themselves as 'modern'.[61] This party, in other words, represented a new political force in Turkish politics with a broad appeal to the former centre-right, centre, nationalist, as well as a significant portion of Islamicist voters.[62]

Not only did Tepe cover the period of the first-term JDP rule, she also made a poignant prediction about the likely electoral fallout for the JDP if the party resorts to classical populism and religious populism, which is relevant to the JDP's second term:

> [t]he ability of the JDP to resist the political lure of resorting to populist policies will determine whether the party can prevent an erosion of its broad electoral coalition and thwart yet another wave of alienation and search for a new political 'outsider'. A failure to capitalize on the favourable constellation of international and domestic factors is likely to amount to missing a unique opportunity to escape the pendulum swings between popular and populist policies and further the consolidation of Turkey's liberal democracy.[63]

Taking the findings of Hazama, Akarca and Ansel, and Tepe together with Çarkoğlu's surveys reveals something rather surprising: the dichotomy thesis appears incapable of explaining the complete transformation of crucial aspects of Turkish political Islam, ranging from embracing EU accession to endorsing a radical free market agenda and globalisation. More Turks today self-identify as 'Muslims' rather than as 'Turks' yet the proportion of the population subscribing to secularism has also grown dramatically. These seemingly incompatible results suggest that Islam and secularism in Turkey are converging or fusing together (in the face of the more conventional assumption of divergence) into a cohesive ideology, which can alternately be described as 'secularising Islam' or 'Islamic secularism'. Importantly, the findings show that since the 1990s, the politics of identity are less determinative of voters' choice than the socio-economic concerns of voters.

In fact, the religious and political views of Turkish voters are conditioned by socio-economic indicators rather than a predisposition towards an Islamicist ideology. According to a survey of the political and religious orientations of the middle classes in Turkey conducted by Hakan Yılmaz, 80 per cent of Turks considered themselves as middle class.[64] It revealed that 43.9 per cent of Turks classify themselves being 'post-right wing', supporting democratic values, and 44.9 per cent say that 'secularism must continue to be implemented without change'; only 12.3 per cent ask for a re-interpretation of secularism in Turkey. As many as 82 per cent do not want a military coup under any circumstances, and 58 per cent support Turkey's accession to the European Union. A total of 62.7 per cent of respondents describe themselves as 'modern conservatives' while 73 per cent of modern conservatives say that wearing a headscarf is not a sign of being pious but of being of good character.

These surveys reveal that the prime drivers of religious opinion are socio-economic, which is contrary to the logic of the 'dichotomy thesis' which suggests that the source of Islamicist leanings in Turkey is ideological. Jeffrey C. Dixon applied statistical methods to the 1999–2002 European and World Value Surveys which obtained responses on social and religious issues in many countries, including Turkey. He concluded:

> [d]espite political rhetoric suggesting otherwise ... Turkish people hold similar evaluations of democracy as people in EU member and candidate states. Other assumptions of cultural difference, though, have some merit: Turkish people are more authoritarian, less secular, and less tolerant than their counterparts in the EU. Where cultural differences between Turkey and EU member and candidate states are apparent, they are not as firmly rooted as some politicians and others suggest. The best explanation for these value differences is not religion, but rather economics. As such, more liberal economic policies may help Turkey change: Based on the results presented here, if Turkey's economic situation improves relative to the average EU candidate or member state, Turkish people will be more democratic than people in an average EU member and candidate state; their anti-authoritarian scores will improve by about half; and, their secularism and tolerance scores will improve by about a third. Turkey's political culture would thus be much more conducive to the liberal-democratic values codified in the Copenhagen criteria.[65]

Frederike Wuermeling carried out a study which revealed that there is a causal link between the rather low level of support for the EU's core principles amongst the Turkish public on the one hand and the country's low GDP and its large Muslim population on the other hand.[66] She found that the 'hypothesis of modernisation' – which assumes that the higher a country's GDP, level of education and degree of urbanisation, the higher the agreement to EU Copenhagen political criteria – prioritises 'state' issues of secularism, rule of law and democracy; socio-economic advancement has twice the impact on those issues than cultural factors. On 'social' matters, namely gender equality and freedom of religion, her analysis supported the 'cultural hypothesis' – which states that the higher the percentage of muslims in a country and the higher the level of individual religious belief, the lower the agreement to EU Copenhagen principles; the influence of Islam is twice as strong as the socio-economic change on those matters. Her study, however, has come under severe criticism from Arzheimer who has argued that it suffers from a whole host of serious methodological and theoretical flaws rendering the core claims of the paper untenable, in particular that Islam is largely responsible for the existing low level of acceptability of European values in Turkish society.[67]

From Dixon's study and the counter-criticism of Wuermeling, it is deducible that Islam–secular convergence is mobilised by the forces of economic modernisation for state-related issues – secularism, democracy and rule – and by the convulsions within Turkish Islam for social issues, notably gender equality and freedom of religion. And for the latter, underscoring the gradual – albeit accelerating – fusion of secularism and Islam, in 2004, under the direction of Mehmet Aydın, the minister responsible for the Diyanet, a group of young theologians at Ankara University initiated a project to transform the way the holy texts of Islam are interpreted. In particular, they aimed to bring to bear contemporary social and ethical values of gender equality and human rights on questions of Islamic morality. Koerner, a German Jesuit priest who is an expert on Turkish Sunni Islam and an advisor to the Diyanet on the changes, described the process thus:

> [t]he [Ankara University] revisionists' vision is still restricted to one type of question: ethics. If they ask only, 'How can we make the Koran ethically acceptable today?', they are selling the Koran under price ... Hermeneutics has then a merely mechanical function: we know what there is in the Koran, ethics; and we know what must come out, modern ethics. The only question left is, how do we get it out? Hermeneutics has become a tin-opener.[68]

Most critical of all the fundamental changes is the rejection of many traditional Islamic theological instruments for interpreting the holy texts and jurisprudence, moving away from legalistic and 'textualist' understandings of religion.

Turkey and the 'market for God'

Kemal Atatürk sought to construct a new Turkish Republic out of the ashes of the collapsed Ottoman Empire, shifting Islam from a primary source of identity into a secondary source coupled with a defensive, reactionary vision of nationalism. This fed the 'Sèvres Syndrome' which originated with the idea that the 1920 Treaty of Sèvres was designed to carve up the remainder of the Ottoman Muslim Empire between the Imperial Christian powers while also creating independent Kurdish and Armenian states. This phobia was nourished and promoted by the state apparatus under the guiding hand of the Kemalist establishment, and the Turkish armed forces: 'Anyone familiar with contemporary Turkey will be aware of the frequency with which Turkish officials, journalists and politicians make reference to the Sèvres Complex'.[69]

Through an analysis of the interpretation of three events covered by the secular and Islamicist press, Guida has demonstrated the extent of 'Sèvres Syndrome', which he terms a 'siege paranoia'.[70] His premise is that the Sèvres Syndrome inevitably compromises Turkish intellectuals' perception of reality and influences their ontological understanding of politics and world affairs. This paranoia also inevitably leads to 'irrational overreactions' and apparently 'irrational behaviours' by the masses and by politicians. Failing to understand this paranoia, he argues, prevents a full comprehension of contemporary Turkish politics.

On the foundations of the Sèvres Syndrome, Atatürk built a Turkish Sunni Islamic identity that glorified Turkey's victory against the Greeks, Armenians, Russians and Imperial Europe leading to the institution of the Republic of Turkey in 1923. Simultaneously, his fascination with secularism and scientific progress denoted a determination to remove the symbols of Islam – such as the fez and the headscarf – from public life, at the same time as engendering European humanist traditions in law, public policy, and education. Therefore, it is not surprising that Republican Turkey manifests features of Islamic nationalism – Sunni Islam firmly integrated with the state – yet laws and public policy are disconnected from Islam. These two ideologies have never co-existed easily throughout Turkey's history. Toprak correctly recognises that the precepts of Turkish Sunni Islamic nationalism demand a complete fusion of Islam and state while secularism posits the opposite.[71] Consequently, the real ideological fracture took the form of a sectarian discourse between Kemalist Islam of the power elites and the more traditional Islam of the masses. Expressed differently, neither the Kemalist Islamicists nor the non-Kemalist Islamicists campaigned to cement Turkey firmly and exclusively on the basis of universal, non-discriminatory and secular citizenship. Both parties welcomed the state's micro-management of its own sectarian version as opposed to the other's sectarian version of Islam.

Exploring the evolution of religious education vividly embodies this point. Between 1927 and 1949, Atatürk's Republican Peoples' Party removed religion classes from the curriculum of primary, secondary and high schools, only to reverse the decision in 1949 and re-establish optional religious classes – permitting an 'opt-out' by parents – in primary education.[72] Thereafter, the expansion of religion classes in schools was unstoppable under different government regimes. During the military coup of 1980–1983, the men-at-arms drafted a constitution replacing optional with mandatory religion (mostly Sunni Islam) classes in schools (article 24(3) of the Constitution of the Republic of Turkey).

Among the chief reasons for Europe's public opposition to Turkey's EU membership is Turkey's Islamic identity. According to a recent survey conducted by Hakan Yılmaz to gauge public opinion in France, Germany, Poland, Spain and the United Kingdom on Turkey joining the EU, '[c]ulture is one of the most important factors that defines perception of Turkey ... The most important argument for those who culturally do not want Turkey in EU is that religion and religion-based differences keep Turkey out of Europe's cultural circle'.[73] Similarly, the Transatlantic Survey by the German Marshall Fund showed that only 34 per cent of Turks believed that they shared common values with the West and a mere 28 per cent were positive on the likelihood of EU membership.[74] These opinion poll results lead us to suggest that the academic contextualisation of Turkey within the prism of secular–Islam divergence have contributed to misperceptions based on religion and religious culture. European opinion sees a 'Muslim Turkey' at variance with democracy and human rights, whereas Turkish opinion is lukewarm, if not sometimes hostile, to 'Christian European' civilisation.

Contrary to the academic definitions of Turkey, the quantitative evidence, quoted previously, is hinting – but only hinting – that the secularisation of Islam is proceeding apace in Turkish society under the impacts of pluralistic politics, quasi-secular traditions, urbanisation, economic globalisation, and EU accession. Socio-economic advancements appear to be the main motor of this secularisation process exemplified by the growth of the middle classes.[75] Secularisation in this context does not necessarily mean 'the transformation of persons, offices, properties, institutions, or matters of an ecclesiastical or spiritual character to a lay, or worldly, position'.[76] Nor does it refer to a social process, which occurs independently of an individual's control.[77] Rather, secularisation is concerned with the differentiation of religious beliefs in line with the modernisation of society, as propounded by Jose Casenova who states that the core thesis of the theory of secularisation is the conceptualisation of the process of societal modernisation as a process of functional differentiation and 'emancipation' of the secular spheres – primarily the state, the economy, and science – from the religious sphere and the concomitant differentiation and specialisation of religion within its own newly found religious sphere.[78]

Turkey may follow the path of India in breaking the link between religion and politics. India, no different than Turkey, is experiencing a considerable growth of religiosity at a period of developing prosperity. Paradoxically, the Hindu-nationalist *Bharatiya Janata Party* (BJP) – arguably a Hindu equivalent of Turkish Sunni Islamic nationalism – has witnessed a steep decline in support. One explanation for this is that in 'the absence of a State Religion, and the freedom to practice any religion, creates a free market of sects that most efficiently caters to this demand. Welcome to this God Market – given that the demand for religion always exists, it is the supply of religious variety that actually increases or decreases religiosity. And countries such as the US and India are prime examples of this trend'.[79] Turkey may be charting a similar course as the developing secularisation and social liberalisation of Turkish Islam eventually filter into the state institutions, thereby lessening the state's impulse to micromanage religious beliefs and enabling in the process more diversity and differentiation of Islamic beliefs – a so-called competitive 'market for God' – to emerge. Such a 'market for God' will offer an array of choice in terms of content, spirituality, morality, relevance to contemporary life and personal fulfilment rather than a one-size-fits-all, monopolistic Islamic belief system.

Concluding thoughts

After 50 years of Turkey–EU relations and 50 years of academic study, are we closer to understanding Turkey's EU trajectory? This chapter has argued that in order to arrive at a sophisticated understanding of the past 50 years we must dispense with some of the most familiar ideas about Turkish politics, and that the idea that Turkey and the European Union share a common postwestern trajectory is a fruitful starting point for further investigation. Postwesternisation does not presume that polarisation in Turkish politics is structural and endemic. This means that the very terms with which we designate groups and their position in Turkish politics needs to be revised: terms such as secularists and Islamicists do not adequately capture the dynamics of contestation. It is for these reasons that scholars have attempted to introduce alternative characterisations: 'conservative globalists' and 'defensive nationalists',[80] and 'third-way Islamicists' and 'secular fundamentalists'.[81]

Turkey is mutating from a Kemalist state – where the central authority imposes a singular form of sectarian Islam – to a state and society of manifold modernities and varying philosophies – a decisive movement from Turkish Islamic Sunni nationalism to a notion of secular citizenship . Postwesternisation provides a pertinent framework with which to map this change in Turkey, not just that initiated at the European level, but also at the level of the state and society. Kemalism cannot accurately be defined in contemporary Turkey as the sole source of legitimacy, but is in fact just one of many competing principles in the marketplace of ideas. Postwesternisation anticipates this sociological transformation; other academic theories and approaches do not even recognise it.

Postwesternisation is also able to link the internal changes in Turkey with the pace and nature of EU–Turkey relations. As Turkey undergoes a shift to secular citizenship, it is natural to presuppose that this dynamic will ease the accession process into the EU given the growing convergence between Turkish and European political and social values. Put simply, both geographic regions have entered a post-ideological era: post-Communist in Europe's case, post-Islamicist and post-Kemalist in Turkey's case. And this reality is itself indicative of the potential for increasing mutual understanding and proximate relations between the two parties provided that – and this is a key condition – bilateral (for example Turkey–Greece) and regional disputes (for example Cyprus) do not hamper Turkey's European perspective. Postwesternisation, at variance with competing scholarly approaches, embraces the key fluidity of Turkey's national identity and its implications for EU–Turkey relations.

Notes

1 Z. Öniş, 'Turkey in the post-cold war era: In search of identity', *The Middle East Journal*, 1995, vol. 49, no. 1, pp. 48–68.
2 Z. Öniş, 'Luxembourg, Helsinki and beyond: Towards an Interpretation of recent Turkey–EU relations', Paper presented at the annual Conference of the British Society for Middle Eastern Studies (BRISMES), University of Cambridge, England, July 2–5, 2000.
3 G. Delanty, 'The making of a post-western Europe: a civilizational analysis', *Thesis Eleven*, 2000, vol. 72, pp. 8–25.
4 cf. H. Kramer, *A Changing Turkey: The Challenge to Europe and the United States*, Washington, DC: Brookings Institution Press, 2000
5 Delanty, 'The making of a post-western Europe'; C. Rumford, 'More than a game: Globalization and the post-Westernization of world cricket', *Global Networks*, 2007a, vol. 7, no. 2, pp. 202–214; G. Therborn, 'Post-Western Europe and the plural Asias', in G. Delanty (ed.), *Europe and Asia beyond East and West: Towards a New Cosmopolitanism*, London: Routledge, 2006.
6 Delanty, 'The making of a post-western Europe'; G. Delanty, 'Introduction: The idea of a post-western Europe' in G. Delanty (ed.), *Europe and Asia beyond East and*

West, pp. 1–8 ; C. Rumford 'More than a game'; C. Rumford, *Cosmopolitan Spaces: Europe, Globalization, Theory*, London: Routledge, 2008.

7 G. Therborn, 'Entangled modernities', *European Journal of Social Theory*, 2003, vol. 6, no. 3, pp. 293–305.

8 G. Delanty, 'The making of a post-western Europe'.

9 Ibid.

10 Delanty, 'The making of a post-western Europe'.

11 C. Rumford, 'Does Europe have cosmopolitan borders?', *Globalizations*, 2007b, vol. 4, no. 3, pp. 327–339.

12 G. Delanty, 2007, 'Peripheries and borders in a post-western Europe', *Eurozine*. Online. Available http://www.eurozine.com/articles/2007-08-29-delanty-en.html

13 U. Beck and E. Grande, *Cosmopolitan Europe*, Cambridge: Polity Press, 2007.

14 Delanty, 'Introduction', in Delanty, *Europe and Asia beyond East and West*, p. 4.

15 Delanty, 'Introduction', in Delanty, *Europe and Asia beyond East and West*, p. 1.

16 G. Delanty and C. Rumford, *Rethinking Europe: Social Theory and the Implications of Europeanization*, London: Routledge, 2005, pp. 106–119.

17 C. Rumford, *Cosmopolitanism and Europe*, Liverpool: Liverpool University Press, 2007c.

18 J. Adler, 'A century of destiny', *Newsweek*, 19 November 2007.

19 G. Therborn, *European Modernity and Beyond: The Trajectory of European Societies 1945–2000*, London: Sage, 1995, p. 360.

20 T. Judt, *Postwar: A History of Europe Since 1945*, London: William Heinemann, p. 295.

21 Judt, *Postwar*, p. 297.

22 Ibid.

23 Therborn, *European Modernity and Beyond*, p. 346.

24 G. Bhambra, 'Postcolonial Europe, or, understanding Europe in the time of the postcolonial' in C. Rumford (ed.), *The Sage Handbook of European Studies*, London: Sage, 2009.

25 J. Borocz and M. Sarkar, 'What is the EU?', *International Sociology*, 2005, vol. 20, no. 2, p.167.

26 D. Pirages, 'Oil industry', in J. Scholte and R. Robertson (eds), *Encyclopaedia of Globalization,*Volume 3, London: Routledge, 2007.

27 Judt, *Postwar*, p. 455.

28 R. Ladrech, 'Historical background' in R. Sakwa and A. Stevens (eds), *Contemporary Europe,* Second Edition, Basingstoke: Palgrave, 2006, p. 44.

29 S. Zubaida, *Islam, the People and the State: Political Ideas and Movements in the Middle East*, London: I. B. Tauris, 1993, p. xix.

30 S. Huntington, *The Clash of Civilizations and the Remaking of World Order*, New York: Simon and Schuster, 1996.

31 H. Kramer, *A Changing Turkey.*

32 G. Delanty, *Europe and Asia beyond East and West.*

33 European Stability Initiative, 'Islamic Calvinists: Change and Conservatism in Central Anatolia', 19 September 2005. Online. Available http://www.esiweb.org/index.php?lang=en&id=156&document_ID=69 (accessed 6 May 2008).

34 S. Tavernise, 'In Turkey's religious heartland, secularism thrives', *International Herald Tribune*, 14 May 2008. Online. Available http://www.iht.com/articles/2007/05/14/europe/turkey.php (accessed 14 May 2008).

35 G. Zengin quoted at http://www.esiweb.org/index.php?lang=en&id=224 (accessed 5 March 2010).

36 A. Lodhi, 'Turkish toil brings new form of faith'. BBC News, 13 March. 2006. Available http://news.bbc.co.uk/2/hi/business/4788712.stm.

37 D. Judson, '"Islamic Calvinism" a paradoxical engine for change in conservative Central Anatolia', *Turkish Daily News*, 30 September 2005.

38 N. Narlı, 'The rise of the Islamist movement in Turkey', *Middle East Review of International Affairs*, 1999, vol. 3, no.3, pp. 38–48.
39 Such as B. Barber, *Jihad vs. McWorld: How Globalism and Tribalism Are Reshaping the World*, New York: Balantine Books, 1995; H. Gülalp, 'Globalising postmodernism: Islamist and Western social theory', *Economy and Society*, 1997, vol. 26, no. 3, pp. 419–433; H. Kramer, *A Changing Turkey*; A. Buğra, 'Labour, capital, and religion: Harmony and conflict among the constituency of political Islam in Turkey', *Middle Eastern Studies*, 2002, vol. 38, no. 2, pp. 187–204 ; A. Kuru, 'Globalization and diversification of Islamic movements: Three Turkish cases', *Political Science Quarterly*, 2005, vol. 120, no. 2, pp. 253–274; H. Yavuz, *Islamic Political Identity in Turkey: Religion and Global Politics*, Oxford and New York: Oxford University Press, 2003; A. Mango, *The Turks Today*, New York: Overlook, 2004; B. Rubin and A. Çarkoğlu, *Religion and Politics in Turkey*, London: Routledge, 2005.
40 S. Mardin, 'Centre–periphery relations: A key to Turkish politics?', *Daedalus*, 1973, vol. 102, no. 1, pp. 169–190.
41 Ibid.
42 M. Heper, 'The European Union, the Turkish military and democracy', *South European Society and Politics*, 2005, vol. 10, no. 1, pp. 33–44.
43 Huntington, *The Clash of Civilizations and the Remaking of World Order.*
44 F. Ahmad, *Turkey: The Quest for Identity*, London: Oneworld Publications, 2004.
45 B. Lewis, *The Emergence of Modern Turkey*, Oxford: Oxford University Press, 1961.
46 B. Toprak, 'Islam and democracy in Turkey', *Turkish Studies*, 2005, vol. 6, no. 2, pp. 167–186.
47 S. Çağaptay, 'Sarkozy's policy on Turkey's E.U. Accession: Bad for France?', *inFocus*, 2007, vol. 1, no. 3. Online. Available http://www.jewishpolicycenter.org/96/sarkozys-policy-on-turkeys-eu-accession-bad-for.
48 Turkish Weekly, 'Without Turkey, EU is Christian club: Turkish Prime Minister', *The Journal of Turkish Weekly*, Friday, 15 May 2009. Online. Available http://www.turkishweekly.net/news/76920/-without-Turkey-EU-is-christian-club-Turkish-prime-minister-.html (accessed 19 January 2010).
49 Toprak, 'Islam and Democracy in Turkey'.
50 A. Kılavuz, 'Adult religious education at the Qur'anic courses in Modern Turkey', *The Journal of International Social Research*, 2009, vol. 2, no. 6, pp. 407–414.
51 Diyanet İşleri Başkanlığı, 'Takdim', 2009. Online. Available http://www.diyanet.gov.tr/turkish/dy/Diyanet-Isleri-Baskanligi-Tanitim-Taktim-3.aspx (accessed 10 January 2010).
52 G. Jenkins, 'Statements by state officials highlight the paradoxes of Turkish secularism', *Eurasia Daily Monitor* Turkey, 2008, vol. 5, no. 10, 17 January 2008. Online. Available http://www.jamestown.org/single/?no_cache=1&tx_ttnews[tt_news]=33307 (accessed 19 January 2010).
53 E. Macar, 'Religious affairs and mandatory religion courses contradict secularism and equality', *Bianet*, 10 November 2008, Online. Available http://bianet.org/english/english/110765-religious-affairs-and-mandatory-religion-courses-contradict-secularism-and-equality (accessed 22 January 2010).
54 Toprak, 'Islam and Democracy in Turkey', pp. 168–169.
55 A. Çarkoğlu and B. Toprak, *Değişen Türkiye'de Din, Toplum ve Siyaset (Religion, Politics, Society in Changing Turkey)*, İstanbul: TESEV Yayınları, 2006; A. Çarkoğlu and B. Toprak, *Türkiye'de Din, Toplum ve Siyaset (Religion, Politics, Society in Turkey)* İstanbul: TESEV Yayınları, 2000.
56 Y. Hazama, *Electoral Volatility in Turkey: Cleavages vs. the Economy*, I.D.E. Occasional Papers Series, 2007. Online. Available http://findarticles.com/p/articles/mi_qa5376/is_200701/ai_n21282802 (accessed 5 May 2008).

57 A. T. Akarca and A. Tansel, 'Economic performance and political outcomes: An analysis of the Turkish parliamentary and local election results between 1950 and 2004', *Public Choice*, 2006, vol. 129, no. 1–2, pp. 77–105.

58 S. Tepe, 'Politics between market and Islam: The electoral puzzles and changing prospects of pro-Islamic parties', *Mediterranean Quarterly*, 2007, vol. 18, no. 2, pp. 107–135.

59 Tepe, 'Politics between market and Islam', p. 126.

60 Tepe, 'Politics between market and Islam', p. 134.

61 B. Akgün, *Türkiye'de Seçmen Davranışı Sistemi ve Sosyal Güven* [*Voter Behaviour and Social Trust in Turkey*], Ankara: Nobel, 2007, p. 205.

62 E. Özbudun, 'Changes and continuities in the Turkish party system', *Representation*, 2006, vol. 42, no. 2, pp. 129–137.

63 Tepe, 'Politics between market and Islam', p. 135.

64 H. Yılmaz, 'In Search of a Turkish Middle Class: Economic Occupations, Political Orientations, Social Life-Styles, Moral Values', Research project co-funded by Open Society Institute and Bogazici University, 2007.

65 J. C. Dixon, 'A clash of civilizations, or differences in economic modernization? Examining liberal–democratic values in Turkey and the European Union', Turkish Industrialists' and Businessmen's Association Washington Office, 22 September 2005, Online. Available http://www.tusiad.us/Content/uploaded/A%20CLASH%20 OF%20CIVILIZATIONS%20OR%20DIFFERENCES%20IN%20ECONOMIC%20 MODERNIZATION%20092105.PDF (accessed 2 March 2008), pp. 5–6.

66 F. Wuermeling, 'Passt die Türkei zur EU und die EU zu Europa?', *Kölner Zeitschrift für Soziologie und Sozialpsychologie*, 2007, vol. 59, pp. 185–214.

67 K. Arzheimer, 'Ein Märchen aus Tausend und einer Nacht? Kommentar zu dem Artikel von Frederike Wuermeling "Passt die Türkei zur EU und die EU zu Europa?"', *Kölner Zeitschrift für Soziologie und Sozialpsychologie.* 2008, vol. 60, pp. 23–135.

68 'Tin-opener theology from Turkey', *Asia Times Online*, 3 June 2008, Online. Available http://www.atimes.com/atimes/Middle_East/JF03Ak02.html (accessed 3 June 2008).

69 B. Park, *Turkey's Policy Towards Northern Iraq: Problems and Perspectives*, London: Routledge, 2005, p. 15.

70 M. Guida, 'The Sèvres syndrome and "komplo" theories in the Islamist and secular press', *Turkish Studies,* 2008, vol. 9, no. 1, pp. 37–52.

71 Toprak, 'Islam and Democracy in Turkey', pp. 167 – 186.

72 H. Adanalı, 'The many dimensions of religious instruction in Turkey, religious education in schools, international association for religious freedom', 2010, Online. Available http://www.iarf.net/REBooklet/Turkey.htm (accessed 25 January 2010).

73 'Young Europeans back Turkey's EU bid more, poll', *Today's Zaman*, 24 January 2010.

74 German Marshal Fund, 'Transatlantic Trends 2009 Partners: Key Findings', 2009. Online. Available http://www.gmfus.org/trends/2009/docs/2009_English_Key.pdf (accessed 2 January 2010).

75 G. B. Özcan and H. Turunc, 'The politics of administrative decentralization in Turkey since 1980', in J. Killian and N. Eklund (eds), *Handbook of Administrative Reform: An International Perspective*, New York: CRC Press, 2008.

76 N. Berkes, *The Development of Secularism in Turkey*, London: Routledge, 1999, p. 5.

77 M. Boroujerdi, 'Can Islam be secularized?', in M. R. Ghanoonparvar and F. Farrokh (eds.), *Transition: Essays on Culture and Identity in the Middle Eastern Society*, Laredo, TX: Texas A&M International University, 1994, pp. 55–64. Online. Available http://faculty.maxwell.syr.edu/mborouje/Documents/English/Secularized.htm (accessed 26 January 2010).

78 J. Casanova, *Public Religions in the Modern World*, Chicago, IL: University of Chicago Press, 1994, p. 19.

79 H. S. Bal, 'God has left politics', *Sri Lanka Guardian*, 13 December 2009. Online. Available http://www.srilankaguardian.org/2009/12/god-has-left-politics.html (accessed 26 October 2010).
80 Z. Öniş, 'Conservative globalists versus defensive nationalists: Political parties and paradoxes of Europeanization in Turkey', *Journal of Southern Europe and the Balkans*, 2007, vol. 9, no. 3, pp. 247–261.
81 C. Rumford, *Cosmopolitan Spaces*.

8   Ethical dimension

Promises, obligations, impatience and delay: Reflections on the ethical aspects of Turkey–EU relations[1]

Thomas Diez

Ambiguity and fear

The Secretariat General for European Union (EU) Affairs within Turkey's Prime Ministerial Office distributed a jacket pin in 2010, showing the EU and Turkish flag merged into each other. It integrated the star in the Turkish crescent and star into the EU ring of twelve stars, and shaped the EU ring of stars in such a way that it looked like an extended half-moon.[2] At first glance, the image provided is one of harmony. We belong together, the pin seems to say. Yet on reflection, one can think of at least two further interpretations. One would emphasise the ambiguity in the picture: Turkey's star is one of Europe's, but its crescent remains outside Europe. The other one would invoke a discourse of fear: The EU stars take on the shape of the crescent – this is what may happen if Turkey became an EU member, critics may say; it will change the shape of the EU. Plus, the crescent looks as if it is threatening to pull out that star, to tear the Union apart.

Ambiguity and fear dominate at least large parts of the public discourse on Turkey–EU relations. There is the ambiguity of whether Turkey belongs to Europe or not: in both Turkey and the EU, the prevailing image is that of Turkey becoming European, rather than that of being European. Then there is ambiguity in the commitment of both sides. On the one hand, they engage in membership negotiations. On the other hand, EU politicians emphasise the open-ended nature of negotiations and float ideas of 'privileged partnerships'.[3] These ideas in themselves are ambiguous in the sense that they suggest that there can be a form of association that goes beyond the rather close association that Turkey already has with the EU but does not amount to membership as such, without clarifying what such a partnership would look like in practice. Meanwhile, on the Turkish side, support for membership seems to wax and wane (which, it should be said, is not unusual for membership candidates during negotiations with the EU), and alternative foreign policy scenarios that emphasise a greater Turkish regional engagement outside Europe keep occurring in the media and political speeches.[4]

Fear also animates the discussion.[5] Among EU member states, those with a relatively high rate of migrants with a Turkish background show a particularly strong tendency to reject Turkish membership, presumably because they fear additional migration.[6] It is against this background that the debates in France and the Netherlands about the initially proposed constitutional treaty for the EU forged links between the treaty and a possible Turkish EU membership. The rejection of the treaty in these two countries consequently came to be seen as a quasi-referendum on Turkish EU membership.[7] Moreover, in 2004 France passed a constitutional amendment to demand a referendum before new member states can be approved. The resulting Article 88 has since been changed so that a referendum does not have to take place if a three-fifths majority in both Senate and National Assembly votes against it, but this does little to deter concerns that Turkish membership is likely to fail at that threshold. There is therefore a securitisation of migration especially from Turkey, in that they represent such migration as an existential threat to the fabric of EU member state societies, legitimising measures such as the need for referendums that would otherwise not seem legitimate.[8] The Turkish debate, too, is not without securitisations, except here, the Kemalist elites that once used to push Westernisation (see the discussion in Rumford and Turunç, this volume), are increasingly constructing EU membership as an existential threat to the state structures that they support and which support them.[9]

What are the possibilities of articulating an ethical position in this context? In what follows, I argue that the case of Turkish–EU relations raises in fact a series of challenges to international ethics in general, and to normative conceptions of the EU in particular. These challenges centre on the question of obligations: who is under which obligation in international relations? And who is in a position to impose obligations? My argument in this contribution is that the core obligation that is justifiable from the position of international ethics is that both sides negotiate within the established routines, rules and procedures of enlargement processes. There is therefore no principled substantive norm that would allow us to decide on Turkish EU membership, and no right to membership, or to deny membership as such. Rather, the obligation is procedural. It also applies to both sides – all too often, participants in the debate lay the blame squarely on the doorstep of either the EU (or individual member states) or Turkey.

I also argue that in fifty years of EU–Turkey relations, we have come from a long period of virtual indifference to increasing impatience over the last twenty years, again on both sides. While this impatience with the lack of progress towards membership is understandable, it is not exactly helpful. For one, impatience diverts attention from obligations. Secondly, it tends to be met with rejection and political controversy. Both of these problems that impatience brings about, I argue, lead to delaying membership rather than expediting it, so that impatience tends to have ironic effects.

In order to develop this argument, I will in the next section first review the role of obligations in international ethics, and in particular discuss to what extent such obligations arise from promises made, for such promises, as we shall see, are the core reference point in the impatience present in the debate. I will then discuss the concrete obligations as I see them arising in the context of Turkey–EU relations. The final section then addresses the problem of impatience and delay. I should stress from the start that I do not wish to make any predictions about the likely outcome of membership negotiations and therefore about the future of relations between the EU and Turkey. Rather, the aim of this chapter is to take a step back and explore a position that allows this relationship to unfold on a defensible basis and without the perpetuation of securitising moves that tap into discourses of fear.

Promises and obligations

Ethics, Mark Amstutz notes, is 'the application of the appropriate moral norms to private and public affairs'.[10] For some, such considerations do not matter in international politics. For a neorealist, for instance, there cannot be any ethics that is relevant to international politics as it is the structure of the system that determines behaviour. In a classic reading of Machiavelli, moral considerations always have to be subjugated to interest.[11] Yet this is not the only interpretation of realism, and the classical, pre-neorealist writers of the twentieth century have displayed a much more attentive attitude to the question of values and norms in international politics.[12] Indeed, one would have to have a highly impoverished notion of statehood and the international system to argue that questions of ethics do not matter. The debates about constructivist and critical approaches in International Relations since the mid-1980s have also re-opened space for probing further into the role of norms in international politics, and have revived the field of international ethics.

Three debates of international ethics are particularly relevant for an exploration of Turkey–EU relations. The first of these is whether normative reasoning should take the form of *consequentialist* or engage in *deontological* reasoning.[13] Consequentialist ethics sets certain goals as the standards to be attained, and sees any means to achieve those standards as justifiable. In contrast, deontological ethics focuses on rules of behaviour, and therefore questions the justifiability of means independent of their goals. This is a debate particularly relevant, for instance, in the question of the legitimacy of war: one may see war as justified on the basis of changes that are hoped to be brought about by the resort to military action, or one may see war in principle as inappropriate behaviour unless there are specific rules accepted by all that allow military means in exceptional cases.[14] That such exceptional cases exist is a sign that in practice, the two forms of ethics are often intertwined.[15] However, I will argue that the case of Turkey and the EU needs to be approached from a deontological perspective, as there are no grounds on which to establish a clear-cut goal in terms of membership.

The second debate in international ethics, and by far the most prominent one, is that between *cosmopolitanism* and *communitarianism*.[16] Cosmopolitanists consider the world as a whole. Their main reference point for ethical judgments is humanity. Communitarianists, in contrast, place value in the existence of a plurality of communities, each with their own identity and prevailing norms. This debate pervades a great number of issues on the agenda of international politics, most prominently on human rights[17] and humanitarian intervention.[18] Again, framing cosmopolitanism and communitarianism in a dichotomy is misplaced, as many arguments voiced for instance by so-called solidarists in the English School will respect some degree of difference while acknowledging the existence of a single human race and globe.[19] The debate does however challenge our conceptions of EU–Turkey relations. I will argue that a communitarian position may all too easily lead to a rejection of Turkey's EU membership bid,[20] while a cosmopolitan position tends to overemphasise the obligations that the EU has towards Turkey, and the rights that Turkey has in terms of membership.

The third debate relevant here concerns the relationship of *promises* and *obligations*. This is admittedly less of a debate in international ethics as such, but it is a theme that is no doubt relevant to Turkey–EU debates. The question, simply put, is whether any obligations arise from promises that have been made in the past. In international law, the principle of *pacta sunt servanda* only applies to treaties as such, which have to be honoured. Yet in any human relationship, we would consider the breaking of promises unacceptable, at least in the absence of good reasons. We can find an indication of this logic being not entirely absent from international relations in the argument that EU enlargement was at least in part a consequence of EU member states having to fulfil promises they made to Central and Eastern European Countries during the Cold War if they were not to lose face.[21] The risk of losing face however only exists if promises do in fact mean something and do create obligations. This is certainly the case in relation to actors, such as the European Union, that consider themselves as exemplary in their conduct in international politics.[22] There are suggestions that the same logic that made the EU enlarge eastwards may also apply to Turkey,[23] yet as I will argue below, in order to assess this, one needs to take a more careful look at which promises have been made and thus which obligations arise.

In the next section, I consider these general issues in international ethics in relation to EU–Turkey relations.

Obligations

Cosmopolitan or communitarian?

In considering the Turkey–EU case, I take the cosmopolitanism versus communitarianism debate first, since the result of this discussion has consequences for the possibility of a consequentalist position. In the public debate, communitarian positions are widespread, especially within EU member states. A commentary taken from one of Germany's main daily newspapers, *Frankfurter Allgemeine Zeitung*, summarises the core of these positions: 'Turkey cannot be found on any of the possible cultural maps of Europe'.[24] In other words, from a communitarian perspective, there is an inherent cultural identity to Europe, which needs to be preserved if one does not want to jeopardise the legitimacy of the entire European integration process.

In its crudest 'Christian Club' version, the communitarian argument relies primarily on religious differences, emphasising the Christian nature of the EU and the Muslim domination of Turkey.[25] Yet there are also more complex notions of the 'Christian nature' of the EU, which do not merely point to religious differences but to different historical experiences and thus social and political identities. German historian Hans-Ulrich Wehler, for instance, argues that Turkey 'has never been part of the historic Europe' and points to the history of war, which was waged by the Ottoman Empire against Christian Europe for 450 years.[26] This historical experience is deeply rooted in the collective minds of Europe and Turkey. In Wehler's view, there is therefore no reason why Turkey should be welcomed in the EU. Indeed, he points out that Turkish politicians themselves see the EU as a 'Christian Club', before he then launches into an attack on Islam, which Wehler claims is the only religion that has in its teaching a deeply rooted hostility against the West. There is no reason, he argues, to accept a huge and powerful Islamic state as member of the EU whereas already Muslim and in particular Turkish immigrants pose a big problem to European societies.[27] Ultimately, his polemic becomes openly securitising: 'Yet Islam alone, it seems, can mobilise a core of religious beliefs, which can be transformed to a radical anti-Western fundamentalism against the threat of succumbing to Western modernity'.[28] Christianity for Wehler does not matter as a religious belief but as part of a historical experience that has shaped Europe.

One should not dismiss the communitarian argument all too easily. Wehler, for one, is concerned that as a consequence of Turkish EU membership, the integration project will derail and antagonistic nationalism will rear its head again.[29] Others see Turkey still in a process of transformation as far as democracy, human rights and the rule of law is concerned, and they are worried about watering down EU standards in these respects.[30] It may well be that these worries are mere rhetoric, and that in fact underlying these positions are concerns about the number of migrants that Turkish EU membership would generate, or other economic or geostrategic concerns.[31] Yet even so, one would first have to say that the fear of immigrants is linked back to the defence of a European community and communities in Europe, and second, that on the level of discursive legitimisation, rhetoric is highly relevant and thus cannot be easily dismissed.

However, the fact that communitarian arguments cannot be rejected as unethical does not make them right. The problem with communitarianism, at least if it is used to legitimise exclusionary social and political practices, is that it takes the nature of political communities as given. While one cannot accuse Wehler and others of following a primordialist position, their political identities are nonetheless forged by material historical forces. They do not therefore take seriously the degree to which such historical forces are themselves contested and narrated in particular ways so as to make it possible to imagine political identities within large territorial spaces.[32] They therefore fall foul to what David Campbell, following Jacques Derrida, has called 'ontopology': the support of a position that attributes highest value to a particular place and treats it as objectively given.[33]

What is the problem with such an approach? In a broader ethical perspective, it not only negates the constructedness of modern political spaces but also leads to exclusionary politics that draws boundaries between people and restricts their freedom both in articulating their identities and in very practical freedom-of-movement terms. In opening up difference, it uses the Other to construct the identity of the Self,[34] and neglects the 'radical interdependence' between Self and Other from which derives a particular responsibility not only to one's own community but also to other communities.[35] Thus, the 'Christian Club' argument for instance is untenable because it is exclusionary, and as such also undermines core Christian values that insist on the openness and the responsibility to others.[36]

Does this lead us directly to adopt a cosmopolitan perspective? The answer, I would argue, is no, but it depends on how one defines cosmopolitanism. There are at least three versions of a cosmopolitan argument relating to Turkey–EU relations: one argument considering the scope of EU institutions, one establishing rights of Turkey towards the EU, and one arguing in favour of what I would call a cosmopolitan ethos.

In terms of the scope of EU institutions, one could make the argument that the EU is a nucleus of a world polity based on federalism and subsidiarity. At a minimum, from such a perspective one would see it as a model for a global federation in which the spirit of universalism and the overcoming of national boundaries is instituted. From this spirit would arise an obligation to take Turkey up as a member, for excluding Turkey would undermine the universalism so central to this view, at least as long as Turkey fulfils basic membership criteria. Yet the question arises whether the EU is in fact such a cosmopolitan institution. Its name and the text of the Treaty on European Union speak against such a view. Article 49 of the Treaty on European Union specifies that 'any European state' that respects EU values can apply to become an EU member state. The EU thus is by definition a regional organisation, as evidenced by the flat-out rejection of Morocco as a possible membership candidate. While it is true that enlargement over time has become a core part of the EU identity, the nearly continuous rounds of enlargement since the early 1970s involved states whose European identity was largely uncontested in public discourse – in contrast to Turkey, whose identity is seen as hybrid, or as one of transforming itself, being 'on the way' to Europe.[37] Because it is defined as a regional organisation, the EU is entitled to define its boundaries in order to be able to say what counts as 'European'; if it did not do so, the whole idea of a *European* Union would become absurd.[38] One may of course question the normative standing of regional organisations as such. David Mitrany, for instance, thought that the European integration process was undermining his ideas of a global functional integration process, as its territorial dimension replicated a core feature of the state system.[39] Yet such an argument would lead to a rejection of the integration process rather than the deduction of specific obligations towards Turkey. Considering the EU as a cosmopolitan institution therefore neglects its character as a regional organisation.

Does cosmopolitanism establish certain rights of Turkey or Turkish citizens towards the EU? Luis Cabrera, for instance, argues that there is a 'natural duty' to enhance individual human rights protection; that EU membership would deliver such enhancement; and that as such, there is a 'human right to accession'.[40] This last step of Cabrera's argument is perhaps purposefully provocative and taking it too far, but the question that he poses is interesting nonetheless. Above all, there is a strong argument that EU membership will lead to greater democracy and human rights protection and strengthen the rule of law in Turkey, as indeed the accession process has already done through a series of constitutional reform packages.[41] Even if one does not see accession as a cause for this transformation process, one will have to acknowledge that the membership prospect has served as an 'anchor' to stabilise the reforms as long as it has been credible.[42] Even before membership, Bahar Rumelili and Fuat Keyman argue, there are certain citizenship rights that Turkish citizens enjoy within the EU on the basis of the association agreement and Turkey's membership of the Council of Europe coupled with the linkage drawn between European Court of Human Rights rulings and the accession process in terms of monitoring human rights standards.[43] Indeed, I have myself argued that the domestic reforms in Turkey are a major argument in favour of membership negotiations.[44] Yet it is one thing to establish a right to negotiation (a position I would like to maintain in what follows), and quite another thing to talk about a right to membership.[45] Cabrera himself notes that such a right can only be a 'qualified' right as the EU cannot be expected to take up any country in the world with immediate effect.[46] In terms of Turkey, he concludes that there are not sufficient arguments to counter membership, but this seems to indicate that the ultimate judgement of how the consequences for domestic reform and thus for individual citizens are to be weighed against other considerations cannot be set in the abstract but must depend on deliberations about the concrete case in question.

The final cosmopolitan argument proposes a cosmopolitan ethos, or a 'cosmopolitan outlook'.[47] Such an ethos would at its core involve a concern towards the overcoming of borders and 'the development of a self-reflexive cultural and political subjectivity'.[48] As Owen Parker notes, such a view does not negate diversity, but tries to combine it with universality in what he terms 'diversality'.[49] I see three problems with this view. Firstly, it seems to me to accept the poststructuralist critique of cosmopolitanism so that the cosmopolitan core is barely recognisable and there are hardly any differences left to what one may label a 'postmodern' position that also tries to negotiate universality and difference.[50] Secondly, and more substantively, I have my doubts about whether the EU indeed has such a cosmopolitan outlook. In line with the view that the EU is a 'normative power',[51] Parker argues that there are what he calls 'cosmopolitan "footholes"' in the 'prevailing EU institutional discourses'.[52] Yet as Parker acknowledges, and as I have argued elsewhere, there are also many aspects of EU practice that redraw boundaries and where it can at least be questioned whether there is any underlying cosmopolitan idea towards the overcoming of borders and greater self-reflexivity.[53] Thirdly, just as in the case of cosmopolitan rights above, I cannot see how a 'cosmopolitan ethos' may result in a specific 'common destiny'; indeed the destiny of EU–Turkey relations seems to be rather open as long as the diversality concern is taken into account.

Consequentialist or deontological?

Neither the communitarian nor the cosmopolitan argument as they are used in the debate about Turkey–EU relations are particularly convincing. I have some sympathies with some of the cosmopolitan arguments, but I am not sure I would call them cosmopolitan any more, and I do not quite see that the consequences postulated in these arguments do necessarily follow from the premises made. A core problem in this discussion however is that cosmopolitan accounts are too focused on Turkish EU membership and therefore take a consequentialist position. Yet for a consequentalist ethics to prevail, it would have to be clear that EU membership is indeed the uncontested aim which we ought to work towards. This, it seems to me, is not the case. While it is true that the EU 'anchor' is likely to stabilise democratic reforms, it is less clear that such reforms would not take place without this anchor.[54] And while it is true that human rights can be bolstered by EU membership, Turkey already is a party to the European Convention of Human Rights, from which arises a set of obligations and citizen rights. Furthermore, Turkish EU membership is contested both in the EU and in Turkey. In such a situation, it seems to me to be problematic, to say the least, to impose a particular aim onto the political debate. Especially within Turkey, the debate needs to be continued on what EU membership would actually mean in terms of policy harmonisation and its effects on different social strata, and whether EU membership on that basis should remain a primary foreign policy goal. While membership negotiations are about *membership* and not alternatives to membership, they also provide the framework to test and assess the effects of membership. Rather than focusing on an ultimate aim, therefore, it is the membership negotiation process that is core to my view of an ethical perspective.

Consequently, I take a deontological position, which argues for fair and proper negotiations within the framework applicable to all candidates. Referenda on Turkish membership are clearly outside this framework. Instead, negotiations should proceed on the 'technical' grounds of the requirements of the *acquis communautaire*, the body of EU legislation and principles, as envisaged in the successive opening, discussion, and closing of chapters that address different aspects of the *acquis*. This is the core of the negotiation process as it has developed in the past. While its rules are technically not of a legal nature, they nonetheless form a set of informal rules that provide a minimum of fairness and guide expectations.[55]

Such a deontological position is also taken by some cosmopolitanists in the Kantian tradition, where the focus is on universal rules to regulate behaviour.[56] In relation to the EU, Erik Oddvar Eriksen has argued that one can conceptualise the EU as a 'cosmopolitan polity' to the extent that it accepts the restrictions of 'higher-ranking law' and that it 'has committed itself to a law-based view of international relations'.[57] Whether any form of law at a higher level satisfies this view is doubtful, but need not interest us here. Likewise, we do not have to engage in a debate whether universal rules are feasible under conditions of diversity. For the argument developed here, it is instead of crucial importance that there are rules; that all sides involved see themselves as bound by these rules; and that they act according to them.

Three counter-arguments spring to mind: Are these rules not a one-sided imposition of the EU? Is this democratic? And, does it work in practice, especially in a contested case such as Turkey?

Are these rules a one-sided imposition? Yes they are, but the counter-question is whether this is a problem. On the one hand, it would of course be a characteristic of an EU that is particularly proud of dialogue and self-reflection if the membership candidates were already involved in setting the rules for membership and membership negotiations. Yet on the other hand, such an involvement also bears the risk of unfairness if it leads to different candidates being judged by different standards. Besides, the EU is an existing organisation with responsibilities towards its members that membership candidates wish to join, in which case it seems appropriate that the EU imposes rules on the membership application process, as long as it sticks to these rules in its own behaviour. And finally, one should note that all rules are an imposition of sorts, which weigh normative standards against each other and against interests and other considerations. It is therefore not the imposition that is the problem, but whether the rules themselves are appropriate. Discussions about appropriateness should however not be taken too lightly, as they undermine the process that should be governed by the rules – in this case, enlargement – and as variation in the rules also brings with it unequal treatment and therefore a problem of fairness.

Is such a process democratic? The short answer is: no. But should it be democratic? One ought to remember Fred Halliday's notes on the events surrounding the World Trade Organisation meeting in Seattle in 1999, hailed by some as the advent of a new, transnational civil society: 'One can only wonder where any of the major peace processes in situations of ethnic conflict of the past ten years would have reached if the protagonists had had to negotiate in public or report routinely to their constituencies; Ireland, South Africa, Palestine would all have remained in the grip of violence.'[58] In other words, there are aspects to international negotiations that make them possible only if public debate, for the duration of the negotiations anyway, is restricted. In fact, some have argued that it is such conditions that facilitate deliberation, largely because negotiators do not have to worry about the next day's news headlines.[59] Of course, such a technocratic view has led to charges of a democratic deficit in the EU. Yet one should not throw out the proverbial baby with the bathwater: important is the possibility of the public to follow the progress of negotiations, and therefore a minimum of transparency. Even the question of whether the negotiation results ought to be democratically approved is already a lot more complex. It seems only reasonable to have a referendum on such results in the membership applicant country, but much less to do so in the existing member states, not only because this would change the established rules and procedures, but also because after the EU has set the rules for negotiating, it cannot make their applicability dependent on the public mood of the day without undermining the spirit of these rules.

One may now finally argue that the rules are only a screen to push through partial interests: does rule-following work in the practice of negotiations, especially regarding Turkey? In the Turkish case, there is for instance the question of the Cyprus conflict. With the Republic of Cyprus now a member of the EU and the still prevailing international legal discourse putting the blame for the continued separation of the island on Turkey's shoulders, it is easy to block negotiations on the grounds that Turkey does not recognise an EU member, which is a formal requirement for membership. Indeed, on this basis Cyprus has been able to prevent more so-called negotiation chapters covering a broader range of policy areas from being opened.[60] Yet while one may question the prudence of taking a divided Cyprus into the EU, both sides now need to live with the fact that the Republic of Cyprus is an EU member. Under these circumstances, it seems to speak against the criterion of fairness to put negotiations on hold, although it is clear that at the end of the day, Turkey will not be able to become a member without it recognising the Republic of Cyprus or another resolution of the conflict having been found. Meanwhile, most chapters within the negotiations are not affected by the recognition issue, and it seems therefore appropriate to continue with negotiations in all policy areas that have no or only a very tenuous link with this problem.

Does the obligation to negotiate in good faith and with the aim of membership introduce consequentialism through the back door in setting a target for negotiations? In my view, there is a crucial difference in the logic of the two arguments. Put in an admittedly crude dichotomy, a consequentialist ethic sees Turkish membership as a right to be attained, and subordinates the mechanisms of the path towards membership to this ultimate aim. In a deontological ethic, the aim of membership does not result from a Turkish right to membership, but is a consequence of past practice, and therefore results out of a procedural logic.

Promises as obligations?

Finally, let us consider the promises involved in Turkey–EU relations. I have argued above that such promises matter. Whether the 'normative entrapment' that promises bring about is an effect of the logic of appropriateness or the logic of consequentiality is not relevant to the present argument[61] – even in the latter case, the calculation of not losing face on the part of those having made promises rests on the norm that it is inappropriate not to keep one's promises. Yet what are the promises at play in Turkey–EU relations?

The literature on normative entrapment in the case of the Central and Eastern European states rests largely on a commitment inherent to European integration to integrate the whole of Europe.[62] There is a communitarian logic to this commitment in that it sees Europe as a distinctive identity, the unity of which needed to be re-established after the Cold War. Therefore, while membership was conditional on the fulfilment of other criteria and the usual screening and negotiations process, the promise was to take these states into the fold of the European Union and to work towards this aim. This is not quite the same for Turkey. In my discussion of cosmopolitanism above I have already noted the construction of Turkey not as an integral part of Europe, but at best as Europeanising and being on the way towards Europe, and at worst as different from Europe, an Other against which European identity is constructed. The promise in Turkey's case can therefore not rest on the aim of re-uniting what once was separated, especially since Turkey was part of the 'Western' world during the Cold War through both NATO and the Council of Europe.

Two counterarguments may be voiced at this juncture: First, has the affirmation of Turkey's candidacy status not constructed Turkey as European? And second, does the Ankara Agreement, through which Turkey became associated with the then European Communities, not already promise membership?

On the first question, it is true that in contrast to Morocco, Turkey has always been deemed eligible for EU membership by EU actors. At the time of the Ankara Agreement, Walter Hallstein declared that 'Turkey is a part of Europe ... geographically, ... historically, ... militarily, politically and economically'.[63] At various points of decision that followed, from accepting Turkey as a membership candidate to opening negotiations, Turkey's eligibility for membership was re-stated. Even at the 1997 Luxembourg European Council, when Turkey's membership bid suffered a temporary setback, the Council confirmed 'Turkey's eligibility for accession to the European Union', and therefore its European credentials.[64] There is therefore a commitment to Turkey that cannot be easily withdrawn. However, this commitment is different from the promises made to the Central and Eastern European states; it concerns Turkey's membership eligibility, not the reunification of a once separated continent. This, it seems to me, is crucial, for a commitment to reunification implies a commitment to membership, whereas in the Turkish case, there is 'merely' a commitment to negotiate membership. In that sense, the promises made in the two cases differ slightly but decisively.

On the question of the Ankara Agreement, the argument that this agreement established a commitment to membership is common, especially in the Turkish debate.[65] It is not correct. Article 28 of the agreement merely states that:

> [a]s soon as the operation of this Agreement has advanced far enough to justify envisaging full acceptance by Turkey of the obligations arising out of the Treaty establishing the Community, the Contracting Parties shall examine the possibility of the accession of Turkey to the Community.[66]

'Examine the possibility of accession' does not, in my view, establish 'an unequivocal membership perspective for Turkey' but a 'rather vague membership commitment' that is vague exactly because the promise is not membership but to *negotiate* membership.[67]

Thus, a consideration of the promises made also leaves the EU with an obligation to negotiate, following the established rules and procedures, about a possible Turkish membership. Nothing more, but nothing less either.

Impatience, delay and faith

For a long time after the association agreement, Turkey–EU relations did not pursue the accession option. For one, progress on the targets set in the agreement proved to be slow, and secondly, the 1974 intervention in Cyprus and the 1980 military coup did not exactly bring the two sides any closer. It was only in 1986 that 'proper' relations were taken up again,[68] and in 1987, Turkey applied for membership. It took Turkey until 1999 to achieve membership status and another six years to actually open negotiations. Since then, negotiations have not progressed as Turkey would have wished, especially because of the refusal to open a number of chapters because of Turkey's refusal to open its sea and airports to vessels and planes registered in the Republic of Cyprus, and therefore acting in breach of the Additional Protocol to the Association Agreement.

To what extent does the evolvement of Turkish–EU relations over the last five decades correspond to the norms identified from an international relations perspective? As far as the period up to 1986 is concerned, one may have wished for both sides to have taken the accession agreement more seriously, although before 1974, there was at least some movement in the agreement of Additional Protocols removing a variety of trade barriers between Turkey and the then European Community.[69] Yet since neither side seemed to have had a strong interest in doing so, there were no particular obligations that would have arisen. Promises need to be activated through invocation in order to generate obligations.

Such activation occurred in 1986 when the EC–Turkey Association Council re-convened after it had been put on ice following the coup d'état in Turkey. For Schimmelfennig, the developments since then, but especially after the change in attitudes leading to the 1999 Helsinki European Council decision to accept Turkey as a membership candidate, show the force of norms generated by the commitments made in the association agreement and in agreeing to the candidate status.[70] In his narration of the story, the EU played by the rules despite massive opposition to Turkish membership. In this view, stalling the negotiations because of the Cyprus recognition issue is in line with these rules and represents a case of 'reverse coherence and entrapment'.[71]

In my view, the assessment is a bit more complex. I accept that the conduct of membership negotiations is a consequence of norm-following, but I would also stress that a number of actors involved have not always acted in good faith, and that the formal procedure of negotiating needs to be accompanied by those involved taking the negotiations seriously. This is particularly important given the absence of a commitment to membership; if in such a case negotiations are only pursued to fulfil the formal obligation to negotiate, they do not fulfil the criterion of responsibility towards each other.

It is in this sense that the introduction of new hurdles, for instance by introducing referendums in EU member states, is problematic, not only because of the general problems of a communitarian approach to decisions that vitally affect others but also because it is outside the established practices of the negotiation process. While member states need to agree to the taking up of new members, most member states have so far not made accession dependent on a national referendum. Likewise, the introduction of alternative models of cooperative relations between Turkey and the EU into the negotiation process would only be defensible once both sides agree that membership is not achievable. And the public insistence on the open nature of the negotiations is either wrong if it implies that membership is not the negotiated object, or it states the obvious if it implies that negotiations can also fail, but then raises questions about the good faith in the negotiations by publicly alluding to such a failure.

I would go even further and contend that the invocation of the Cyprus conflict to prevent the opening of new chapters and the closure of already opened chapters is problematic. Formally, this does play by the accession rules. Yet the problem is that it interferes with the ongoing negotiations about a solution on the island and follows a particular construction of the Cyprus conflict that squarely puts the blame on Turkey.[72] Giving in on this point would amount to a recognition of the Republic of Cyprus by Turkey and thus potentially undermine the position of Turkish Cypriots and the possibility of a constitutional solution that would be based on the principles of a bizonal, bicommunal federation as interpreted in the UN-sponsored, so-called Annan Plan that proposed a United Cyprus Republic with a new constitution and was rejected by Greek Cypriots in a referendum in April 2004.[73] I have argued above that the main mistake in this respect was taking up Cyprus without a solution in the first instance, and that its membership now means that on the one hand, Turkey cannot be taken up as a member before this issue is solved, but that on the other hand the stalling of membership negotiations because of the conflict is unfair. In effect, the problem is one of contending rules and norms. On the one hand there are the narrow rules of the negotiations, on the other hand there are the broader norms of international conduct. Even the latter are problematic in this case; already in relation to Cypriot membership, the EU was trapped between a commitment to conflict resolution and a commitment to international law, which in this case, for historical reasons that cannot be explored here, and in the form of UN resolutions and European Court of Human Rights and European Court of Justice judgements based on these resolutions, largely followed the Greek-Cypriot representation of the conflict.[74]

In this sense, taking up Cyprus, and the insistence of Cyprus on membership, displayed a first form of impatience in the course of Turkey–EU relations. Likewise, writing Turkey off because of a lack of progress in domestic reforms is either motivated by insincerity about Turkey's membership prospects, or again displays considerable impatience given the time that such reforms take. Yet the impatience is not only on the EU side, but also on the Turkish side, where an interpretation of the promise made in the Ankara Agreement prevails and is used to put pressure on the EU, but which, as argued above, is untenable, especially when it is coupled with an outdated, 1960s conception of European integration that does not fully realise the degree to which the EU governance structures challenge member states' sovereignty.[75]

Such impatience leads to outside pressures put on the negotiation process that raise questions about the good faith with which negotiations ought to be conducted, and which undermine the spirit of negotiations. In doing so, impatience ironically tends to lead to delays, partly because the negotiations cannot focus on what they ought to focus on, and the deliberative processes that are supposed to guide them are undermined; partly because impatience often results in adverse reactions from those made responsible for a lack of progress.

It would be part of a larger empirical project to trace the interplay of promises, obligations, impatience and delay in this case. The purpose of this chapter was primarily to explore the obligations that are involved in Turkey–EU relations, particularly on the EU side. I have argued that these do not arise from a commitment to membership, but rather from a commitment to proper negotiations conducted in good faith, which arises partly out of the applicability of rules that have been formed in various accession rounds over time, and partly out of promises made from the Ankara Agreement to the decision to accept Turkey as a membership candidate.

Notes

1 Thanks go to Jerome Kuchejda and Signe Scheid for research assistance, as well as Nathalie Tocci and Armağan Emre Çakır for comments on a draft version of this chapter.
2 Thanks to Bahar Rumelili for bringing this pin as a present to the 2010 ISA conference in New Orleans!
3 G. Aybet, 'Turkey and the EU after the first year of negotiations: Reconciling internal and external policy challenges', *Security Dialogue*, 2006, vol. 37, no. 4, pp. 529–549; F. Schimmelfennig, 'Entrapped again: the way to EU membership negotiations with Turkey', *International Politics*, 2009, vol. 46, no. 4, pp. 413–431.
4 See among others M. Zeynalov, 'Turkey Gains New Vision in Foreign Affairs Under Davutoğlu', *Sunday's Zaman,* 13 September 2009, Online. Available http://www.sundayszaman.com/sunday/detaylar.do?load=detay&link=186955 (accessed 5 March 2010); R. Muzalevsky, 'Kazakhstan offers to hold joint military exercises with Turkey', *Eurasia Daily Monitor*, 2 February 2010, vol. 7 no. 22. Online. Available http://eurodialogue.org/osce/Kazakhstan-Offers-to-Hold-Joint-Military-Exercises-With-Turkey (accessed 5 March 2010); A. Davutoğlu, 'Turkey's foreign policy vision: An assessment of 2007', *Insight Turkey* 2008, vol. 10, no. 1, pp. 77–96.
5 L.-A. Glyptis, 'Which side of the fence? Turkey's uncertain place in the EU', *Alternatives: Turkish Journal of International Relations*, 2005, vol. 4, no. 3, p. 117.
6 M. S. Teitelbaum and P. Martin, 'Is Turkey ready for Europe?', *Foreign Affairs*, 2003, vol. 82, no. 3, pp. 104–105. For an overview of Turkey–EU migration, see P. Martin, E. Midgley, and M. Teitelbaum, 'Best practice options: Turkey', *International Migration*, 2002, vol. 40, no. 3, pp. 119–131.
7 On the role of Turkey's prospective membership in the referendum see G. Ivaldi, 'Beyond France's 2005 referendum on the European Constitutional Treaty', *West European Politics*, 2006, p. 10; K. Archick and D. Mix, 'The European Union's reform process: The Lisbon Treaty', *CRS Report for Congress 21618*, 2009, pp. 1–6; N. de Boisgroiller, 'The European disunion', *Survival*, 2005, vol. 47, no. 3, p. 58.
8 On this notion of securitisation, see B. Buzan, O. Wæver and J. de Wilde, *Security: A New Framework for Analysis,* Boulder, CO: Lynne Rienner, 1998, pp. 23–26; and, especially in relation to migration, O. Wæver *et al.*, *Identity, Migration and the New Security Order in Europe*, London: Pinter, 1993.
9 I. Ermagan, 'EU-Skeptizismus in der türkischen Politik', *Aus Politik und Zeitgeschichte*, 2009, no. 39–40, pp. 18–19. For an excellent analysis of the construction of Europe within Turkish debates, see B. Alpan, 'Demarcating Political Frontiers in Turkey: Discourses on Europe after 1999', PhD thesis, University of Birmingham, 2010.
10 M. Amstutz, *International Ethics: Concepts, Theories, and Cases in Global Politics*, second edition, London: Routledge, 2005, p. 9.

11 S. Forde, 'Classical realism', in T. Nardin and D. R. Mapel (eds), *Traditions of International Ethics*, Cambridge: Cambridge University Press, 1993, p. 65.

12 J. Donnelly, 'Twentieth-century realism', in T. Nardin and D. R. Mapel (eds), *Traditions of International Ethics*, Cambridge: Cambridge University Press, 1993, pp. 94–99; J. Donnelly, 'The ethics of realism', in C. Reus-Smit and D. Snidal (eds), *The Oxford Handbook of International Relations*, Oxford: Oxford University Press, 2008, pp. 150–162; A. Murray, 'The moral politics of Hans Morgenthau', *The Review of Politics*, 1996, vol. 58, no. 1, pp. 81–107; and of course Richard K. Ashley's critical exploration of realism in 'The poverty of neorealism', *International Organization*, 1984, vol. 38, no. 2, pp. 225–286.

13 R. Shapcott, 'International ethics' in J. Baylis, S. Smith and P. Owens (eds), *The Globalization of World Politics: An Introduction to International Relations*, fourth edition, Oxford: Oxford University Press, 2008, p. 194.

14 M. Fixdal and D. Smith, 'Humanitarian intervention and just war', *Mershon International Studies Review*, 1998, vol. 42, no. 2, p. 287.

15 M. Walzer, 'Words of war: Challenges to the just war theory', *Harvard International Review* 2004, vol. 26, pp. 36–38.

16 Among many others, see O. O'Neill, 'Bounded and cosmopolitan justice', *Review of International Studies*, 2000, vol. 26, no. 5, pp. 45–60.

17 For example T. Dunne and N. J. Wheeler, 'Introduction: Human rights and the fifty years' crisis', in T. Dunne and N. J. Wheeler (eds), *Human Rights in Global Politics*, Cambridge: Cambridge University Press, 1999.

18 For example A. J. Bellamy, 'Pragmatic solidarism and the dilemmas of humanitarian intervention', *Millennium: Journal of International Studies*, 2002, vol. 31, no. 3, pp. 475–479.

19 On the problems of the communitarian–cosmopolitan 'impasse', see among others, M. Cochran, *Normative Theory in International Relations: A Pragmatic Approach*, Cambridge: Cambridge University Press, 1999, and R. Shapcott, *Justice, Community and Dialogue in International Relations*, Cambridge: Cambridge University Press, 2001. On the pluralist–solidarist debate in the English School, see B. Buzan, *From International to World Society? English School Theory and the Social Structure of Globalisation*, Cambridge: Cambridge University Press, 2004, pp. 45–62 and 139–160, as well as A. Linklater and H. Suganami, *The English School of International Relations: A Contemporary Reassessment*, Cambridge: Cambridge University Press, 2006.

20 Although one should note that this is not a necessary consequence of taking a communitarian position, as one may also argue that an EU organised according to the principle of unity in diversity should be able to accommodate and indeed welcome Turkey as a member in the name of cultural richness.

21 K. M. Fierke and A. Wiener, 'Constructing institutional interests: EU and NATO enlargement', in T. Christiansen, K. E. Jørgensen and A. Wiener (eds), *The Social Construction of Europe*, London: Sage, 2001, pp. 121–139 and F. Schimmelfennig, 'The community trap: liberal norms, rhetorical action, and Eastern enlargement of the European Union', *International Organization*, 2001, vol. 55, no. 1, pp. 47–80.

22 M. Pace, 'The construction of EU normative power', *Journal of Common Market Studies*, 2007, vol. 45, no. 5, pp. 1041–1064.

23 Schimmelfennig, 'Entrapped again'; A. Bürgin, 'Can the EU accession process of Turkey be reversed? The strategies of the Turkey sceptics and their impact on Turkey's membership process', paper presented at the 2010 Annual Convention of the International Studies Association, New Orleans.

24 L. Jäger, 'Auf allen Karten abseits. Europa und die Türkei: Die Unlogik der Beitrittsverhandlungen', *Frankfurter Allgemeine Zeitung*, 14 August 2002, reprinted in C. Leggewie (ed.), *Die Türkei und Europa: Die Positionen*, Frankfurt am Main: Suhrkamp, 2004, p. 31, my translation. For anyone reading German, Leggewie's book

provides an excellent overview of the positions in the public debate on a possible Turkish EU membership.

25 B. Rumelili, *Constructing Regional Community and Order in Europe and Southeast Asia*, Basingstoke: Palgrave, 2007, p. 89. For a summary of such an argument and its relevance in French and German debates in particular, see A. Wimmel, *Transnationale Diskurse in Europa: Der Streit um den Türkei-Beitritt in Deutschland, Frankreich und Großbritannien*, Frankfurt am Main: Campus, 2006. See also M. Müftüler-Bac, 'Through the looking glass: Turkey in Europe', *Turkish Studies*, 2000, vol. 1, no. 1, p. 26. For a historical perspective, see Y. A. Stivachtis, 'Europe and the 'Turk': An English School approach to the study of EU–Turkey relations', in M. Müftüler-Baç and Y. A. Stivachtis (eds), *Turkey–EUropean Union Relations: Dilemmas, Opportunities, and Constraints*, Lanham, MD: Lexington Books, pp. 23–28.

26 H.-U. Wehler, 'Die türkische Frage: Europas Bürger müssen entscheiden', *Frankfurter Allgemeine Zeitung*, 19 December 2003, p. 35, my translation.

27 H.-U. Wehler, *Konflikte zu Beginn des 21. Jahrhunderts: Essays*. München: Beck, 2003, pp. 46–49.

28 Wehler, 'Die türkische Frage', my translation.

29 H.-U. Wehler, 'Soll Europa künftig an den Irak grenzen?', in C. Leggewie (ed.), *Die Türkei und Europa: Die Positionen*, Frankfurt am Main: Suhrkamp, 2004, p. 272.

30 For instance O. Höffe, 'Das Übermorgenland: So schnell wird die Türkei nicht europäisch', in C. Leggewie (ed.), *Die Türkei und Europa: Die Positionen*, Frankfurt am Main: Suhrkamp, 2004, pp. 175–179.

31 L. M. McLaren, 'Explaining opposition to Turkish membership of the EU', *European Union Politics*, 2007, vol. 8, pp. 251–278.

32 B. Anderson, *Imagined Communities: Reflections on the Origin and Spread of Nationalism*, second edition, London: Verso, 1991.

33 D. Campbell, *National Deconstruction: Violence, Identity, and Justice in Bosnia*, Minneapolis, MN: University of Minnesota Press, 1998, pp. 80–81.

34 Among many others, R. B. J. Walker, *Inside/Outside: International Relations as Political Theory*, Cambridge: Cambridge University Press, 1993; W. Connolly, *Identity/Difference: Democratic Negotiations of Political Paradox*, Ithaca, NY: Cornell University Press, 1991.

35 D. Campbell, *Politics without Principle: Sovereignty, Ethics, and the Narratives of the Gulf War*, Boulder, CO: Lynne Rienner, 1993, pp. 92–93.

36 K.-J. Kuschel, 'Die "christliche Identität" Europas und die Zukunft der Türkei', in C. Leggewie (ed.), *Die Türkei und Europa: Die Positionen*, Frankfurt am Main: Suhrkamp, 2004, pp. 89–94; T. Diez and M. Barbato, 'Christianity, Christendom, Europe: On the role of religion in European integration', *Arès*, 2008, vol. 23, no. 1, pp. 28–29.

37 Rumelili, *Constructing Regional Community*, pp. 82–88.

38 It is interesting in this context to note the efforts of the Republic of Cyprus to present itself as European in the run-up to its membership campaign, and thus not to emphasise its Eastern-Orthodox tradition, but its classical Hellenic heritage; see, for instance, T. Diez, 'Identity matters: Cyprus, Turkey and the European Union', in B. Dunér (ed.) *Turkey: the Road Ahead?*, Stockholm: The Swedish Institute of International Affairs, p. 44.

39 See B. Rosamond, *Theories of European Integration*, Basingstoke: Palgrave, 2000, pp. 36–37.

40 L. Cabrera, 'Is there a human right to accession? The Turkish case', Paper prepared for presentation at the SHUR meeting, Rome, June 2009. Online. Available http:// www.luiss.it/shur/wp-content/uploads/2009/05/cabrera.pdf (accessed 3 March 2010).

41 M. Müftüler-Baç, 'Turkey's political reforms and the impact of the European Union', *South European Society & Politics*, 2005, vol. 10, no. 1, pp. 17–31.

42 N. Tocci, 'Europeanization in Turkey: Trigger or anchor for reform?', *South European Society & Politics*, 2005, vol. 10, no. 1, pp. 73–83. The anchor metaphor is taken from M. Uğur, *The European Union and Turkey: An Anchor/Credibility Dilemma*, Aldershot: Ashgate, 1999.

43 B. Rumelili and F. Keyman, 'Transnational spaces of democratic participation in EU accession politics: Turks and the practice of multi-layered citizenship', paper prepared for presentation at the 51st annual convention of the International Studies Association, New Orleans, LA, 17–20 February 2010. Online. Available http://www.allacademic.com/one/isa/isa10/index.php?click_key=1&PHPSESSID=0c068e50350 6124847b6c51ec3c83ae9 (accessed 3 March 2010).

44 T. Diez, 'Turkey, the European Union and security complexes revisited', *Mediterranean Politics*, 2005, vol. 10, no. 2, pp. 176–177, and T. Diez and B. Rumelili, 'Turkey and the EU: Open the door', *The World Today*, 2004, vol. 60, no. 4, pp. 33–35.

45 See the discussion in the section on 'Promises as Obligations' below for the argument that the Ankara Agreement establishes such a right to accession.

46 Cabrera, 'Is there a human right'.

47 O. Parker, "Cosmopolitan Europe' and the EU–Turkey question: the politics of a 'common destiny", *Journal of European Public Policy*, 2009, vol. 16, no. 7, p. 1088, citing U. Beck, *Cosmopolitan Vision*, Cambridge: Polity, 2006.

48 Parker, "Cosmopolitan Europe", p. 1088.

49 Parker, "Cosmopolitan Europe", citing W. D. Mignolo, 'The many faces of cosmopolis: border thinking and critical cosmopolitanism', *Public Culture*, 2000, vol. 12, no. 3, p. 743. See for a similar position A. Linklater, 'Dialogic politics and the civilising process', *Review of International Studies*, 2005, vol. 31, no. 1, pp. 141–154.

50 For such a position, see the exemplary R. B. J. Walker, *One World, Many Worlds: Struggles for a Just World Peace*, London: Zed Books, 1988.

51 I. Manners, 'Normative power Europe: a contradiction in terms?', *Journal of Common Market Studies*, 2002, vol. 40, no. 2, pp. 235–258.

52 Parker, 'Cosmopolitan Europe', p. 1089.

53 T. Diez, 'Constructing the Self and Changing Others: Problematising the Concept of 'Normative Power Europe", *Millennium: Journal of International Studies*, 2005, vol. 33, no. 3, pp. 613–636, and T. Diez, 'Europe's Others and the Return of Geopolitics', *Cambridge Review of International Affairs*, 2004, vol. 17, no. 2, pp. 319–335.

54 Tocci, 'Europeanization in Turkey'.

55 A. Michalski, 'The enlarging European Union', in D. Dinan (ed.), *Origins and Evolution of the European Union*, Oxford: Oxford University Press, 2006, p. 276.

56 But see the critical engagement by R. Marchetti, 'Consequentialist cosmopolitanism and global political agency', in J. Eade and D. O'Byrne (eds), *Global Ethics and Civil Society*, Aldershot: Ashgate, 2005, pp. 57–73.

57 E.O. Eriksen, 'The EU – a cosmopolitan polity?', *Journal of European Public Policy*, 2006, vol. 13, no. 2, pp. 253, 264.

58 F. Halliday, 'Getting Real About Seattle', *Millennium: Journal of International Studies,* 2000, vol. 29, no. 1 p. 128.

59 C. Joerges and J. Neyer, 'Transforming strategic interaction into deliberative problem-solving: European comitology in the foodstuffs sector', *Journal of European Public Policy*, 1997, vol. 4, no. 1, pp. 609–625.

60 The immediate issue is the refusal of Turkey to open its ports and airports to vessels and airplanes registered in the Republic of Cyprus as part of the already existing customs union between Turkey and the EU. Behind this, however, is the problem that this is seen on both sides as an act of recognition, which the Republic of Cyprus wants to achieve and Turkey wants to avoid.

61 The classic work on this distinction is J. G. March and J. P. Olsen, *Rediscovering Institutions: The Organizational Base of Politics*, New York: Free Press, 1989.

62 On this issue see also the chapter by A. E. Çakır in this volume.
63 Cited in Schimmelfennig, 'Entrapped again', p. 420.
64 European Council, Presidency Conclusions, 12/13 December 1997, pt. 31. Online. Available http://www.consilium.europa.eu/ueDocs/cms_Data/docs/pressData/en/ec/032a0008.htm (accessed 4 March 2010).
65 M. Müftüler-Baç and Y. A. Stivachtis, 'Introduction', in M. Müftüler-Baç and Y. A. Stivachtis (eds), *Turkey–EUropean Union Relations: Dilemmas, Opportunities, and Constraints*, Lanham, MD: Lexington Books, p. 3.
66 Agreement Establishing an Association between the European Economic Community and Turkey (signed in Ankara, 1 September 1963). Online. Available http://www.abgs.gov.tr/index.php?p=117&l=2
67 Both citations are from Schimmelfennig, 'Entrapped again', p. 420 and p. 424 respectively.
68 Müftüler-Baç and Stivachtis, 'Introduction', p. 4.
69 Z. Öniş, 'Luxembourg, Helsinki and beyond: towards an interpretation of recent Turkey–EU relations', *Government and Opposition*, 2003, vol. 35, no. 4, p. 467.
70 Schimmelfennig, 'Entrapped again'
71 Schimmelfennig, 'Entrapped again', p. 428.
72 On the various perspectives on the Cyprus conflict, both theoretically and politically, see T. Diez and N. Tocci (eds), *Cyprus: A Conflict at the Crossroads*, Manchester: Manchester University Press, 2009.
73 On the problem of state succession and the failure of the Annan Plan, see A. Sözen and K. Özersay, 'The Annan Plan: State succession or continuity', *Middle Eastern Studies*, 2007, vol. 43, no. 1, pp. 125–141. On the negotiations since the Annan Plan, see H. Faustmann, 'History in the making? A new drive for a solution to the Cyprus problem', *Mediterranean Politics*, 2008, vol. 13, no. 3, pp. 453–458.
74 See T. Diez and M. Pace, 'Normative Power Europe and conflict transformation', in R. G. Whitman (ed.), *Normative Power Europe: Empirical and Theoretical Perspectives*, Basingstoke: Palgrave, forthcoming.
75 Öniş, 'Luxembourg, Helsinki', p. 465.

9   Conclusion

Armağan Emre Çakır

The period 1959–2009 has certainly been a process of tribulation and embarrassment for Turks and Europeans alike. Yet for us, students of European politics, this fifty-year timespan is a rare and spectacular phenomenon to examine; in front of our eyes Sisyphus is rolling his boulder up the hill, only to watch it roll back down, and to repeat this for decades.

Neither the individual chapters nor the whole of this book claim to have solved the mystery of the relations between Turkey and the EU. Nevertheless, the authors provide some fresh insights into this half-a-century-old vicious circle, provide their own answers to some long-awaited questions, but also come up with new puzzles. They all depart from the conviction that superficial explanations and quick diagnoses that prevail in the literature are far from being satisfactory; the narrative of these fifty years cannot consist only of 'a Turkey that does not do its homework' and 'a European Union that does not give Turkey its due'.

Çakır's chapter is based on a denial of analyses that reduce EU–Turkey relations to a sum of the reciprocal moves of the EU and Turkey in a bilateral game. Instead, the chapter provides a triangular model where Turkey, its rivals and the EU interact. Over these fifty years, Turkey sometimes focuses too much on its rivals and sometimes completely neglects them, whereas the rivals sometimes positively affect Turkey by inspiring and motivating it, but in most cases act against its interests and maximise their gains from the EU at Turkey's expense. Meanwhile, the EU mostly shows a predilection for Turkey's rivals. This analysis evidences the multitude of actors in EU–Turkey relations, and is a call for further studies that would cover other actors than Turkey's rivals that have had considerable influence on EU–Turkey relations.

For Nas, these fifty years were not entirely wasted. Turkey may not have progressed as quickly and as much as it could have towards full membership. Yet, its economic gains in the course of accession cannot be denied. The motivation arising from the prospect of membership, the stimulation brought about by the competitive atmosphere of the Customs Union, and the higher standards emanating from the portions of the *acquis* incorporated into Turkish law have all contributed to the improvement of Turkish economy. This approach, which focuses on the 'process' of relations between the EU and Turkey rather than become preoccupied by the possible 'outcome' seems innovative and is a plausible alternative to that of the body of teleological and pessimistic writings that resort to economic analyses only to demonstrate Turkey's losses and/or poor economic performance in its relations with the EU.

Bilgin sheds light on the security dimension, one of the fuzziest realms of EU–Turkey relations. She hypothesises that the respective security cultures of Turkey and the EU have been constructed along different paths since the beginning of EU–Turkey relations. Although transformed over the years, Turkey's security culture has remained dependent on military means, whereas the EU has constructed a 'security community' through the adoption of broader conceptions and non-military practices. This divergence meant a gradual erosion of Turkey's role as a 'security provider' for Europe. Despite the fact that it was possible for Turkey to reclaim its sercirty provider status in its neighbourhood in times of crisis. Turkey has been relegated to the position of a source of insecurity which 'exports' its societal, political and economic problems to Europe via such media as migrant workers or political asylum seekers. Thus, Turkey's aspiration for EU membership is also a quest for security as much as it is for other gains such as economic benefits.

Tocci challenges the truism that for European elites EU–Turkey relations have always been a crucial concern. Elite debates, she claims, rarely focused on EU–Turkey relations until the 2000s unless an important event related to Turkey such as Turkey's military intervention in Cyprus occurred, whereas in the 2000s elite debates at European level seemed to include EU–Turkey relations. A closer look through Tocci's lenses, however, reveals that even in this later period, 'EU–Turkey relations' were a mere subset of larger discussions on international or European issues such as the future structure or international role of the EU. Likewise, elite debates at the level of Member States were shaped mainly by interests of the respective states or the EU rather than by EU–Turkey relations themselves. Furthermore, in both of these cases, most of the time, elites focused either on Turkey or the EU in isolation but not the relations between these two entities. Misperceptions, prejudices, ignorance and neglect have been the natural by-products of these fallacious debates, and had a significant contribution to the delay in Turkey's accession to the EU. As such, Tocci's reasoning emphasises the concept of 'elite debates' as an important parameter in the study of EU–Turkey relations.

Canan-Sokullu and Kentmen undertake the daunting task of taking stock of and analysing the changing patterns in European public opinion on Turkey's accession to the EU. Their analysis starts with the year 1988 when the Europeans were for the first time asked in the Eurobarometer poll explicitly about their opinion on whether Turkey should be admitted to the EC, and concludes with the year 2008. In particular, the 2000–2008 interval in this period is examined through multinomial logistic regression analysis. Whilst some findings of their study corroborate the common-sensical claim that improvements in macro-economic indicators in the EU increase the support of the European public for Turkey's accession, some other findings disconfirm some fundamental axioms of the literature on EU–Turkey relations such as personal employment concerns or religion playing a substantial role in shaping European public opinion about Turkey's accession to the EU. This study by Canan-Sokullu and Kentmen is also an invitation for more empirical research on EU–Turkey relations which, just like the relations themselves, have so far been misguided by rhetoric and sensationalism.

Rumford and Turunç offer us an analysis of the EU–Turkey relations by using the concept of 'Postwesternisation'. Fifty years ago, with its application to the EEC, Turkey's journey started as a project of Westernisation, and many take it for granted that Turkey's accession to the EU will mean the completion of this project. However, as Rumford and Turunç argue, the 'place of destination' of this journey has moved elsewhere. By incorporating new ideological, cultural and geopolitical elements, Europe has become a different blend than it was fifty years ago, and its co-ordinates in the Western space have changed as well. Turkey itself has also undergone a radical transformation in politics: traditional concepts and categorisations used to describe the political life in Turkey have recently lost their meaning. Thus, although Turkey has not been able to realise its dream of acceding to the EU, with their respective transformation processes, the EU and Turkey have already met on the large and slippery ground of the Postwesternisation era. This line of argument by Rumford and Turunç may be the sign of a paradigmatic change in the study of EU–Turkey relations.

Diez's contribution is a call-to-reason in EU–Turkey relations. With reference to some key debates in international ethics, he concludes that the discourses of the parties should be divested of their value-laden overtones. Established routines, rules and procedures of enlargement processes should be the only guide for the negotiations between the EU and Turkey as well as the only source of rights and obligations of the parties. Inventing new rules or procedures, or developing unfounded expectations, rights or obligations in the process of these negotiations is against the fundamentals of international ethics. Diez argues that it is not possible to say that Turkey has a vested right to membership that can be derived from this procedural complex governing the modus operandi of enlargement. However, in his opinion, Turkey does have a right to pursue its negotiations with a membership prospect, and parties to these negotiations have to act with a bona fide intent. The indifference, impatience or blaming that sometimes overshadow EU–Turkey relations are nothing other than counter-productive, and contribute further to the delay in Turkey's accession as well as lead to rejection and controversy. This analysis by Diez is not only one of the first applications of international ethics to EU–Turkey relations, but also a compelling critique of some of the fundamentals of international ethics itself.

When we bring these individual chapters together, we get a bigger picture which contains important messages for academics and policy-makers alike.

For academics, EU–Turkey relations, in the way they are covered in this book, contain important theoretical clues as well as challenges. The whole of these relations make up a colossal and intricate conglomerate, many parts of which have been only superficially studied. This whole defies reductionism which is an inevitable element of our scientific toolkit: in Çakır's chapter we see that third parties in these relations are variables difficult to leave out of our formulae, and

Nas demonstrates that the mostly neglected conditioning effect of the EU is in fact an important parameter. Bilgin as well as Rumford and Turunç draw our attention to the significance of grasping transformation, relativity and contingency: while Bilgin claims that identity, interests and insecurity constitute each other and that 'cultures of insecurity' are continuously reproduced, by demonstrating the changing meaning of the concept of Westernisation, Rumford and Turunç question the limits of constancy assumption which has been an important foothold so far in international studies. Diez reminds us how important the mostly neglected concept of ethics is in studying international relations. The collective myopia of European elites towards Turkey, exposed by Tocci, as well as the value-laden nature of EU–Turkey relations brought to light by Diez defies the premises of rational choice theory. Canan-Sokullu and Kentmen's contribution contains suggestions to cope with the difficulty of designing empirical research for such a long period with so many different variables and with so little standard data available.

For policy-makers, each chapter of the book offers some valuable recommendations. Turks should get over their preoccupation with full membership and try also to appreciate and enjoy the other fruits of the relations such as the ones Nas emphasises. As Diez states, charging too much emotion into the process of accession of Turkey is counter-productive whereas following the path of established procedures is the surest way. In the light of the arguments put forward by Rumford and Turunç, Turkish policy-makers have to consider the fact that neither Turkey nor the EU bears the same identity as they did fifty years ago. The discourse of 'Turkey's accession as a Westernisation project' has to be revised. Another discourse that now needs revision is Turkey's potential role as a security provider for the EU. As Bilgin suggests, in the present context of the security culture of the EU, some circles see Turkey as a country that exports insecurity to Europe via, among other channels, migrant workers and political asylum seekers. Whereas the governing elites of Turkey should amend their strategies towards the EU accordingly, those in the EU should try to understand the different ecurity culture of Turkey and its needs that arise therefrom. Governing elites in Turkey should also admit that besides paying attention to the technical aspects of EU–Turkey relations, they should spend some time and effort to influence their European counterparts and, as Tocci implies, try to divert their attention from Turkey itself to the relations between the EU and Turkey. In line with Canan-Sokullu and Kentmen's study, Turkish politicians should keep in mind that the support Turkey gets from the European public is also connected to the EU's own economic performance. They should advertise that empirical studies do not support the hearsay that European citizens are concerned that their job market will be flooded with cheap Turkish labour. Contrary to the assumptions of many, religion, democracy or human rights are not among the core concepts that shape the views of the European public towards Turkey. As Çakır suggests, in formulating their moves in EU–Turkey relations Turkish policy-makers should not forget about the rivals of Turkey. European policy-makers, on the other hand, should not discriminate between Turkey and its rivals; as Tocci and Diez's respective texts indicate, those policy-makers should consider Turkey's performance in the relations and negotiations rather than secondary details such as Turkey's cultural characteristics.

The variety of arguments and data presented in this volume allows readers to draw their own lessons from and conclusions for this Sisyphean story.

Does our protagonist deserve his ordeal? Perhaps, yes … Because, similar to the mischievous nature and wrongdoings of Sisyphus, Turkey has some inherent problems and peculiarities that adversely affect her relations with the EU, as well as having made a number of faulty moves in the history of EU–Turkey relations. Or perhaps, no … Because the ceaseless and otiose toil of Turkey is imposed based rather on prejudices, quick judgements, generalisations, ignorance, and discrimination than discernment and fairness.

Does our protagonist suffer? Perhaps, yes … In his *The Myth of Sisyphus* Camus says that 'the struggle itself towards the heights is enough to fill a man's heart. We have to imagine Sisyphus happy'. This may not be true in the case of Turkey though. This fifty-year wait of the successor of the mighty Ottoman Empire at the door of Europe must be embarrassing, and knocking on the door continuously must be exhausting. Or perhaps, no … Maybe for Turkey, accession to the EU is not so important as it seems. Seeing the declining popular support for EU membership and the confusing political signals from politicians, one may surmise that Turkey may be happy in flirting with the West and the East at the same time, while reaping the benefits of its candidacy status (upgrading its laws, liberalising its economy, benefitting from some funds and programmes of the EU) without the confines of a matrimonial yoke.

Is the ordeal of our protagonist really endless? Perhaps, yes … The chapters of the acquis Turkey has to adopt may be left open or frozen indefinitely. If the 'end' in this story means Turkey's accession to the EU, first, Turkey's withdrawal from this process, secondly, the EU's imposition of alternatives (such as privileged partnership) to Turkey's membership, or thirdly, the EU's demise are among possible scenarios that may also leave this story endless. Or perhaps, no … Because, while for its own reputation the EU cannot make Turkey wait for ever, on its part Turkey has progressed a long way towards achieving its goal. Apart from all complicated arguments, a mere extrapolation of this progression may lead us to assume that sooner or later Turkey will attain EU membership.

Index